Interpersonal
Communication
in the
Modern Organization

Interpersonal Communication in the Modern Organization

―――――――――――――――**Second Edition**―――――――――――――――

ERNEST G. BORMANN

University of Minnesota

RALPH G. NICHOLS

University of Minnesota, Emeritus

WILLIAM S. HOWELL

University of Minnesota

GEORGE L. SHAPIRO

University of Minnesota

Prentice-Hall, Inc., Englewood Cliffs, New Jersey 07632

Library of Congress Cataloging in Publication Data

Main entry under title:
Interpersonal communication in the modern organization.

     Includes index.
     1. Communication in organizations.   I. Bormann, Ernest G.
HF5549.5.C6I57 1982   658.4'5   81-13927
ISBN   0-13-475061-6   AACR2

© 1982, 1969 by Prentice-Hall, Inc., Englewood Cliffs, New Jersey 07632

Printed in the United States of America

10 9 8 7 6 5 4 3 2 1

Editorial/production supervision by Paul Spencer
Cover design by Wanda Lubelska Design
Interior design by Paul Spencer
Manufacturing buyer: Edmund W. Leone

ISBN 0-13-475061-6

Prentice-Hall International, Inc., *London*
Prentice Hall of Australia Pty. Limited, *Sydney*
Prentice Hall of Canada, Ltd., *Toronto*
Prentice Hall of India Private Limited, *New Delhi*
Prentice Hall of Japan, Inc., *Tokyo*
Prentice Hall of Southeast Asia Pte. Ltd., *Singapore*
Whitehall Books Limited, *Wellington, New Zealand*

Contents

PART TWO

Learning to Communicate as a Subordinate

PART THREE

Learning to Communicate as a Manager

Preface

The first edition of *Interpersonal Communication in the Modern Organization* was aimed at people who were already actively involved in organizations. In the preface to that edition we explained that "The book is intended for individuals and groups involved in the gamut of organizational activities. It is designed to supply theory and techniques to aid in solving the problems of interpersonal communication that crop up in the context of the modern organization. It deals with both verbal and nonverbal elements of human interaction."

The revised edition continues the emphasis on supplying theory and techniques to foster better communication skills within the organizational context, but the material has been adapted to the requirements of instructors teaching courses in organizational communication in community and four-year colleges. The book seeks to meet the career needs of students who are in vocational and technical training courses and programs which lead to positions within organizations.

The major focus of the treatment is upon the student as a person who is or will be actively "involved in the gamut" of organizational communication.

Each chapter is divided into two parts. The first section deals with a concrete classroom assignment and contains basic advice on how to develop specific skills related to the laboratory application. The material in these laboratory application sections is essentially new in the second edition. The second section develops the theory to support the laboratory application.

The book leads the student in logical fashion through the communication system of the organization as a participant, beginning with joining the organization and then going on to learning to communicate as a subordinate and learning to communicate as a manager.

We have based this revision on the latest findings of research in organizational communication and on the latest developments in teaching applied courses for undergraduates. The book is divided into three parts. Part One deals with joining the organization and presents the basics of making a job application, preparing a resume, and participating in a job interview. It also discusses the use of informal conversation in learning about human relationships and the formal and informal communication channels and networks. The first part also presents the basics of the communication process and participating in the social and work groups of an organization. Part One ends with a chapter reporting the latest findings on research in communication and organizational culture.

Part Two consists of three chapters related to "Learning to Communicate as a Subordinate." The chapters discuss communication networks and flow, listening, and the evaluation interview.

Part Three discusses "Learning to Communicate as a Manager" and deals with nonverbal communication, leading group meetings, making organizational presentations, persuasion, theories of management, and developing and sustaining a productive and satisfying communication climate.

The book's organization moves from simpler concepts as the newcomers get acquainted with the communication practices of an organization through the more complicated communicative needs of upper management. Our organizing principle in deciding which skills to include in the section for subordinates and which in the part for managers has been the move from the more basic to the more advanced. Of course both subordinates and managers need similar communication skills and knowledge. Our point in dealing with listening in the section on communicating as a subordinate is not that listening is unimportant for managers, but that it is particularly important for subordinates and that the student who has studied listening early in the term will have that background when moving on to study managerial communication. In some instances we have dealt with similar communication contexts from both perspectives. For example, in Part Two we deal with the basics of participating in organizational group meetings and in Part Three we deal with leadership communication as it relates to managing small groups.

We wish to express our appreciation to the following persons who reviewed the manuscript of the revised edition and offered valuable suggestions: Professors Eldon Baker, University of Montana; William Donohue, Michigan State University; Clarence Edney, Florida State University; James Lahiff, University of Georgia; Ben Morse, University of Miami; Patricia Smith-Pierce, William Rainey Harper College; Debra A. Strugar, University of Arizona; Robert K. White, Black Hawk College; and Alan Zaremba, State University of New York at Fredonia.

The case study of the new breakfast cereal in Chapter 12 was modified and adapted from William S. Howell and Ernest G. Bormann, *Presentational Speaking for Business and the Professions* (New York: Harper & Row, 1971), pages 3-7.

Interpersonal
Communication
in the
Modern Organization

Part One
Joining the Organization

Part One

Joining the Organization

1

Getting a Job

———————————— **Laboratory Application** ————————————

THE JOB INTERVIEW

People have been talking their way into and out of good jobs forever. Vice-presidents have fired sons and presidents have groomed daughters to take over business empires, but for most of us nowadays, the way into a good position is through some sort of job interview.

Much of this book will be concerned with the communication situations involved with successfully engaging in organizational interactions, even including those skills necessary for gracefully terminating one's association with a company, but first you have to be hired.

Many of us spend a large part of our waking hours at work in order to earn a living. Sometimes we take a job in a haphazard, almost accidental way because we hear of an opening or because someone we know suggests we apply for a position. Why would someone follow the path of least resistance and slip into paths that might lead to dissatisfaction with a career? Deciding what we want to do a large part of every working day for the rest of our lives is so important we find making a career decision very threatening. We can slide into "just a job" and tell ourselves that what we are doing is "just for now," something temporary.

Taking a job on a temporary basis is fine unless it is a symptom that you are failing to face the issue of what you want to do on a long-time basis.

3

For the purpose of this laboratory application, assume that you have come to the point where you want to make a career choice. Do not fall into the trap of thinking that this sort of careful analysis is something that you only do once or twice during your working career. Actually the more times you do this the better for your career. The search for new opportunities is an ongoing process which will be useful throughout your life.

To be successful you need to make an analysis of your goals and skills. What do you want to do? What have you learned to do? What talents do you have? What are you good at? What are your interests? How can you put this all together to create a meaningful work situation for yourself?

Know Yourself. Begin your preparation by examining your personal priorities. Ask yourself questions such as the following: What would you like to be doing five years from now? Ten years? How would you measure success? Is money important? Peer approval? Social relevance? Leisure time activities? Personal relationships? Where would you like to work? Would you like a job that allows you to stay in the same location or would you prefer travelling? Do you want to live in a large city? A small community? A rural area? Do you like to organize people? Deal with information? Do you prefer creating ideas, projects, products? Do you like working in private or do you prefer working on a team? Would you prefer a mixture of both working situations? Do you like to deal with people individually or in large groups? As a supervisor or as a teammate, an equal? Do you like to make decisions and assume responsibility or do you prefer someone else to have the final responsibility?

Sometimes if you are unsure about the answers to such questions you can get help by going to your college counseling office and asking to take vocational and personal interest and aptitude tests. Another good method to help answer such questions is to write a brief history of your activities (paid and unpaid) which includes what you liked and disliked about each.

Know the Market. Having made a survey of your career hopes and aptitudes, you need to match your self assessment with openings in the current labor market. You should find out where organizations advertise positions of the sort you wish to find. More and more firms are advertising their positions in order to live up to governmental guidelines dealing with equal opportunities for women and minorities. Sometimes the advertisements are in general circulation newspapers and sometimes in more specialized journals, but a few hours in a public library or your college library can provide you with substantial information. You should make a list of the most promising leads and map a plan to approach them in some regular order. When making your survey remember that you will usually not find exactly the job you want at the entry level. What you often need to do is to find some good career paths to the job you eventually want.

The Resume. A key opening step to joining the organization is the careful preparation of a resume of your education, training, and experience for a possible job. Your resume is an important message designed to help you get a chance for a job interview. Certain basic information is necessary for every good resume. The resume should include a description of the kind of position or positions you want, basic personal information, a summary of your educational background, and an outline of your work experiences.

A good resume is brief. If you can provide the necessary information in a one-page resume, great. That is ideal. If you have held a number of jobs and find one page too limiting, you could expand the resume to two pages, but you should resist adding any more. Too often a person writing a resume will put down everything that comes to mind. When you include unimportant as well as important accomplishments, a reader may get the impression that you are padding your resume in order to hide the fact that the main features are not strong.

The resume could include personal information such as your name, address, telephone numbers, marital status, age, health, number of children. You should provide the names of the educational institutions you attended after high school, dates you were there, degrees received, and major areas of study. List these items in order, beginning with the most recent school and degree first, then working backwards. Finally, summarize your work experiences with dates, employers, titles, responsibilities, and accomplishments.

Frequently you will want to include certain information, in addition to the basic core discussed above, because of your special background or because you are applying for a position with a particular organization and a particular hobby, travel experience, or honor will make you a more attractive applicant.

Figure 1 presents a sample to guide you in the preparation of your own resume. Remember the sample is only a guide; make any creative adaptations you can to present yourself in the best possible light. When preparing your own resume, take special care to make it look professional—make it concise, attractive in layout, and without errors in spelling or typing or grammar.

If you are sending out a number of applications you may not need or have the time to tailor each resume for each position. Individual adaptation is an excellent idea, however, and for particularly attractive jobs you should modify and individualize your resume, type a fresh copy, and tailor it to the specific position and organization.

Before writing the cover letter, spend some time in analyzing the

Martin S. Gordon
203-A Highland Hall
State College
Central City, MN 55624

(412) 385-9731

<u>Professional objectives</u>:	Corporate management in medium-sized company in electronic or computing industry.
<u>Education</u>:	BA, State College, Central City, Minnesota. Major: Business Administration--concentrating on management, marketing, and information systems.
<u>Employment history</u>:	
Present	Assistant Manager, student coop bookstore, State College Union Hall. Supervise sales force.
Present	Undergraduate dormitory counselor, Highland Hall (office: Office of Housing, State College). Responsible for managing section of large coed dormitory.
1980 (summer)	Intern program, Information Systems Corporation, Minneapolis, MN. Position included working in personnel with a management training program.
1978/79	Asst. Manager, Central City Big Burger food outlet. Supervised hiring and personnel and managed overall operations for evening shift.
1977/78	Cook for Big Burger, Central City.
<u>Additional information</u>:	1980/81 member, Omicron Delta Upsilon (National Economics Honor Society), member Board of Governors, Student Union, and member, Student Senate, State College, Central City.
	1980/81 member of Committee for Homecoming Parade, reporter for <u>Business Review</u> student magazine of State College of Business Administration.
<u>References</u>:	Recommendations **and** personal references available from the State College School of Business Administration, 1819 College Avenue, Central City, MN 55624.

Figure 1. Sample Job Resume

company or firm or institution and include some specifics about it as well as some personal touches about yourself that might be of particular interest to the personnel specialists who will read your material.

When you write the cover letter express your ideas in clear and complete sentences. Do not indulge in fancy writing. Good writing that is direct and brief suggests that you have communication skills that are important for every member of an organization. Type each letter and address it to an individual rather than to a title or an organizational division.

You should mention the specific job or, if your query is more general, the kind of employment you are seeking. Explain your interest in the organization and the positions you understand are available. Feature your most attractive qualities and experience for the position; do not simply repeat what is in your resume. Here is the place for a few personal touches. Be sure to ask for an interview. Indicate when you would be available for it. Figure 2 presents a sample cover letter.

To this point you have made an assessment of your personal abilities and experiences and preferences; you have searched for an organization to join and have made an analysis of the organization, and you have prepared and submitted a resume and cover letter. All of this is but preparation for the job interview. Your well-prepared resume and attractive cover letter can get you an interview, but they will not land the job for you. How you communicate in the job interview will be the deciding factor in whether or not you are invited to join the organization.

The interviewer will have the information from your resume and cover letter plus any other application questionnaires that you have filled out for the organization. Still, the interviewer will want to check out this information in the face-to-face situation for more details and greater understanding. This face-to-face checking out and the non-verbal as well as verbal communication that go along with it often make the difference between getting hired or rejected. "She looked good on paper, but . . ." If the interviewer knows that you have the necessary professional or technical skills, then the way you dress and communicate becomes highlighted.

Planning the Interview. Only by planning and anticipating what will happen can you present yourself in the proper light, namely, as a person who knows his or her assets and career goals.

Information About the Organization. As you begin your planning, gather information about the organization. Collect as much written and promotional material as you can before the interview. Read recruitment brochures, annual reports, and—this is particularly important—get a table of organization or a description of the formal structure of the organization. If possible, visit the organization and look around at how offices are laid out and at outward shows of status and authority such as job titles. In the theoretical rationale section of this chapter we will explain how an analysis of the formal communication channels and structure of the organization can aid you in planning your communication with members of the organization.

```
Month date, Year

Ms. Marilyn Crockett,
Personnel Director
Data Systems, Inc.
3050 Madison Crossway
Minneapolis, MN  55104

Dear Ms. Crockett:

(PURPOSE OF PARAGRAPH: WHY I AM WRITING YOU THIS LETTER)
I am writing to apply for the opening in your management
training program at Data Systems, Inc., listed with the College
of Business Administration Placement Service at State College
in Central City.

(WHY YOUR ORGANIZATION AND THIS PARTICULAR JOB LOOK GOOD TO ME)
Your management training program is exactly what I am looking
for.  Data Systems, Inc. is a healthy, progressive company and
I would be proud to be associated with it.  I spent a summer
internship working in the personnel department of Information
Systems, Inc. in Minneapolis.  I love the area.  While the
summer job experience was invaluable, I found that I felt
somewhat uncomfortable in such a large organization, one that
makes a practice of rapid turnover in terms of assignments.
I feel that Data Systems, Inc., smaller, and with an excellent
record of employee commitment and stability, is just the kind
of organization I would find both challenging and supportive.

(WHY I SHOULD LOOK GOOD TO YOU AS AN EMPLOYEE)
My vita is enclosed.  I have majored in management and economics
at State College.  Working part-time as a student, I was made
assistant manager of the Central City Big Burger after working
eight months as a cook.  I served as undergraduate dorm counselor
my senior year.  After working at Big Burger two years, I began
assisting the manager of the student cooperative bookstore in
Union Hall, which I will conclude when I graduate this June.

(WHY YOUR JOB, YOUR ORGANIZATION, AND I SHOULD BE A 'GOOD FIT')
Your job description, "someone with a knowledge of sound business
practices and a keen interest in personnel management" caught
my eye immediately.  I am a good worker, but I have found my best
skills and the greatest challenges in helping other employees
utilize their abilities best.  I like to know the people who
work with me.  I like to help them find the job that both
stretches and satisfies them.
```

Figure 2. Sample Letter of Application (page 1)

Pre-interview Visit. In a visit you should also note such things as how employees dress, how formal the communicative atmosphere seems to be, and the general air of organized chaos, boisterous interaction, quiet formality, or tense interchange which characterizes the way people interact. In the late 1960s and early 1970s some organizations adopted what was then called a "laid back" or "mellow" style of organizational norms including scruffy clothing and informality of communication. By contrast, some organizations have clothing

```
                          - 2 -
    (REQUEST FOR AN INTERVIEW OR WHATEVER NEXT STEP IS NECESSARY
    IN ORDER TO BE CONSIDERED FOR THE JOB - PLUS - BRIEF THANKYOU
    FOR CONSIDERING MY APPLICATION)
    If you would please contact me, I can be in Minneapolis for
    an interview at your convenience.  My address and telephone
    number are below.  I appreciate your consideration of my
    application.

    Sincerely yours,

    (SIGNATURE)

    Martin S. Gordon
    203-A Highland Hall
    State College
    Central City, MN 55624

    Area code 412,  telephone 385-9731



       encl: Vita
```

Figure 2. Sample Letter of Application (page 2)

norms that stress conservative dress, with both men and women tending to wear suits. All organizations have a "uniform," even though it may range from actual uniforms to obvious conformity to highly individualized apparel where distinctiveness is the norm. Clearly, how you dress for your interview should reflect your analysis of the tone and personality of the organization. If you appear at an organization with a formal style of communicating and conservative dress norms in torn blue-jeans and a T-shirt adorned with suggestive slogans front and back, the interviewer may be so startled by your appearance that he or she fails to hear much of what you say. Probably the wisest thing is not to approximate the dress norms closely, but dress more casually for informal organizations and more conservatively for the formal. You are not a member of the organization at the time of your interview but you should look as though you could fit in if hired.

Your Appearance. Popular writers and lecturers on how to conduct yourself during the interview often make it sound like all that matters is the way you dress and greet the interviewer. They make such strong statements as "You get the job within the first two minutes of the interview [some say it is a matter of seconds only] and it all depends on how you dress, how firmly you shake the interviewer's hand, and whether or not you look the interviewer right in the eye with a steady and sincere gaze." Such oversimplification of a communicative process as complex and important as the job interview is dangerous. Still, the point is worth making that a little preliminary study and analysis can help you dress and act in a way that smooths your chances to communicate effectively during the interview. Your appearance, at any rate, should not be a distraction for the interviewer.

Interviewer's Questions. Generally, interviewers come to have certain things they try to do in the conference and certain things they look for. Interviewers often look for answers to questions such as these: Have you had a pattern of success in school, in extracurricular activities, in the community, and in other organizations and clubs? Are you effective as a communicator in interpersonal relations? Are you flexible? Can you adapt and perform in unfamiliar settings? Is what you say and how you appear in line with what is on your resume? (The interviewee who lists on the resume membership in the debating club, then mumbles and cannot give clear answers to a number of questions will raise doubts in the interviewer's mind.)

Your Objectives. You should plan your objectives before the interview. What would be the most desirable outcome in your mind? The least desirable? The minimum acceptable outcome? Would pushing for the most desirable outcome force a decision that might bring about the least desirable? (If you want the job and you push the employer for an immediate decision, might that result in a negative decision? Would leaving the outcome for a second interview or for sometime in the future be more in your favor? We cannot stress too strongly how often job applicants have assured us after an interview that they *know* they did not do well and they will not be called back, only to tell us later, jubilantly, "I got the job!" Nervousness impairs judgment in tense situations. You also do not have the interviewer's perspective; you do not see the other interviews.)

Here are some questions to keep in mind as you plan the specific details of the interview:

What can I do to help create a comfortable social climate to aid in getting the information I need?

Do we have common ground that can serve as a topic for opening the conversation?

What should my overall tone be? Should I be serious, solemn, friendly, light-hearted?

What major points about my background, education, desires, hopes, ability and interest in working with people should I try to make?

What information about the job, working conditions, pay, fringe benefits, and so forth do I need to know?

If the interviewer asks me an open-ended question and gives me a chance to take over the order of topics, what are the points that I should try to make and how should I arrange them?

How is the interviewer likely to respond to my main objective for the meeting? What resistance can I anticipate?

A good way to plan the details of the interview is to try to put yourself in the interviewer's position. How will you appear to the interviewer? What will he or she be looking for? The interviewer will often try to find out how dependable you are. Will you show loyalty to the job or are you self-centered and looking out for yourself? Do you really want this particular job and, if so, why? Is an association between you and this organization likely to be good for both you and the organization? Sometimes the interviewer will ask you directly about these matters, but often he or she gets an impression which provides answers from the subtle nonverbal cues you exchange while talking with one another.

The interviewer will usually ask some questions that let you point out your strong points, but sometimes an interviewer will pose some tougher questions. How about: What is your greatest weakness? or, Can you tell me about an important mistake you made and what you learned from it? Thinking up some likely questions while you are imagining yourself in the interviewer's role and then thinking up some good answers is an excellent way to prepare in detail for your interview.

Here is a list of some questions which often come up in job interviews:

> Why did you apply for this position?
> What do you know about our organization?
> Why should we hire you?
> What are the most important rewards that you hope to gain from working with us?
> How has your college career helped prepare you for this position?
> Why did you pick your major field of study?
> What two or three things that you have done gave you the most satisfaction? Why?
> How would you describe your ideal job?
> Where would you like to be in terms of a career five years from now?
> What goals do you have for the next five years outside your job?
> Which of your previous jobs did you find most satisfying? Why? Which least? Why?
> How would you describe yourself?
> What kind of a working environment do you like?
> What kind of relationship would you prefer with a supervisor?
> What do you think are your greatest strengths?
> What is your greatest weakness?

If you are asked to discuss your greatest weakness, you should not only identify it but discuss steps you are taking to overcome it if possible. For example, you might say something like, "I have had some trouble with time management, particularly in my first term at college, and as a result I often had to scramble to get my work in on time. The last few terms I have set myself earlier deadlines and although I haven't always stuck to them I have not had an incomplete for two terms; giving myself more lead time has resulted in better work. If you notice on my transcript, my grades have improved steadily." The interviewer has weaknesses, too. Telling anyone you are perfect raises suspicions! On the other hand, the organization is not hiring you for your good; it is hiring you for its good—hopefully, for your mutual benefit. Do not belabor your weaknesses or problems either. Optimistic honesty looks good to most employers.

Directive, Non-directive. The interviewer may select one of two general strategies in conducting the interview. The first is a directive approach in which the interviewer takes control and asks the questions and decides when to start and stop discussion of each topic. The second is a non-directive approach in which the interviewer asks open-ended questions and allows you to take a more active part in deciding what is to be talked about and when. For most interviews, the employer will keep some balance between the directive and non-directive approaches. At some point, you can expect the employer to ask if you have any questions. Very likely you will have.

Details on Organization. You have every right to ask for information about the organization which will help you decide whether or not to join it, should you be offered the job. Do not ask for information which has been covered adequately in the company's written material for job applicants. But a more detailed explanation of the job itself, opportunities for growth or advancement, information about fringe benefits, are certainly justifiable areas for questions.

Nonverbal Communication. Be aware of your nonverbal communication as the interview proceeds. Such things as the shaking of the head, nodding, frowning, smiling, looking puzzled, exhibiting interest and enthusiam—all communicate a great deal about both particpants. The amount and nature of eye contact must be decided during the interview. The nonverbal aspects of the interview are as important as what you say to one another. If the interviewer is shuffling papers, gazing around the room, you may be off on the wrong tack. Be careful of talking too much. You have one job interview with this employer and it is vital to your interests. The interviewer may have a number of interviews during the week and because of the volume of such communication events each becomes more routine for the employer. Usually the interviewer will feel more pressed for time than you do. Often the interview will last for less than an hour. You can offset a generally good impression and twenty good minutes of an interview by talking too much at the end. Bring your part of the interview to a successful close by indicating again your interest in the job, asking about how to follow up, and thanking the interviewer for the opportunity to be considered.

Money Matters. Salary considerations are often touchy topics in job interviews in our culture. Since monetary matters are important not only in terms of subsistence but also in terms of reward and confirmation of our worth to an organization, the question of salary and fringe benefits becomes symbolically important. Touchy topics are usually put off until near the end of the interview. Salary is important and you have a right to a full discussion of such matters. You should raise the issue if the interviewer does not. Ask enough questions to get the information you need to make a wise decision. Payment can come in a number of ways including a straight salary, commissions, bonuses, medical benefits, company cars, expense accounts, opportunities to buy products or services at a discount, and so forth. You should not appear overly concerned about money but, on the other hand, the employer is undoubtedly concerned about it and will respect your need for information.

One additional consideration is this: interviewers vary in skill and experience. You may be more comfortable than the interviewer. This is rare, but it does happen, particularly if the interviewer, though capable in other duties in the organization, does little interviewing and approaches the session less prepared and knowledgeable about the process than you. If you feel such is the case, you can at least make an effort to ease the situation by relaxing yourself and including the necessary interchanges without appearing to "take over" the interview.

ASSIGNMENT: The Job Interview

Your instructor will (1) have you find job openings in your community in which you are interested and arrange for an interview, or (2) invite several personnel officers to your class to conduct simulated job interviews, or (3) divide the class into pairs and have you take turns being the employer and the applicant. If the assignment is a simulation during class time you will be recorded either on audiotape or videotape.

You will prepare a resume for the position and a cover letter. You will also write a brief paper evaluating the interview itself. In the case of the classroom simulations, you will use the recordings to aid you in the evaluations.

―――――――――――――**Theoretical Rationale**――――――――――――

The theoretical rationale relating to the job interview provides a perspective and some technical concepts about the communicative process and about the organization as a message processing system.

With a little time and effort you can usually get written material relating to such things as the mission, function, official identity, and formal structure of an organization. We begin this section with a description of the communicative process in task-oriented meetings and then examine the influence of the formal structure of the organization on communication.

THE ORGANIZATION AS A MESSAGE-PROCESSING SYSTEM

The modern organization is a message-processing system. A table of organization is an anatomical drawing that indicates the formal channel through which flow official and unofficial messages. Around the formal structure is an ever-changing and complicated network of informal communication channels. Through these veins flows the information that achieves a community of understanding to provide objectives, divide the work, develop morale, evaluate performance, and mobilize the resources of the organization. If the circulation of messages is good and the level of understanding high, the organization will be more effective.

Within the formal divisions, departments, projects, and units of an organization—whether it be governmental, commercial, industrial, scientific, educational, or religious—there are supervisors who must organize and divide the work for their people. These supervisors do not manhandle their subordinates and push them around. Supervision consists primarily of speaking and listening.

The smaller units within an organization are gathered together in larger clusters, and middle management divides the work of these larger units. The middle manager, too, must rely on speech-communication to do much of his job. Finally, all the parts of the organization must mesh together and upper management must organize the work of all and bring the resources of the total organization to bear upon the outside world. How well the organization meets the challenges posed by competition of similar groups and the pressures of other organizations is largely determined by the skill with which the total group handles information.

Every communication situation poses a challenge to those involved in it. Too often we face those challenges without thinking, relying on our habitual patterns of communication to help us muddle through. Yet, every organizational setting provides an opportunity for vital choices in deciding how best to achieve results from our communicating. The possibility of choice creates the opportunity for rational decisions, the development of skills and competence, and the conscious attainment of effectiveness. If we are to deal effectively with communication in the modern organization, we must understand the organizational structure that underlies it.

THE STRUCTURE OF THE MODERN ORGANIZATION

Modern organizations have certain similarities whether they are concerned with producing a product for profit, conducting government business, running a charitable enterprise, educating students, treating the ill, or defending a country. Every manager must see that objectives are set, work clarified, performance reviewed, and problems solved. The manager's problems and the skills he or she needs to meet them remain essentially the same, thus it is not surprising that a successful army general often becomes a successful corporation president or that a successful corporation president often becomes a productive official of the Federal government.

Formal Organizational Structure. What are the essential features that most organizations have in common? Organizations typically have a *formal* division of labor, authority, and responsibility; associated with the division of labor they have a *formal* division of status and prestige. Both sets of formal divisions are reflected in a hierarchical structure. That is, not only is the labor divided but some of the labor is formally judged to be more important to the organization, and hence is given a higher or more important place in the structure.

Figure 3 presents a typical anatomical diagram of the formal structure of an organization. Each block represents a *formal position* within the organization. The size and position of the block indicate its relative place in the hierarchy. The larger the block and the closer to the top of the diagram, the more important and influential the position, regardless of the abilities of the individual who might, at a given moment, be occupying it. Blocks of the same size located at the same level of the diagram are judged equal in prestige, status, and importance. The anatomy of a typical organization also includes a formal specification of the share of the labor, responsibilities, and authority assigned to each position.

The blocks in Figure 3 are connected with heavy black lines that indicate not only who works for whom but also who reports to whom, who gets directions and orders from whom; in short, these lines indicate the formal channels set up by the structure to guide the flow of messages. Typically, a person in a block at the third level (e.g., C) is not allowed by the formal structure to talk about official matters to the top person (A). Rather, person C is supposed to go "through channels" and transmit official messages through his or her immediate superior (B) to

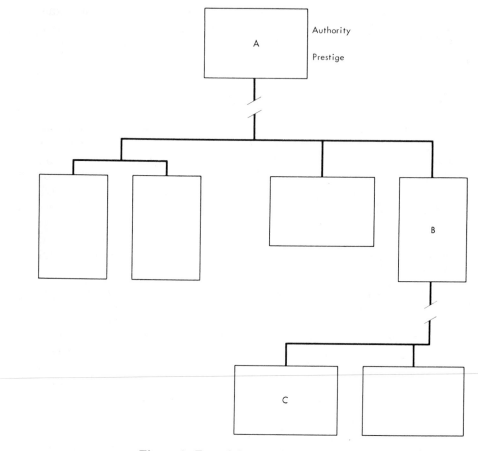

Figure 3. Formal Organizational Structure

upper management. Sending messages through channels assures that the individual at position B is informed of developments in the unit.

The Formal Position. What the organization expects from a given member and what that member can expect from the organization are spelled out in the formal position. Sometimes these precepts are written out and codified. The duties and responsibilities of the sales manager, for example, might be written up. For other members of the organiza= tion, particularly for new people on the production line, duties may be outlined by the supervisor in an interview. Because a member holds a *formal position* he knows what he is supposed to do. The status relationships of the various positions may be indicated in the table of organization as well. The production supervisor has a higher status position than the line supervisor. The line supervisor has a higher status than the workers on the production line.

One way to look at an effort to communicate is to think of it as an attempt to predict response. The formal structure of an organization provides information that can help an individual predict the response to a given bit of communication. If the communicator knows the formal structure of Invention Incorporated, she can infer some things about the responses inherent in each position, *regardless of who is filling the position at a given time.* Of course, to make a complete prediction she would need to know the informal roles of the members within the work groups. However, many members of the organization cannot know of the informal structure, and the formal organization then becomes indispensable as an aid to communication.

Each position in the table of organization has certain tasks associated with it. These may include such things as dividing up the work and making task assignments. The position may carry with it the selection of new members and the removal of old members—hiring and firing. Quite often the position carries with it certain sanctions—rewards and punishments—to aid in performing these duties. Typically there is a rigidity in the formal position. Some things the member occupying that position may do and some things he may not do. Whether he fails to do what he must do or does things he must not do, the organization will punish or remove him in either case, because he is not doing his job or has overstepped the bounds. The duties required by the formal position can be thought of as *responsibilities.* If these duties are not taken care of, the individual occupying the position will be called to an accounting.

Despite the rigidity of the clearly spelled-out responsibilities each position has a certain amount of inherent flexibility. The organization simply cannot list *all* of the "must do's" and the "must not do's," and so there are some "may do" and "may not do" opportunities. This flexibility explains the development of informal roles with the work groups. The natural tendency of every small group to have its members specialize and develop roles is given an opportunity to develop—somewhat restricted by the formal organization—because the responsibilities of each position cannot be completely specified. Organizations, of course, differ as to the amount of flexibility their formal structure will allow. Where the list of "must do's" and "must not do's" for each position is long and clearly specified, the development of informal role structures is hindered to a greater degree than in those organizations where duties are less clearly defined.

Associated with the duties and sanctions of each position is a certain amount of *authority.* If you know and understand the formal structure of the organization, you can predict the amount of *authority* any individual has by finding out what position the person fills. The authority goes with the position. If you know that you are talking to the president of the company or to the plant manager, you can estimate the authority of that individual no matter *who* the president happens to be or who holds the position of plant manager. The authority inherent in the position of sales manager remains the same, even though three people hold the position over a period of years.

Predicting Behavior on the Basis of the Formal Position. If you are to communicate with an individual within your own organization or within another organization and you know very little about the individual, you can often discover something about the basic organization. You should be alert to the cues that reflect status. In general you must be careful not to communicate, either verbally or nonverbally, that you feel the receiver has more authority than he does, in fact, have. The wise communicator, therefore, makes a careful estimate as to the authority inherent in the position before she begins to talk to the person holding that position. The vice-president who is called "president" or treated as though he were the president will be irritated. The infantry captain who is called "colonel" will soon grow angry. Members of organizations expect to be treated in a way commensurate with their position, but not as though they had more authority than they actually have. Perhaps treating people with too much deference makes them think the speaker is making fun of them. Perhaps they are reminded that they do not have as much authority, in fact, as they wish they had. At any rate, the wise communicator estimates the amount of authority in a given position and communicates with the person in that position with that in mind.

Even more dangerous for the success of the communication is the situation where the speaker gives the receiver of the message the impression that his or her actual authority is not recognized. The recruit who approaches his company commander and asks to see the major because he wants to talk to "somebody with some authority around here" soon learns this lesson on KP.

Formal Channels. The formal channels influence the nature of messages in several important ways. Organizations tend to specify the nature of the messages that flow through formal channels. They may even be routinized to such an extent that they are expected at a given time of the month or that they are to be presented on a standardized form. If they are speech-communication messages they may be expected on certain set occasions (department heads make oral reports in a monthly meeting with the plant manager), they may be restricted as to time (10 to 15 minutes), and they may be in a certain form (an oral presentation with slides, charts, etc., and a period for questions following). Messages sent through formal channels are often given greater consideration and more careful examination. They often take much longer to reach their destinations, and as they move from individual to individual up the levels they often experience the distortions common to messages handed on from one person to another. It is not uncommon for a person to wish that he might talk directly to someone several levels up the hierarchy rather than having to "work" through channels. Much of the so-called red tape and the delay that inhibits quick and decisive action in an organization stems from the cumbersome necessity of sending messages through formal channels.

Communication in a Hierarchy. Successful communication among equals is difficult enough, but when a formal status ladder is clearly established and emphasized the difficulty is increased. We need not write an essay on the sociology of status and the indications of status in organizations because the subject is by now hackneyed. It has been discussed in industrial magazines, satirized in motion pictures (the key to the executive washroom), and studied by industrial psychologists. The reader will have no trouble listing the status indicators in a given organization. Location of the office, rugs and other furnishings, number of secretaries, eating and washing privileges, and the proper dress—all may serve to point up differences in status. Silly as some of these practices may seem to the outsider, to the insider they are useful clues to the prestige and status of others. In large organizations where a person needs to deal with other members who are relative strangers such clues are helpful in structuring the communication.

Nonetheless, *speech-communication among people with different organizational status is inhibited by that difference.* Good communication among equals is often characterized by honesty, ease, consideration of all relevant information, and a high level of feedback. But when a supervisor has a conference with subordinates, honest, complete, easy communication with adequate feedback is difficult to achieve simply because one person has authority over others and because the supervisor is in a position to control their fate.

SUMMARY

The modern organization is a message-processing system. The table of organization indicates the public, planned formal channels of communication. If we are to deal effectively with the communication in a given organization we must understand the organizational structure that furnishes its formal channels of communication.

Organizations typically have a formal division of labor, authority, and responsibility. Often the formal structures are hierarchical. The structure is composed of formal positions connected by formal channels of communication. The structure provides information that can help an individual predict the response to messages.

Each position has certain tasks associated with it. The duties required by the formal position are called responsibilities. Associated with the responsibilities of each position is a certain amount of authority.

In examining the formal positions you should be alert to indicators of status. Be careful not to communicate either verbally or nonverbally that you feel the other person has either more or less formal status than is the case. Members of organizations expect to be talked to in ways commensurate with their positions.

The formal channels influence the nature of messages in terms of specifying such things as their nature, their timing, and their form and content. Formal messages are often given more careful consideration than informal ones and generally take longer to reach their destinations.

Successful communication among equals is difficult enough but formal status differences add still more problems. When there is a difference in the formal status of the positions held by two people they often have difficulty communicating in an honest easy way with adequate give-and-take to achieve understanding because one of them is in the position to control the fate of the other.

QUESTIONS FOR DISCUSSION AND REVIEW

1. What are some of the things you can do to help analyze your goals and skills in order to help decide on a career?
2. How can you best go about finding suitable job openings?
3. What basic information should go into a good job resume?
4. What major points should you keep in mind in planning for a job interview?
5. What should you look for when making a visit to an organization prior to the job interview?
6. Explain how the organization can be considered as a message-processing system.
7. What are the essential features of a formal position?
8. How can knowledge of the formal position help in communicating with the person who holds that position?
9. How do formal channels relate to the nature of organizational communication?
10. How does formal status influence communication within the organization?

REFERENCES AND SUGGESTED READINGS

Blau, P. M. and W. R. Scott. *Formal Organizations*. San Francisco: Chandler Publishing, 1962.

Etzioni, A. *Modern Organizations*. Englewood Cliffs, N.J.: Prentice-Hall, 1964.

Goldhaber, G. M. *Organizational Communication,* 2nd. ed. Dubuque, Iowa: Wm. C. Brown, 1979.

Katz, D. and R. Kahn. *The Social Psychology of Organizations*. New York: Wiley, 1966.

March, J. G. and H. A. Simon. *Organizations*. New York: Wiley, 1958.

2

Learning About Human Relationships

———————————— **Laboratory Application** ————————————

THE INFORMAL CONVERSATION

When you join the ongoing organization as a new member you find yourself on unfamiliar ground. No matter how well you analyzed the organization in preparation for your job interview and no matter how thoroughly you understand the formal map (table of organization) of the territory, nonetheless, once you start to work you come face-to-face with the people whose actions and talk define the social reality of the organization.

People quite often act in ways you would not expect, given their formal positions. The supervisor may not act like a supervisor. A secretary may talk less like your stereotype of a secretary and more like your notion of how a supervisor communicates. You notice that some people greet each other warmly in the morning and drift off for coffee together. You notice that other people only nod to each other coolly. You may try to strike up a conversation with a fellow worker and get little response. You may hear a ruckus down the hall and discover that someone is speaking in a loud and apparently angry voice and everyone around you gets very tense.

You may feel uneasy during your first few days in a new job because you do not know the informal procedures that the old-timers use in doing things. You do not know the people who like each other and those who dislike each other. You do not know the stories from the past that

21

many of the people who have been working in the organization for a longer period of time know. These stories relate to which members of the group are hoping for promotion and therefore feuding or which members are sexually involved with each other or which members have had long-standing conflicts or allegiances. Until you get a reading on interpersonal relationships among your fellow workers you feel unsure about how to react during the conversations that take place as you go about your job.

You do not know about other sorts of relationships such as power, influence, dominance, and political connections. Who, in fact, can get things done? If you need help to do your job you may discover that the person you expect should give you help (according to the table of organization) is not able to do so but that someone else can smooth the way and get results with a single telephone call.

You learn about the informal organizing behavior largely by observing the communication patterns and content and by participating in informal conversations that are only partly devoted to the work of your group. You pass the time of day with a fellow employee and find you have some similar interests and feel attracted to that person; you overhear a conversation between two people in your work group and find they have some interests that are strange to you and you are fascinated to learn more about their activities with, say, a hang-gliding club. Perhaps you ask a question about a task and soon you are involved in a three-way conversation which veers off into interests and activities unrelated to your work.

ASSIGNMENT: Getting Acquainted

Your instructor will (1) have you find a stranger and strike up an informal conversation with the person in another class or on the job or at a social event or (2) divide the class into pairs and have each pair go out for coffee or a Coke and spend an hour getting acquainted.

You will write a paper in which you discuss the conversation in terms of getting to know one another, developing interpersonal trust, self-disclosure, and openness.

──────────────── **Theoretical Rationale** ────────────────

The theoretical rationale that relates to learning to get acquainted with the people of the organization provides a perspective and some technical concepts about interpersonal or relationship communication and about the informal and dynamic communication system that evolves as people go about trying to work cooperatively for common goals.

RELATIONSHIP COMMUNICATION

Every time you communicate with other people, the personal relationships that are being created or have been established play an important part in what happens. If on your first day at the job the supervisor explains your duties and takes you around to show the job layout you will come to form a personal relationship of some sort during the tour. You may think the supervisor is likeable, warm, open, physically attractive or cold, distant, and unattractive. During the course of the talk you may feel a spark of mutual acceptance and respect or begin to have an uneasy stomach at the thought of working with this person.

When we have a good personal relationship with another person we can usually talk more openly, express our feelings without fear of the consequences, and reveal some of our important hopes and interests because we come to trust that person. Good personal relationships make for better task-oriented communication in that the participants can express disagreements, confront conflicts, and hammer out decisions.

Much of the communication in an organization is clearly task-oriented. We attend a meeting called to deal with a crisis in the production department. We are asked to meet with our supervisor to find out about our next assignment. We are having difficulty completing a job and we call people in two other divisions of the organization to try to clear roadblocks and obtain needed resources. Although the emphasis is upon business-like communication, *the personal relationships are always there,* perhaps under the surface, but nonetheless affecting the quality of the communication.

Oftentimes in task-oriented conferences the relationship dimension is communicated nonverbally. While the words being spoken deal almost exclusively with the business at hand, the vocal intonations, gestures, eye movements and so forth may be commenting about what the people involved think of one another and how they are relating to each other.

Not every conversation in your new work setting is task-oriented, of course. Much of the informal and passing-the-time-of-day talk is social and emphasizes getting acquainted with your fellow workers and establishing personal relationships with them.

Good relationship communication is characterized by a lack of defensiveness (the participants do not have to feel continually on guard), an openness on the part of the people involved (they have learned they can be candid), and the development of a feeling of mutual trust (no one is going to use their openness then or later to hurt them).

The term *disclosure* has always had the meaning that what is being said is important information. In terms of interpersonal or relationship communication, the term self-disclosure has come to mean the important reciprocal function of revealing information about one's self so that one person can become known to another. In terms of learning about human relationships in the organization, two types of disclosure messages are important. The first is self-disclosure, by which the people involved grow to know and trust one another gradually. The second is organizational-disclosure, by which a newcomer is slowly brought into the social reality of the organization as he or she is told about the inner workings, the informal ways of proceeding, the stories, the legends, the folk tales which make up the organizational oral history.

Self-disclosure is an important part of relationship communication. Some of the typical stock get-acquainted questions include:

> Where are you from?
> Do you know Jimmy Jones? He lives there.
> Where did you go to school?

Questions such as these are essentially attempts to get other persons to reveal something about themselves, although such self-disclosure is at a relatively superficial and nonthreatening level.

We find it difficult to get to know people who are close-mouthed about themselves and who do not reveal much about their personal lives, interests, hobbies, troubles and triumphs.

As time goes on we may speak with the other person and test our growing relationship by more significant self-disclosure to see how the person responds. If he in turn reveals more of himself and uses the information that we have risked telling him in a responsible and supportive way, we begin to develop trust in him. As self-disclosure proceeds, a reciprocal cycle of greater trust, more willingness to take risk, further supportive communication, and even greater trust may develop. Of course we all have many opportunities to develop deep personal relationships in our lives other than those we establish in our job-related organization. We may, indeed, prefer not to establish close relationships on the job. Such a right to privacy on the job is very important and we can often work cooperatively with others without long deep conversations about our personal lives. Still, the odds are that you will develop closer relationships with some of your fellow workers than with others and it is from these people that you will learn more of the inside story of what has happened and what is going on in the organization.

When you have established a trusting relationship with a fellow worker so that person begins to tell you important information about the informal structure of the organization, you begin to join the organization symbolically as well as formally. You start to share a common past, common heroes and villains, and common organizational values. Frequently insiders are secretive about matters relating to past feuds, actual power bases, emergent as opposed to formal leadership, sexual liaisons, jurisdictional disputes, and in-jokes.

Information about the informal dynamic of the organization is power. People who have it can get things done and avoid getting sidetracked. They often do not want to share such information with others, particularly outsiders. "We should not wash our dirty linen in public," is an old saying which makes the point. The organization's members often feel that if the public "really knew what was going on around here, it would be bad for the organization," and perhaps embarrassing. You are a newcomer, still unknown, untried; you might make the information public. The insiders will have to test you and decide they can trust you before they will disclose the inner workings of the organization.

Insiders may also feel that a newcomer should go through a period of hazing. College fraternities used to have a formal period of hazing for new pledges which lasted for several months and peaked with a "hell week" of intensive harassment. Hell week served largely to test how much the pledge wanted to become a full member. It probably also helped increase the commitment of those who succeeded and the overall cohesiveness of the organization.

Instead of hazing, as a newcomer to the organization you will more likely be treated with a hands-off policy, which allows you to break the organization's rules and norms without receiving any coaching about what they are and how to deal with them. Usually you make mistakes that are embarrassing, though not of lasting significance.

When people in the organization fail to disclose either organizational or personal matters of consequence, the hidden material can cause communication problems. Sometimes people really want to talk about something but because of fear, tension, worry about saving face, and so forth they do not do so. We call these undisclosed items which are important to the communication the *hidden agenda* of the meeting.

Hidden Agenda. In most discussions the participants acknowledge the purpose of the interchange and talk about topics openly. A superior may call a subordinate into his office for a brief talk about scheduling the subordinate's vacation. In all such situations at least one and perhaps more topics of concern to the participants are not discussed directly but nonetheless play an important part. The topics of concern that are not openly discussed constitute a *hidden agenda*.

In every situation one important hidden agenda item relates to the establishment, protection, and enhancement of each individual's self-image. Whenever a party to the communication feels his desired image of himself is threatened, the climate is conducive to disruptive disagreement. Figure 4 depicts the typical situation. While two people ostensibly talk over a common problem, they are simultaneously projecting and protecting their desired image. In an important way we all have potentially split personalities when we talk to others. Each of us is divided at least four ways, and thus in every interpersonal communication eight personalities are interacting.

You have a private image of yourself. Sometimes people develop defenses to insulate themselves from the kind of person they really are. The old Greek saying that was said to be the key to all knowledge was, Know thyself! The imperative wisely reflects that so often human beings blind themselves to what they really are.

A second important image is the picture a person would like others to have. Many relationships in everyday life have probably made the reader aware that a desire to project a favorable image is inherent in all of us.

A third estimate of self comes from a person's impression of how the other individual in the communication situation sees him. An influential school of sociologists finds the estimate of others such an important factor in the development of roles in society that they call the general impression a person has of how other people view him the *generalized other*. They would explain much social behavior on the basis that an individual develops a realistic impression of himself from the communication, verbal and nonverbal, that he gets from other people.

Finally, the other person's actual estimate of an individual is one of the social realities of every communication situation. Quite often the transformers within the other person distort reality, and her image of the first individual is not much more accurate than his private image of himself.

On rare occasions the various pictures that the participants have

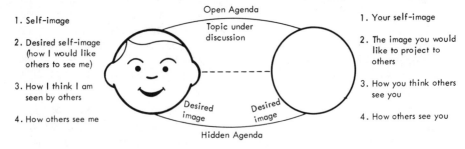

Figure 4. Images of Self That Act as Variables in Communication

about an individual, for example the speaker, may be in substantial agreement. That is, in these instances, the speaker's image of himself, his desired image, how he thinks the listener sees him, and how the listener, in fact, does see him are much the same. Under these ideal conditions disruptive disagreements are minimized. Quite often, however, the pictures do not match. When discrepancies occur disruptive disagreements often follow.

Discrepancies Between Self-Image and Desired Image. A person with a low opinion of himself may still want others to have a high opinion of him. Such a person will be insecure in the organizational setting. Take the case of Henry Wolfson at Information Systems. Henry rose so rapidly to a managerial position that he *never proved his ability to himself.* His self-image therefore did not include the ability to do the important job of managing the procurement and personnel division. Yet Henry enjoyed the rewards that the position gave him. He wanted to keep his job. Therefore, he wanted others to see him as an efficient and capable manager. He lived in dread that any moment might bring the fact of his incompetence to the attention of both his subordinates and his superiors.

A person who thinks she is not respected as she would like to be is likely to respond with hostility. The person who wants to be seen as an authority and instead is viewed by and treated by her associates as an equal often becomes antagonistic and hostile.

Discrepancies Between Desired Image and Public Image. Another type of communication problem stems from differences between the image a person wishes to project and the one his listeners actually have of him. Take the case of the supervisor who is seen by her subordinates as an authoritative expert with all the answers. She decides many of her administrative problems stem from her public image. She would like to be seen as a coordinator and equal. When she begins to communicate to her subordinates in ways intended to change her public image *they* can become insecure.

Many subordinates like to look to the boss as the woman with the answers. Particularly when a necessary decision is unpopular, unpleasant, and painful, individuals are relieved if they can avoid the responsibility. Many religious leaders today are trying to get the members of their congregations to assume responsibility for church activities. However, many of the church members typically feel uncomfortable and insecure in assuming responsibilities formerly delegated to leaders.

Messages that ask for action that threatens the desired image also tend to cause disagreements. For example, a conscientious mother attended a meeting for parents of children about to enter kindergarten. She returned home full of enthusiasm and information that she wished to share with her five-year-old son. Communication with her boy, however, did not go as she planned; the child was apparently uninterested in kindergarten. He tried to change the subject and, obviously uncomfortable, became very fidgety. His lack of interest irritated his mother; she interpreted his response as an attack on her self-image as a good mother. As the argument between mother and son got under way, a third person asked, "Jeffrey, are you a little afraid of going to school?" That simple question released a veritable fountain of communication.

Jeffrey was afraid of the challenge and responsibility facing him. School was six blocks away. Could he find it? It was a long walk; would he arrive on time or would he be punished for being late? Would he have any friends at kindergarten? Jeff viewed his mother's messages as an attack on the maintenance of his self-image. The action she was calling for was very threatening, and the threat was so strong that their conversation was disrupted.

Types of Messages That Attack the Self-Image. Jack Gibb reports the results of research indicating that six specific message-perceptions often cause defensive reactions. These are messages that are interpreted as: (1) the speaker making an evaluation of the listener as a person rather than of his or her performance; (2) the speaker attempting to exert control over the listener; (3) the speaker attempting to use strategy on the listener; (4) the speaker being disinterested in the listener; (5) the speaker feeling superior to the listener; and (6) the speaker being dogmatic and arbitrary.

On occasion the above perceptions might not result in the listener becoming defensive. For example, a person may not react negatively to an evaluation of himself if he feels it is presented from a point of view of equality rather than superiority, and if it seems to concentrate on a problem rather than on the speaker's control of the listener. Generally speaking, however, messages interpreted in any of Gibb's six categories produce defensive reactions and thus often lead to disruptive disagreements.

The best general solution to the problem of interpersonal clash is to acknowledge it and try to redirect the communication to the open agenda items. Very often the "rational" problems cannot be solved until the personal differences are openly acknowledged, discussed, and accepted, eliminated, or compromised.

THE INFORMAL COMMUNICATION SYSTEM

As you get acquainted with people in the organization and they begin to tell you about how things are done and what kind of a place it is you can speed up your understanding by looking out for the informal organizational structure and the informal communication system.

The Human Factor. When one studies the diagram of the structure of an institution he or she learns something about its operation and about the communication patterns that accompany its function. Yet it is one thing to study the anatomy of the heart, and another to study a given individual and discover the way *his* heart functions, for it must be considered that he will have a unique history and hereditary background. Variables such as age, as well as the health, activity, and condition of other organs, will affect the functioning of the heart. Similarly, when an organization's formal structure is activated by a given complement of people, a new dimension is evident.

Figure 5 shows the addition of the human element. When individuals are placed within the formal positions, they begin to exercise their authority and thereby exert *power*. *Power* is the effective use of authority. Theoretically the allocation of authority in the formal

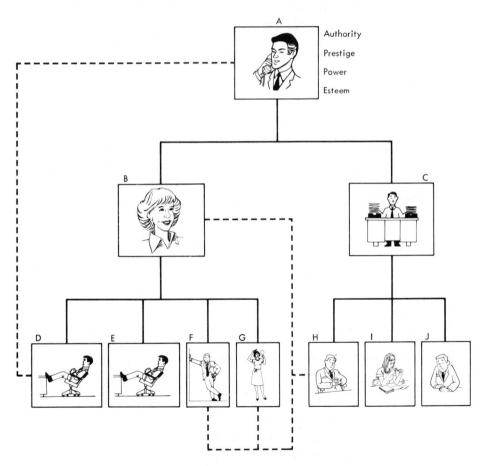

Figure 5. Formal Organizational Structure Modified by Characteristics of the Personnel

structure divides the power as well, but actually it is the interaction and communication of given individuals with certain amounts of assigned authority that determines how power is divided. Conceivably, a person in position B may have more or less power than she has authority.

Esteem is also associated with persons. Prestige is influenced by location in the formal structure, but esteem is earned by the person who occupies a formal position. Again it is possible that a person in block B may have more or less esteem than she has prestige and status.

Figure 5 also indicates by the dotted lines that when the static structure of an organization is set in motion with a given complement of workers and managers, informal channels of communication develop. These channels may stem from a host of factors, such as previous acquaintance, familial ties, common hobbies and interests, shared irritations, sexual attraction, and congenial temperaments. If the individual in position D is the son-in-law of the member in block A, an important informal communication channel between the two may be established. If the persons in blocks B, F, G, and H frequently take coffee breaks together, they may establish another informal communication network.

Gatekeepers. Figure 6 adds an important factor to the communication channels, in this instance, a formal position called *administrative assistant.* This person's duties include the sifting of messages for individuals in positions A, B, and C. The *administrative assistant* position shows how some people can act as valves turning off or on the flow of messages through the formal channels. Almost any person may do somewhat the same with the messages that flow through the informal networks, although some may be more adept and more highly motivated to ferret out rumors and information and thus play the informal role of gatekeepers. Other formal positions may afford a good opportunity to facilitate or impede communication, but few offer more such opportunities than does the position of assistant. The assistant may open the boss's mail and decide which letters need immediate attention. She may also control the supervisor's appointment schedule and thus determine who gets in to talk to her. She may filter the telephone messages. Informally she is in an excellent position to establish lines of communication. If she has lunch with other gatekeepers in the organization, they can keep each other posted on what is going on.

A good deal of research has investigated the relationship between the flow of communication and the growth of influence in small laboratory groups. One of the implications of research into communication networks is that the individual who receives and controls communication grows in importance and influence in the group. Thus, if an artificial network is established as in Figure 7 so that all members

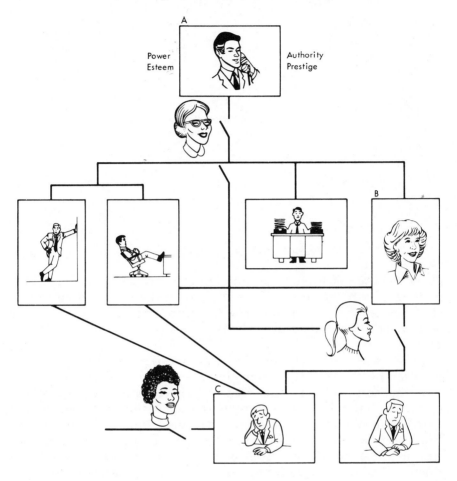

Figure 6. Gatekeepers and Informal Channels of Communication

can talk to A, and A can talk to all members, but no one else in the group can talk to anyone else, A soon becomes a key person. To some extent the gatekeeper in an organizational communication network experiences a similar increase in influence. The oft-noted instance where the "old man's secretary really runs things around here" illustrates the phenomenon.

The Grapevine. The *grapevine telegraph* has come to mean a person-to-person method of conveying information, often secret, which cannot be gained from formal channels. The term may have originated in the Civil War when intelligence telegraph lines were strung from tree to tree like grapevines. Often today we drop the term *telegraph* and simply refer to the *grapevine* as the source of informal information

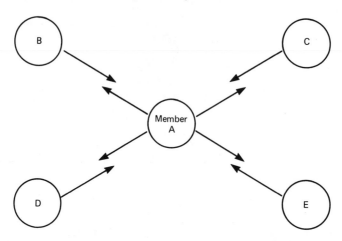

Figure 7. Restricted Communication Net

about the organization. Often the information relates to important matters of concern to employees that they cannot get from formal channels. As you get acquainted with the informal dimension of your organization, it is a good idea to be alert for ways to get connected to the grapevine.

The small world problem. Scholars investigating the small world problem want to know: how many links would it take to connect you to any other citizen of the United States? To investigate such a question I might give a number of randomly chosen people the assignment to find a certain person such as a marathon runner named Pfister in San Francisco. Each subject is directed to try to contact an acquaintance who might either know Pfister or know someone who would know Pfister. Thus from acquaintance to acquaintance, the messages would go along until, for those subjects who succeed, the final link would connect with the target, Pfister. The research question might be, how many links are required for those subjects who succeed?

The small world problem might be focused more narrowly and become the small organization problem in terms of how many links would it take to connect you by person-to-person communication with any other member of the organization.

In general, the small world problem turns up a smaller number of links than you might at first think in terms of connecting you to other people in the country. The number of links within a small or medium-sized organization might be quite small indeed.

A number of investigators have studied the grapevine in organization contexts and, although a dictionary definition of the grapevine telegraph often includes the notion that the messages are unauthenticated and rumors, the research results indicate that the grapevine is

often accurate. They have discovered accuracy rates as high as 80 to 90 percent. Goldhaber did a study which found that employees in sixteen organizations got more information than they wanted from the grapevine and that they evaluated the grapevine as often-used, fast, but not accurate. He concluded that the perception of inaccuracy might come from the fact that when the grapevine was wrong, it was sometimes dramatically wrong about very important information.

The grapevine is, indeed, a rapid method for transmitting information. The grapevine may spread messages through your organization within a matter of hours whereas the same message travelling through formal channels might take days or weeks before it reached you in official form.

Information magnets. Some people become information magnets within the grapevine. You can think of them as telegraph operators within the grapevine telegraph. They are interested in rumors, gossip, official developments, and personal affairs of others. They seek out such information and actively send messages along the line. They often have locations where they set up their information exchanges. Perhaps they go for coffee break to the same table in the cafeteria or stop by the same bar every evening after work. They may have a desk in line with considerable office traffic or stand in their office doorway or in other ways indicate nonverbally a willingness to break off working in order to socialize and have a conversation. They develop regular "customers" for information who drop by every day at approximately the same time to "pass the time of day" and, incidentally, report any information they have picked up in exchange for the latest messages from the grapevine.

People who serve the function of information magnets gain power because of their possession of information even though their formal organizational positions may not indicate such power. They also do much to set the tone for the social dimension of the organization's life.

As you seek to know and understand the informal communication and organizing behavior that characterizes your organization, you might try to identify the people who are information magnets ("Ask Eddie; *he'll* know") and become acquainted with them in order to plug into the grapevine telegraph.

SUMMARY

Personal relationships play an important role in organizational communication. People who have good personal relationships with one another talk openly, express feelings, and disclose their important hopes and interests. Such open talk builds trust and makes for better task-oriented communication.

The topics of concern that are not openly discussed in a communication

episode constitute the *hidden agenda.* In almost every situation one hidden agenda item relates to the establishment, protection, and enhancement of the participants' self-images.

Messages that attack the self-image tend to result in defensive communication. Often the best solution to the problem of interpersonal conflict is to acknowledge it and try to work it through. Task-oriented problems can seldom be solved until personal relationships are satisfactory.

The informal structure plays an important part in the organization's communication system. When individuals are placed in formal positions they begin to exercise their *authority.* How successful they are in exercising this authority depends on how others respond to their efforts. *Power* is the effective use of authority. *Prestige,* like authority, is associated with the position no matter who holds it; while *esteem,* like power, must be earned by the person who holds the position.

Gatekeepers can act as valves turning off or on the flow of messages through formal channels. Informal gatekeepers do the same for informal networks. One of the implications of the research in communication networks is that the individual who receives and controls communication grows in influence in the group.

The *grapevine* is a person-to-person method of conveying information which cannot be gained through formal channels. The grapevine transmits information rapidly and—usually—accurately. Some people become *information magnets* within the grapevine and, as a result, are more influential than one would expect from their formal position. Their communication also helps set the tone for the social dimension of the organization's life.

QUESTIONS FOR DISCUSSION AND REVIEW

1. What is the nature of good relationship communication?
2. What is meant by *self-disclosure* and how does it influence relationship communication?
3. What is interpersonal trust and how can it be developed?
4. What is the hidden agenda and how does it relate to interpersonal communication?
5. What is a person's self-image and how does it relate to interpersonal communication?
6. What are some typical messages which attack the self-image?
7. How do the concepts of power and esteem relate to the informal communication system of an organization?
8. What are communication gatekeepers and how do they influence the communication flow?
9. What is the organizational grapevine and what are its typical characteristics?
10. What are information magnets and how do they influence the informal communication grapevine?

REFERENCES AND SUGGESTED READINGS

Bormann, E. G. and N. C. Bormann. *Speech Communication: A Basic Approach,* 3rd ed. New York: Harper and Row, 1981.

Gibb, J. "Defensive Communication," *Journal of Communication.* 11 (1961), 141–48.

Goldhaber, G. M. *Organizational Communication,* 2nd ed. Dubuque, Iowa: Wm. C. Brown, 1979.

Jourard, S. *The Transparent Self,* 2nd ed. New York: Van Nostrand Reinhold, 1971.

Leavitt, H. *Managerial Psychology,* 3rd. ed. Chicago: University of Chicago Press, 1972.

Rosenblatt, S. B., T. R. Cheatham, and J. T. Watt. *Communication in Business.* Englewood Cliffs, N.J.: Prentice-Hall, 1977.

Weaver, R. L., II. *Understanding Interpersonal Communication.* Glenview, Illinois: Scott, Foresman, 1978.

3

Using the Information Systems

―――――――――――――― **Laboratory Application** ――――――――――――――

THE TWO-PERSON BUSINESS CONFERENCE

Much of the actual organizing that goes on in an organization takes place in direct face-to-face communication where the people concerned with doing the work discuss how best to do it.

From the first day you join the organization you will be talking with others about what you are to do and how you are to do it. Since you are new on the job you will often have to ask about details of your work, about where you can get supplies, and about all sorts of other things you need to know to complete tasks. As you go about your work, unexpected things will happen and you will have to make spur-of-the-minute checks directly and often face-to-face with someone who can help you solve problems or make decisions.

Those two-person business conferences may be spontaneous and informal. Something suddenly goes wrong with a piece of equipment and you have to find someone to help. You may have to interrupt another conversation or disturb a fellow worker who is doing another task in order to get the information you need to deal with the faulty equipment. Your work group may be planning a new procedure or a new project. If you see one of the group in the hall, she may ask you about some detail, or you may seek information or resource material informally as you wait in the cafeteria line.

Often your task-oriented conferences are more carefully scheduled and organized. Supervisors and middle and upper managers are often confronted with communication overload; many people want to check with them or get their approval for various projects. Supervisors often manage their time by using a schedule which cues up the people who wish to speak to them. (The cueing may not be an actual line in the waiting room outside the office but nonetheless you have to make an appointment with the manager that allows you, say, fifteen minutes for your conference a week from Tuesday.) Under such circumstances you know when you will get your conference and you often will want to plan ahead to make the best use you can of your chance to talk to the person directly.

Since two-person business discussions resemble the informal social conversations we analyzed in Chapter 2, many people feel they can deal with them in the same spontaneous way. Far too often they strike up a business conversation at a poor time and in a poor place. Just because you see someone you have been meaning to talk to is no reason to assume you can make life easier by plunging into a discussion of business matters. The "as long as you are here there is something I have been meaning to talk to you about" approach to business conferences often leads to hasty agreements and sometimes to irritation on the part of the person you trap in such a fashion. You should be particularly careful about broaching such subjects with managers who have higher organizational status than you do. If you keep finding yourself in conversations with supervisory personnel which end with the supervisor saying, "I tell you what—call my secretary and make an appointment and we will go into this in detail next week," they are signalling that the time or place you have chosen to discuss business is inappropriate.

In planning discussions about matters relating to your job you should consider finding a suitable place and time and plan how you will conduct the meeting. Even though you wish to talk to a supervisor, you can still often decide where you will try to have the conversation. You may want to hold the conference outside the organizational environment in order to relax the formal communication boundaries and reduce the effect of status differences on communication. Our point above was that you should make such a decision only after careful consideration and then assure that the place is one that the other person will find satisfactory. Timing is equally important. Often people have difficulty fitting conferences into their schedules. Showing consideration for such time problems may put the other person in a better mood for the discussion. Finally, you should think through how you plan to conduct your part of the conference.

HOW TO PLAN PERSON-TO-PERSON COMMUNICATION

The person planning any significant communication should use the following checklist of questions to guide his preparation.

1. What do I wish to accomplish as a result of this communication? (More specifically, what response do I want the other persons to make as a result of the messages that I send them?)
2. Do the others have the ability, the motivation, and power (not just authority) to make the responses that I desire?
3. Am I the best person to help these people make the desired response? Are my relationships with them such that it might be better to turn to a third party to implement the communication? (One of the well documented results of communication research is that the very same message will get a different response if it is attributed to varied sources. Thus, the same message attributed to the receptionist, the sales manager, or the plant manager will have a different impact.)
4. What resistance might there be because of the listeners' interests, needs, and so forth? Will response be influenced by the receivers' physical condition? Emotional condition? What do I know about their knowledge, past experiences, goals, and values? (Whenever we communicate we make some important guesses. We hypothesize that our objective is possible. We predict that our message is such that it will accomplish the objective. We predict that our choice of inputs and channels is optimum.)

ASSIGNMENT: The Task-Oriented Conference

Your instructor will divide the class into pairs and have you take turns first being the employee discussing a job related matter with a supervisor and then being the supervisor. The focus is on the employee as planning and conducting the conference. You will either (1) role play the conference in front of the class with class discussion and evaluation of the employee's communication or (2) role play the conference at a scheduled out-of-class time for audio or video recording. In either case your instructor may ask you to write a brief paper evaluating the level of information transmission and evaluation.

──────────────── **Theoretical Rationale** ────────────────

The theoretical rationale relating to the task-oriented business conference provides a perspective and a model of effective message communication. It also includes an analysis of individual psychological processes which need to be coordinated in order to increase understanding.

THE PROCESS OF SPEECH-COMMUNICATION

Most of us think of talking to another human being as an elementary, mechanical operation. We put an idea into vocalized words; the other person picks up the message and is thereby informed. Visualizing the sending and receiving of spoken messages in this fashion seems sensible but amounts to a drastic and deceptive oversimplification. The necessary further dimensions of the act of spoken communication can be seen in a model that represents *purposeful* use of speech from the point of view of the person with the message, the speaker. We wish to make clear that this is a PRESCRIPTIVE model, one that suggests what ought to be planned and implemented for optimum results. While the model is source-oriented, it may be said to be receiver-centered.

First let us look at the parts of our model in Figure 8 and their relations to each other. In the left margin are the three physical components involved in an act of communication, the SOURCE (speaker), the CHANNEL (speaking directly to the listeners with or without eye contact, public address system, telephone, radio, TV, and so forth), and the RECEIVER (the individual or group that is to hear the message and whose behavior or attitude is to be modified).

The Source. The direction of the solid arrows indicates both time sequence and the direction of development and movement of the message. Events in the "universe of ever-changing things, events, and people" bring to the conscious mind of the communicator a need to communicate. Changing conditions produce events that create the desire to share goals and action. The source begins the process of communicating by identifying an INTENT in the form of a statement of what he wishes to accomplish by the message. This purpose is as definite as he can make it, considering the situation, the person or persons who will receive it, and their attitudes, knowledge, and

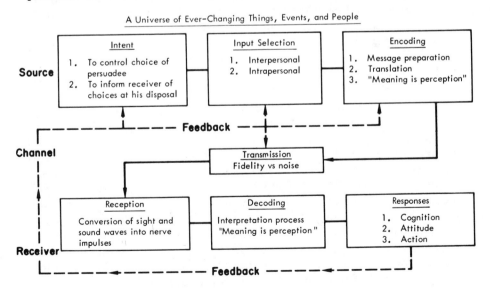

Figure 8. Model of the Communication Process

capabilities. If he wishes to produce an action response, his INTENT can be stated specifically in terms of what he wants them to do.

Input Selection. Once her purpose is clear, the speaker plans the "inputs" for her message. She must make at least two strategy decisions: how she will transmit her message by light, sound, or electronic waves or telephone lines to her listener, and how her message will be conveyed from the ear and eye of the receiver to the audience member's centers of response and understanding. The first elements of input we will call *interpersonal.* The second series is *intrapersonal.* Interpersonally, a message source will choose among media. She may prefer to talk face-to-face, or use the telephone, or she may decide that this message can be best transmitted by radio, intercom system, or open- or closed-circuit television. She may go through formal channels or she may choose informal communication networks. If she decides to use a two-person or small group situation, she must decide how formal her structure of interpersonal interaction should be. For example, should she call a meeting in the board room or arrange a golf game? With telephone or intercom, should she plan to talk with the individuals separately or use a conference call?

Intrapersonally, she should make a choice that is not as obvious but is equally real and, perhaps, even more important. Human beings can be reached with messages that produce response through their critical faculties or via their conditioned responses (habits). In a present instance, does the speaker prefer to have her receivers deliberate about the facts of the case, about her recommendations, or would she consider it more effective to bypass critical responses to a large degree and settle for more automated, routine reactions?

Encoding. Never forgetting the unique individuals to whom she will speak, and being guided by her INTENT and choice of interpersonal and intrapersonal CONTEXT, the speaker ENCODES her message. She plans the main and supporting points she will make, the facts and illustrations she will use, and the language that will be most meaningful to her listeners. She adjusts to time limitations. Ordinarily, all encoding is tentative, amounting to a list of possibilities that the speaker can draw upon and rearrange during transmission. Only in the exceptional case does she write out the complete message, for she recognizes the rigidity a script imposes upon communications, as well as her own inability to predict how well her listeners will understand her and how soon they will be ready to advance from point to point.

The "person with the message" is guided by two utilitarian concepts: the notion that she is *translating,* and the realization that whatever she wishes to send to another person is limited by the most basic principle of communication, *meaning is perception.* Because her listener attaches his or her own meanings to words of the source, the sender must translate what she would communicate into what the receiver knows or is interested in. This is often as significant a change in the message as putting it into Chinese. And when her message is decoded, all results depend upon what the listener perceives, the meaning he or she thinks is there, no matter what the source intended. Thus selection of language and content in encoding are shaped largely by considerations of translation into terms the receiver is likely to interpret in predictable perceptions.

Transmission. The message becomes an event during TRANSMISSION. Sounds and visual stimuli are emitted by the speaker, and via selected channels either or both are conveyed to the receiver(s). The speaker's main concern is with "high fidelity" TRANSMISSION. If the speaker talks so softly that the listener cannot hear her clearly, the receiver may misunderstand the message. Obviously, to the extent that fidelity is inadequate, communication fails.

A major problem in TRANSMISSION is noise. *Noise* is any physical or psychological distraction at the time of transmission that reduces the ability of the receiver to get the message. Speakers should assign a high priority to the control or elimination of *noise*.

The Receiver. The RECEIVER includes three discrete functions of message reception. Each function poses a different problem for the communicator. RECEPTION is satisfactory when a faithful copy of the message enters the nervous system of the listener. (If a source says "Wash out the lazy workers," and the receiver hears "Watch out for the daisy workers" the reception is poor.) RECEPTION depends upon the availability of above-threshold, high fidelity sights and sounds, plus properly functioning eyes and ears, plus the attention of the receiver on the message.

DECODING takes place in the brain of the receiver. Nervous impulses trigger habit and thinking activities necessary to the creation of meaning. When meanings are attached to sights and sounds received from a source, the listener has perceived the message. This fact accounts for the somewhat perplexing truism that "meaning lies not in the word, but in the mind of the hearer." Thus, the manager who hears her boss say, "Watch out for the daisy workers" and perceives that the meaning she attached to that sentence makes absolutely no sense in the context of the situation is likely to ask for clarification.

Only after meaning is developed is RESPONSE possible. If we respond to the meaning resulting from a unit of communication either by changing our opinion or by believing a controversial statement even more firmly than before, our response is one of *attitude*. If we do something we would not have done in the absence of the communication, our response is *action*. Change in attitude and action often indicates the impact of communication.

But much effective communication produces negligible attitude or action response. Information may be assimilated and understandings increased without the listener modifying any opinions or doing anything about it. *Cognition* refers to the acquisition of knowledge, the discovery of insights, and the extension of awareness. Cognition in and of itself is often a desired response of organizational communication.

Feedback. FEEDBACK, represented in Figure 8 by the long, broken arrow connecting RESPONSE to INTENT, INPUTS, ENCODING, and TRANSMISSION, consists of collecting information about the receiver's reactions to the message and using that information to modify a current or subsequent message to make it more effective. "Feedback" is a term borrowed for our model from modern control systems. A simple example is furnished by the thermostat that controls the level of temperature in the room. Someone decides upon the desired level of temperature (intent) and sets the thermostat at that level. The thermostat takes a continuous reading on the actual level and feeds the information back to the furnace when the temperature departs from the desired level. This information causes the furnace to modify its behavior and turn off or on depending upon the information it receives from the thermostat. In this way the actual level of the temperature is brought on target to approximate the desired level. In the same way, the source of a message should take a reading on its effect on the receiver and modify subsequent stimuli.

In speech-communication almost continuous FEEDBACK is possible and desirable. The speaker can never know enough about the moment-to-moment reactions of her audience. Consequently, she becomes a "feedback detective," sensitive to all clues that tell her how her listeners are reacting.

Along with continuous monitoring of the receiver(s) comes equally continuous modification of the message. Even the INTENT, what the speaker thought she could accomplish, may need to be revised in light of receiver reactions. The context, encoding, and transmission operations, all are candidates for change to better meet the current needs of particular listeners.

Delayed feedback, collecting information about response after the communication is complete, is useful to the planning of future messages, but too late to help a given communication event. Obviously, building continuous feedback mechanisms into a unit of communication becomes exceedingly important.

Our entire source-oriented process of communication is enclosed in a *Universe of Ever-Changing Things, Events and People*. This reminds us that the human and inanimate contexts of communication are never twice the same, that which comes before and after an act of communication may profoundly influence its outcome.

Our model of the process of speech-communication is necessary because it makes clear all of the significant parts and shows their interrelationships. The able practitioner of the process accounts for every element of the model in her planning. During the communication event she modifies various elements appropriately through continuous feedback. When communication fails she uses the model as an aid to diagnosis of the trouble. Usually one or two elements in the model will account for much of the failure. She can then modify her strategy for the next effort to correct the malfunctions and thus avoid repeating her mistakes. Occasionally the student of organizational communication will use the model to evaluate her successes not only for the personal gratification she receives from a good job but also because she can learn from success as well as from failure.

Our model of the process of communication is a very general one and can be used to study a host of communication situations within as well as outside organizational settings. Now we must place the model within the context of the complicated message-processing system of the modern organization. When two members of an organization speak to one another, the very fact that they are members of a common structure influences the sending and receiving of messages, the fidelity of transmission, the perception that gives meaning to the message, and the cognitions that result. The organization also provides conditions that facilitate or impede feedback.

It may facilitate communication when two people are members of the same organization. Their shared experience in similar communicative situations often insures accurate reception of messages. If a person expects the message on the intercom to relate to the committee meeting, he is likely to decipher the words "Committee moved to room eight" properly rather than to receive them as "Committee moved to ruminate."

In the same fashion, a common jargon may standardize the meanings associated with certain terms so that the perception of the message is close to intent. The use of letters of the alphabet to designate groups within the organization, or different product lines, illustrates one such practice. In short, some of the organization's habits and traditions increase the fidelity of message transmission and promote effective feedback.

A number of factors in organizations inhibit communication, and these organizational barriers should be understood. To do so we need to examine both the anatomy and physiology of organizations. Anatomy separates the parts (organs) and discovers their position, relations, structure, and functions. Physiology, on the other hand, deals with the processes and dynamic interactions associated with the life of the organism. It relates to the various organs as they do their work in cooperation with all the other parts of the body.

SPEECH-COMMUNICATION AND THE PSYCHOLOGY OF THE INDIVIDUAL

In our basic model of the process of speech-communication we begin with an individual who wishes to initiate communication. A number of events have occurred that arouse in the source a desire to send a message. For example, there is a new sales quota and procedures must be changed to meet it, or a new production deadline is set, or new people have been hired and they must be trained. Perhaps the person initiating the message is trying to persuade his organization to expand its functions.

Transformers. An electric transformer is an instrument that modifies current and voltage. The transformer reshapes in important ways the electricity that passes through it. Individuals, too, have "transformers" analogous to the electrical transformer that reshape their perceptions. Because of a person's intellectual capacity, emotional development, and experience he or she sees the world and responds to messages in his or her own peculiar way.

In the process of communication both listener and speaker bring sets of transformers to the transaction. Each passes symbols and other stimuli through these transformers that give expression and interpretation of messages an individual, sometimes even unique, meaning.

Physical Condition as a Transformer. An important factor in human perception and response is the physical condition of the individual. We can all recall times when we have been ill and our response to messages was influenced by our sickness. We can think of occasions when we were tired and our ability to speak or listen was impaired. A number of studies have investigated the energy level of people as related to their behavior. The research reveals that human beings have a changing profile that represents their energy levels throughout the 24-hour day. An individual's energy curve affects her communication pattern. She would be wise to plan her activities to exploit the peaks of energy.

Emotional Mood as a Transformer. People are happy at times and sad at others. Sometimes they are angry, sometimes frightened. The emotional condition of an individual at a particular moment affects how he perceives the world and how he responds to it. For example, frightened people cannot work consistently at the peak of their ability; they tend to search messages for ominous hidden meanings.

Intellectual Capacity as a Transformer. Psychologists have discovered that the greater the intellectual capacity of an individual, the more stimuli the person receives and the larger her repertoire of responses. Certainly, human speech is one of the most complicated of enterprises. One of the big differences between humans and other species is that humans are able to use connected speech to discuss time in three dimensions—past, present, and future—as it relates to themselves and their environment.

Past Experience as a Transformer. A fourth transformer is a person's experience in the form of learned behavior. An individual's history has a great deal to do with his attitudes toward himself, toward others, and toward organizations. The interpretation of an event by people with specialized interests—for example, the description of an automobile accident given by a doctor, a lawyer, and an automobile mechanic—illustrates this point. The doctor concentrates on the injuries to the participants, the lawyer on the assessment of liability, and the mechanic on the damage to the machines: Each is responding in a manner that is consistent with his or her experience, training, and resultant interests.

Language plays an important role in the way an individual interprets and shapes experience. One learns the language common to his culture. Persons who share a language usually perceive the world in a similar way so that they will find it less difficult to come to an understanding. In addition, every individual learns a vocabulary and a way of speaking that is his own.

Without language the world impinges upon our senses as a kaleidoscope of changing shapes and colors and a hum and buzzing of noises. With language, however, we impose order and system on the flow of stimuli that reach us. We begin to discern patterns in our surroundings, and our language furnishes us with words to name the patterns. All individuals transform their experience according to the language they learned and the emotional aura surrounding the way they learned it. Word connotations are highly individual and varied.

Clyde Kluckhohn in the "Gift of Tongues" from *Mirrors for Man* points out that language does more than convey ideas, arouse feelings, and provide self-expression. Language serves to categorize experience. Every person selects from his surroundings certain items to attend to and certain others to ignore. Some things a person highlights and others he neglects. Every culture has its own characteristic categories in which it "pigeonholes" its collective experience. Each community's experience helps form the language that orders its world and each new member is, in turn, indoctrinated into the culture by learning its language and with it the community's world view. For example, certain cultures in the polar regions developed languages with different words for the experience that is called, in English, "snow." Similarly, cultures in the tropical region have few, if any, categories for that phenomenon.

In most organizations the work groups and formal subdivisions develop their own special language or jargon. These technical languages often reflect the interests and specializations of the units, but they may become blinders to perception and hinder the inter-group communication. In addition, the group may protect their expertness by the use of a technical vocabulary. One organization attempted to get each unit to define their 100 most often used "technical" terms for a projected dictionary to facilitate inter-group communication. Some units resisted the attempt to get them to release "lodge secrets." Apparently some of their members were using language to establish prestige and control others.

A person responds to his environment like a computer, which will process data according to the way it has been programmed. An individual's experience, although infinitely more complex, serves somewhat the same function as a computer program. The person will respond and process data the same way he has learned to respond by past experience.

Individual and Group Goals as Transformers. The last set of transformers consists of the goals toward which a person is directed. What an individual holds important and significant and will strive to achieve shapes interpretation of messages.

Goals differ in importance and complexity. Some goals are personal, trivial, and transitory; others are personal but important and long-term. Some long-term goals may be so important that an individual will dedicate his or her life to them. Still other goals are shared by a group and may be important to the welfare of a number of people. People communicate for many different reasons. Sometimes they simply wish to make contact with other human beings, sometimes they talk in order to express their feelings, sometimes to give or get information, and sometimes to persuade or be persuaded. Within the context of a given communication event each participant will have some particular intent to fulfill.

In addition to the enhancement of self, most individuals will have other goals important to them, such as the education of children, the protection of the family, and the building of an organizational empire. Other goals such as the improvement of the neighborhood or backing a political candidate may be less self-centered.

Some goals of importance to individuals are actually or ostensibly shared by all members of a group. For example, the goals of the sales department, although related, may be different from the goals of the production division. Sometimes individuals within a group supposedly sharing common goals actually have different goals. Such a situation may interfere with the communicative process because people assume that goals are identical and cannot understand why messages are perceived so differently.

An example of this problem is furnished by six engineers who were working together on a project. They experienced such a severe breakdown in communication that they sought help from a consultant. The consultant asked, "What are the goals of your particular operation?" They scoffed at the question and answered, "The goals are obvious." But he persisted. "No, let's get them down on paper." The engineers finally consented to write down a list of goals. They all mentioned three important objectives in producing the product: (1) meeting the target date, (2) meeting quality standards, and (3) staying within the budget.

Next the communication consultant asked the engineers to list the three goals *in order of importance.* The six engineers ordered the three goals in three different ways. Two said that turning the product out within the budget was the most important objective; two said "meeting the deadline"; and the remaining two said that meeting the quality standards held top priority. While all six agreed on the three most important objectives, the differing view of their relative importance served as transformers to shape both encoding and decoding. Since they were unaware of their differences they found varying responses to the same communication frustrating and confusing.

TRANSFORMERS AND THE PROCESS OF COMMUNICATION

Although we have concentrated on verbal codes, in the broadest sense of the term, communication may take place through a wide variety of nonverbal messages as well. Some of the nonverbal elements in the speech-communication situation add meanings to the spoken messages and need to be included in the basic model of speech-communication.

Variations in vocal inflection, loudness patterns, and the rate of speech are, of course, an integral part of the speech-communication process. Receivers often interpret the speaker's sincerity, intent, emotion, and attitude from clues contained in the *way* the words are spoken. Generally, people believe the manner rather than the matter. It is not difficult to say, "Have you seen the new supervisor? Wow!" in such a way that the listener may interpret the message as meaning: The speaker thinks the new woman is attractive sexually. Nor is it difficult to say the very same words in such a way that the listener decides the speaker thinks the new supervisor is an extremely able executive.

Variations in pitch, inflection, loudness, and rate of speech also furnish emphasis and oral punctuation. Thus, by pausing at the proper place and using the proper pitch inflection a sentence like, "Woman without her man is a beast," can be spoken so that the listener understands it to mean something about a woman's need for a man, or with different pauses and inflections to imply that it means something about man's need for woman. Because visual stimuli are absent, telephoned messages are heavily dependent upon pauses, inflections, and the quality of the voice.

Although gestures and facial expressions are filtered out of messages transmitted by telephone or radio, they are a part of much face-to-face verbal communication. The person who sits slouched in his chair at a meeting, doodling on the pad before him, apparently unaware of the discussion, is sending a nonverbal message to the others. As with vocal inflections, the receiver tends to believe the gesture rather than the word. If a person leans his face in his hand with a sigh and says with a tired expression, "I am very excited about the new line," his listeners are not likely to believe him.

Many managers use the arrangement of furniture in their offices to communicate. A supervisor has two chairs for visitors. One is opposite her desk and the other beside it. When she wants to stress a formal relationship in which her status is emphasized, she has the visitor sit in the chair opposite the desk. The desk then serves to suggest a professional distance. On the other hand, when she wishes to establish an informal relationship and to minimize any status differences, she has her guest sit beside her with no object between them.

The superintendent of a state psychiatric hospital received word of a surprise inspection tour by a group of state legislators. He knew that the lawmakers would want to interview some patients about the conditions in the hospital, so he called his staff together and asked their advice about a suitable candidate for such an interview. They decided on a patient who had no history of violence and who was in a relatively euphoric state, hence unlikely to complain about the food or the living conditions.

In due course the inspection of the grounds, the wards, and the kitchen was complete, and one of the legislators asked to talk with an inmate. He was given an opportunity to interview the euphoric patient. After conversing with him for a bit, the legislator started to leave the room. At that point the patient leaped upon the legislator, grabbed him by the throat, and wrestled him to the floor. The cries of the victim brought the attendants on the run and they separated patient and visitor. After the superintendent had calmed the lawmaker as best he could and the inspection party had departed, he asked that the patient be brought to him.

"What in the world happened?" he asked. "You have been quiet and relatively satisfied here. What caused you to attack that man?"

"Oh," the patient replied, "he expected me to."

The nonverbal components in the speech situation were interpreted by the patient. Because he *knew* that the legislator expected inmates to be violent and dangerous, the patient's transformers interpreted the legislator's actions to meet his own expectations.

The process of speech-communication includes an individual with a set of transformers (physical condition, emotional state, intellectual capacity, past experience, goals) interpreting a series of events and responding to these stimuli by deciding to initiate communication. She begins with an intent (immediate goal) and encodes a message that she transmits to the receiver. The message is transmitted by the spoken word with its inflections, by gesture, by behavior, and by the manipulation of things in the environment.

The receiver interprets the message in terms of his own transformers and part of his response becomes a reciprocal message for the source who started the communication. That is, when the original message is received the listener may react by speaking, gesturing, or moving in a significant way. The person who began the interchange then becomes the receiver for the messages encoded by the original listener, starting the feedback cycle.

If one views the entire communicative event from a perspective that includes internal transformers, organizational and small group context, and verbal as well as nonverbal messages, one is impressed by its complexity. No wonder misunderstandings arise from even the simplest attempts to communicate.

Communication is not a simple matter of a sender transmitting a message to a receiver. Realistically, it is a reciprocal interaction, a give-and-take in which each party must participate actively. Each alternates from sender to receiver and back to sender again. The good communicator is aware of the reciprocal interaction and the transformers that always modify the interpretation and expression of messages, and plans communication to allow for and take advantage of the transformers.

THE BASIC REALITIES OF COMMUNICATION

We can best illustrate the complexities of person-to-person communication and suggest the attitudes and knowledge required to accommodate to them by stating the five basic realities of communication.

1. Many times others interpret something a person says or does or *fails to say or do* as a message when the person did not consciously intend it to be one.

2. Meanings are in people not in words. A receiver interprets a message by attaching his own meanings to it. The person who is unaware of the fact that meanings are in people often ends up crying, "But I told them!"

3. The ability to communicate is a learned behavior and, as in all learning, reward and punishment determine how the individual behaves. People tend to send those messages which they think will maximize their rewards and minimize their punishment. The manager who is unaware of this reality is told only the "good news." "How are things going?" she may ask. "Fine, boss." Only when the crisis reaches such a proportion that it can no longer be concealed does the manager discover the trouble and she reproaches the subordinate: "But why didn't you tell me?"

4. The normal result of an attempt to communicate is a partial misunderstanding. The great enemy of successful communication is the illusion that we have achieved it. Every attempt to communicate results in the arousal of somewhat different meanings on the part of the source and the receiver. The question becomes how large a margin of difference can be tolerated in a given case. For example, if the supervisor asks for a "model job," and the employee returns with a small working model when the manager wanted a production model, the difference is great enough to make a difference. In the mental institution the psychiatrist may say to the attendant, "I want you to be in control at all times." To the doctor the message means the attendant must maintain self-control, but if the attendant interprets the message to mean rigid discipline in restricting the behavior of the patients, the difference again is significant. But most misunderstandings are not of this magnitude. The main point is that a certain amount of misunderstanding in the initial stages of communication is normal, not pathological. Through feedback, necessary corrections can be made.

5. When communication breaks down, a normal response is to ask, "Whose fault is it?" The person assigned the blame denies it, and time and energy are expended in defense and attack. If you are aware of this reality you have just as many initial misunderstandings in your communication, but because you are results-oriented your first question is, "What do we need to do to achieve sufficient understanding to accomplish our objectives?"

SUMMARY

Two-person business conferences may be spontaneous and informal or carefully scheduled and organized. In planning discussions about matters relating to your job you should consider such things as finding a suitable place for the meeting and planning how you will conduct your part of the interview.

A prescriptive communication model can aid understanding by providing a graphic presentation of the parts of the event. Such a model includes a *source* (speaker), a *message,* a *channel* (or channels), and a *receiver* (listener). The message becomes an event during transmission. The speaker encodes the message into verbal and nonverbal elements which are transmitted to the receiver. Feedback is the process by which listeners react to the message and the speaker collects information about that reaction. The source uses feedback to modify current or subsequent messages to achieve the purpose of the communication.

Both listener and speaker bring sets of transformers to the process of communication. These transformers give a unique meaning to the way people express and interpret messages. Transformers often inhibit the effective transmission of information. Among the important individual transformers which influence communicators are their physical conditions, emotional moods, intellectual capacities, past experiences, and their individual and group goals.

In studying the process of communication we must remember that nonverbal elements such as variations in vocal inflections, loudness patterns, and the rate of speaking are important. Although gestures and facial expressions are filtered out of telephone messages, they are a vital part of face-to-face communication. In many instances the listener will choose to believe the nonverbal communication rather than the words if they are in conflict.

Placing the entire communication event into a context of organizational and small group factors and considering both the verbal and nonverbal messages as well as the influence of individual transformers reveals the complexity of the process.

QUESTIONS FOR DISCUSSION AND REVIEW

1. What are some of the things to keep in mind when planning a person-to-person communication?
2. What are the main elements in the model of the communication process?
3. What is the meaning of *feedback?*
4. What is involved in the encoding and decoding processes?
5. How do individual transformers shape perceptions and influence the communication process?
6. What are the important transformers listed in the chapter and how do they work?
7. How does language influence our perceptions?
8. How do nonverbal elements enter into the communication process?

REFERENCES AND SUGGESTED READINGS

Berlo, D. K. *The Process of Communication.* New York: Holt, Rinehart, and Winston, 1960.

Bormann, E. G. *Communication Theory.* New York: Holt, Rinehart, and Winston, 1980.

Kluckhohn, C. *Mirrors for Man.* New York: McGraw-Hill, 1948.

Knapp, M. L. *Nonverbal Communication in Human Interaction.* 2nd ed. New York: Holt, Rinehart, and Winston, 1978.

Stewart, C. J. and W. B. Cash. *Interviewing: Principles and Practice.* Dubuque, Iowa: Wm. C. Brown, 1974.

4
Taking Part in Basic Social and Work Groups

———————————— Laboratory Application ————————————

THE ORGANIZATIONAL MEETING

Members of the modern corporate organization do most of their work in small task-oriented group meetings. The organizational setting brings together people who have been deeply but narrowly trained in various specialized fields, allows them to study the ins-and-outs of a question, and then gives them a chance to sit around a table and arrive at an understanding and make decisions. By means of small group meetings they can pool their specialized knowledge and training in order to do large-scale projects.

The modern organization is essentially a pyramid of committees in which those concerned with a task or problem make decisions which are forwarded to other responsible groups for final approval and implementation. We often dramatize the workings of a large institution as the action of a well-known individual or several individuals. Thus we may say that the president or provost created the budget for our college or university. We often talk as though the president of the United States took action about energy or about the Federal budget. What typically happens, however, is that many members of the organization, meeting for weeks or months in small groups in many different divisions of the college administration or the executive branch of the government, make the decisions and take the actions we attribute to one person.

You will probably find yourself attending meetings as soon as you join the organization. These meetings may be informal and essentially social in tone. They just seem to happen as people take a coffee break and assemble in the cafeteria at the same table and start talking about any topic that interests them at the moment.

The informal social groups that emerge from people getting acquainted on the job are important to the workings of the organization. In the course of these meetings some people emerge as natural leaders who often represent the others in the group in terms of responses to management programs and policies, attitudes towards productivity, and general morale. If the group develops a norm which sets a high achievement level, the productivity of the section will often rise. If the informal group sets a moderate or low level of production as a norm it will be very difficult for management to change the level.

The informal social groupings also contribute to how much you will enjoy your work. If you find congenial people and are accepted in the groups you will get more social rewards and these will supplement whatever achievement rewards you receive from the job. If the job itself turns out to be unrewarding you might still enjoy the organization because of the social rewards you receive from the other organization members.

The informal social groups can also provide you with much information about the workings of the organization of the same kind we discussed in Chapter 2 in our consideration of the informal two-person conversation.

The formal task-oriented group meeting is an opportunity to discuss issues and make decisions in a binding way. Many of the other formal channels are restricted in terms of the flow of messages. If you have to talk first to your supervisor and ask for permission before you can officially talk to the unit chief, or if you have to write a memo first to your supervisor and then have the supervisor send it on to the unit chief, communication is often time-consuming and unsatisfactory. We use the term "red tape" for the idea that going through formal channels results in delays, false starts, seeing the wrong person and being sent to other channels. Most students have to go through formal channels to register for their courses and they then experience directly some of the typical problems that people run into when they use formal channels of communication.

The business meeting, however, provides a setting in which the people involved in a task or a decision can get together to talk face-to-face in a give-and-take fashion with maximum opportunity for direct and continuous feedback. Such meetings can also cut through status boundaries so people from several different levels of management may attend the same meeting as the people doing the work.

In this application section of this chapter we concentrate on the organizational meeting, but the theoretical rationale which follows later applies to the informal groups as well.

ABUSES OF ORGANIZATIONAL MEETINGS

Clearly, the organizational conference is suited to serve a number of important purposes. Yet, members of organizations repeatedly testify to the abuse of meetings. The paradox is explained by the fact that too many meetings are badly organized, badly conducted, and totally useless. Meetings in which little communication takes place are time-wasters.

It is even more ironic that often the time-wasting meeting results from the desire to save time. The conference leader bustles in with everything planned and opens the meeting with an apology for having called it. He assures the group that the meeting will halt promptly at the end of the hour. He knows that a number of people have other appointments, and he too has to attend another meeting shortly. His entire manner communicates haste. He glances at his watch from time to time. When a discussion develops he cuts it off with a reminder that a number of things have to be covered, and time is short. The member who raises a question or makes a comment in such a meeting is a brave person. Soon it becomes apparent that speed is more important than getting work done. The leader goes through the motion of mentioning the items on the agenda, asking for questions or comments, but no real communication takes place. Feedback is stifled by the drive to cover the agenda in the specified time. The meeting is useless; it could have been eliminated; it is a real time-waster.

Some organizations continue to hold regularly scheduled meetings although they are no longer necessary. Originally the meetings met a need, but as time passed the circumstances changed and the meeting lost its purpose. However, because the members are in the habit of holding the meeting, they continue to do so. Such meetings are also time-wasters.

Meetings may be used as administrative dodges in the political infighting that occurs in most organizations. The inter-group conflict stemming from empire building or buck-passing may spawn such abuses. One way for cagy administrators to handle a touchy issue that they do not want to deal with personally is to "bury it" in committee. In some organizations the *ad hoc* committees seldom serve any purpose other than to postpone action or to kill a proposal.

The administrator may use the meeting to conceal her decision. That is, she has already made up her mind but she pretends that the meeting has been called to discuss the problem and arrive at a solution. After a time the people in the organization catch on to what she is doing and come to realize that the meeting is a sham and that the supervisor has already made up her mind and that nothing said in the meeting will change it.

When the people who call a meeting have a genuine need to communicate they should organize and plan in such a way that they have enough time to do the job. They must assure a climate conducive to feedback if the session is to be successful. Such a meeting will run overtime and may not cover the entire agenda, but members will say that it was a good meeting, that it accomplished something, and that "we ought to have *more* meetings like this one." Such meetings are not time-wasters.

PROPER USES OF MEETINGS

A Ritual. Every organization has some meetings that are used primarily as rituals. The department heads may always present their yearly budgets in a meeting attended by all the vice-presidents. Each person may have only five minutes to discuss a complicated budget. A brief question and answer period may follow the presentation. Auditors, accountants, the vice-president in charge of the department, as well as the president have carefully screened the budgets before the presentation. The meeting puts a rubber stamp on the decisions already made. Still, the organization goes through the yearly ritual of presenting the budgets. Some "Young Turk" may challenge the usefulness of the meeting. He asserts that nothing is accomplished. The meeting is a waste of time. He is voted down and the organization continues to use the meeting as a ritual. He misjudged the meeting because he did not understand its purpose.

In addition to adding to the cohesiveness of the organization, the ritualistic meeting often assures that hurt feelings do not impede efficiency. If the proponents of policy or proposals fail to have a ritualistic meeting in which all people of authority are informed about developments, they may suddenly find many roadblocks in their way. The person of authority who feels slighted in this regard can throw his weight around. A much wiser course is to call a meeting designed primarily to keep the interdepartmental fences mended. The only requirements for such a meeting are that the proper forms are recognized and it is conducted in the expected way.

The Briefing. A conference that often looks like a ritualistic meeting but really is quite different is the briefing session. The purpose of this meeting is to provide members of the organization with the information they need to carry out a program. The general objective is clear. The basic decisions have been made and the plans to accomplish this objective are drawn up. Now the people responsible for doing the job must be told what their task is to be and how they are to do it. The meeting is crucial to the task efficiency of the organization and must be carefully planned and conducted.

Instruction. Organizations often use meetings to develop their members, to make them more proficient on their jobs, or to provide them with information that will enable them to work with greater understanding. As in the briefing meeting, the instructional session is built around the individuals who have the knowledge and must impart or teach that knowledge to the other members of the group.

Creative. On occasion a meeting is set up to "brainstorm" new ideas, techniques, or procedures. The purpose of the creative meeting is to stimulate members of the organization to think up new approaches and solutions. On occasion new ideas are developed during the course of the meeting. Frequently, however, the meeting serves as a stimulus to the creativity of the members and helps them to develop new ideas prior to or after the actual brainstorming session.

Decision-Making. The most difficult and yet one of the most useful meetings is the session designed to make plans and decisions. Such meetings have both the responsibility and authority to solve important problems facing the organizations.

Consultative. The consultation resembles a decision-making meeting but does not have the authority or responsibility for the decision. The person responsible for the decision does not delegate these powers to the group. Rather he or she asks for their advice and suggestions before personally coming to a decision.

PLANNING THE MEETING

1. *Be sure meeting is absolutely necessary.* Meetings are the heavy artillery of organizational communication. The wise general uses the big guns sparingly because they are expensive and difficult to maneuver. On the other hand, there really is no satisfactory substitute for them and so the general must use them on occasion. If the communication can be accomplished through individual conferences or by other techniques, the meeting is probably unnecessary.

2. *Make sure that it accomplishes its objective.* The members of the organization must treat the meeting as an important occasion if it is to do the job. They must prepare for the meeting carefully. They must have sufficient time for preparation. They must create a group climate that encourages maximum feedback.

3. *Determine the purpose of the meeting.* If the purpose of the meeting is ritualistic, then it should be treated and judged as such. If the meeting is consultative, this should be made very clear to the members. Nothing is harder on the effectiveness of such a meeting than to have the members think it is to be a decision-making session and then discover that the decision will be made later. Always make absolutely certain that all the members understand the purpose of the meeting. If they come to the session hoping to accomplish other purposes, they often become disillusioned with the meeting and after a time with all organizational meetings.

4. *Plan the meeting to achieve the purpose.* What is the best place to hold the meeting? If it is a ritualistic meeting, perhaps the most impressive conference room in the organization should be used. The board room might be an appropriate place for this meeting. Select a classroom with audiovisual aids and desks and blackboards for the instructional conference. Do not hold a decision-making meeting in the office of a high status member. The plush board room may inhibit the kind of communication required for a decision-making session. Choose a small simple meeting room with few distractions where the members can sit close together.

Which type of meeting format will best achieve the purpose of the group? A series of short presentations with little interruption is sufficient to achieve ritualistic ends. Once the proper salute to author-ity has been made, the members appreciate short speeches and a quick conclusion to the ritualistic meeting. For a briefing session or an instructional meeting a lecture using the latest presentational tech-niques including overhead projectors, filmstrips, flannel boards, flip charts, graphs, blackboards, charts, and other visual aids may be the best procedure. Even so, there must be provision for feedback from the members attending the meeting. Perhaps a series of short presenta-tions with plenty of time for questions and discussions is the way to organize some of these meetings. For the creative meeting the less formal the structure the better. Status differences must not be stressed. Informality should be the keynote; the atmosphere of the meeting must be social, relaxed, and agreeable. For the consultative meeting and the decision-making session an agenda is often useful but set speeches should be discouraged. Everyone should have an equal opportunity to take part.

Who should attend the meeting? This is a crucial question for the ritualistic session. The purpose of such a meeting is to ensure that people in authority, who expect to be consulted and informed, will feel that their position is recognized. Therefore the selection of participants must proceed with this in mind. Who would feel left out and hurt? Who could jeopardize the project if they were not informed? In the briefing session often the only people who need to attend are the members who will implement the plan. For instructional conferences the question is simple. Who needs the information or skill that will be taught in the meeting? For creative conferences talent as well as understanding and authority should be considered. Sometimes, if one or more persons *not concerned* with the organization take part in the meeting, they will contribute some fresh ideas. Planners of decision-making and consultative meetings should include those members who have the necessary information and the proper status.

Who should be the leader? For a ritualistic meeting the leader should have high status if possible. The president of the organization, for example, is a good person to preside over an important ritualistic meeting. For briefing sessions and instructional conferences leadership often can be furnished by the person doing the briefing or by the teacher of the class. For the creative meeting status should be discounted. Therefore, the leadership of the meeting should be unobtrusive, preferably by someone with the same status as most of the other members. A meeting of peers is more likely to be free and easy. The decision-making and consultative meetings require more direction. Again the meeting should be planned so that status differences do not inhibit honest discussion of important questions. If people of differing status must take part, every effort should be made to reduce the differences in the choice of meeting place, in the formality of the meeting, and in *the manner and attitude of high status members.*

5. *Do your homework.* A successful meeting requires time and effort in the planning stages. A certain amount of administrative detail must be taken care of if the meeting is to run smoothly. Attention to small details such as pads and pencils for the participants, coffee at break time, chalk for the instructors, or a well-lighted, well-ventilated, and well-heated room all contribute to the success of the meeting. When such details are carefully handled, the members get the impression that this meeting is important and will accomplish something worthwhile. When they are not attended to, the members get a negative impression of the meeting.

The authors have participated in innumerable instructional sessions. Often these meetings get off to a bad start because some small detail was not handled properly. Perhaps the door to the meeting room was locked and a janitor had to be found before the meeting could get underway. On occasion the room's temperature was uncomfortable. Frequently the planners forgot to check on possible distractions, and the meeting was interrupted by the whine of a floor-buffing machine or the sound of a jackhammer on the floor below. If the tape recorder does not work or the light in an overhead projector is burned out, the interruption and distraction can reduce the effectiveness of the meeting.

More importantly, the planner should specify in concrete terms the outcome of the meeting. The outcome should be distinguished from the purpose. If a decision is to be reached, how is this decision to be developed? In general outline? In specific detail? When is this final decision to be reached?

Do the participants require briefing before the meeting? How will this be done? Will they be furnished with information ahead of time? Will they receive instructions as to how to prepare for the meeting? How will this be accomplished? Too many meetings are held off the top of the head. If a meeting is required, particularly a decision-making or consultative meeting, then all participants should be knowledgeable and have thought through to some extent their ideas on the topic under discussion.

How will the proceedings and results be recorded? Will a secretary be appointed from among the members of the meeting? Will a professional secretary keep a record in shorthand? Would it be better to keep a tape recording of the entire meeting and have it transcribed later? Who will prepare the agenda? Will everyone get a copy prior to the meeting? Would it be better to have the group formulate its own agenda?

6. *Evaluate results and follow-up.* Some time should be spent after the meeting to evaluate its effectiveness in a systematic way. Of course the members usually make an informal evaluation of the meeting as they walk away from it. They may think or say to their friends that it was a good meeting or that they talked all around the subject or that they wasted a lot of time and nothing was accomplished. The organization will benefit from more organized and systematic evaluation of meetings. Some member of the group should collect impressions of the strengths and weaknesses of each meeting. These evaluations should be fed back to the participants to upgrade future meetings.

One of the striking things about meetings is that members seldom spend any time talking about the group and how it functions. When groups do spend short periods after a meeting talking about it, the cohesiveness and effectiveness of the group is often increased.

Formal techniques for evaluation of meetings usually save time in the long run. The results of the meeting should be utilized to their fullest. What can be done to follow up and apply the results of the conference? Do not let the matter drop at the end of the meeting.

CHECKLIST FOR PLANNING A MEETING

The members planning a meeting should use the following checklist of questions to guide them.

1. What is the purpose of the meeting? Ritual? Briefing? Instruction? Creative development? Decision-making? Consultative?
2. What outcomes are to emerge from the meeting? When should these goals be reached?
3. What type of conference will best achieve the meeting's purpose? Lecture and discussion? Short presentations by several people, followed by a discussion period? Round-table discussion? Other?
4. Who will participate? Have we left out someone who should be invited? Have we included someone who need not be involved?
5. Who will serve as leader?
6. What is the best place to hold the meeting? What is a good time? How long should the meeting last?
7. How and when will the participants be briefed on the meeting and given directions for preparing to take part?
8. What physical details need to be taken care of? Will the room be ready and open? Ventilation and heating? Audiovisual aids? Can we guard against unnecessary distractions?
9. How will the proceedings and results be recorded?
10. Who will prepare the agenda? Will it be circulated in advance?
11. How will the conference be evaluated?
12. What will be done to follow up and apply the results of the meeting?

ASSIGNMENT: A Business Meeting

Your instructor will assign you to a task force group and give you a topic to study and report on. You will have time during your regularly scheduled class hours for meetings and are free to meet outside of class if you wish. You will record your meetings on either audio or videotape. After you finish your report you will have some time to discuss what happened with your group and how well you did in terms of the theoretical rationale which follows.

————————————— **Theoretical Rationale** —————————————

THE LEADERLESS GROUP AS A RESEARCH TOOL

One of the most interesting ways in which the investigators discovered the basic dynamics of the work group was by means of the leaderless group discussion. The studies in group process, communication, and leadership at the University of Minnesota, which provided much of the material for this chapter, used the technique of the leaderless group discussion extensively. The leaderless group is essentially a test-tube situation in which people who do not know one another are placed in a work group and given a specified amount of time to do a job. The group has no formal structure. The investigators do not appoint any member as leader, moderator, manager, supervisor, or spokesman. Every member of the leaderless group discussion is equal. No one is looked down upon and no one is looked up to at the start. Also each can perform any or all of the jobs that the group needs to have done to succeed.

In this test tube the normal operations of everyday work groups are speeded up and the basic patterns of group process are easy to observe and study. The amazing thing is that at the end of several hours the members of the group begin to specialize and some members are looked up to and some are looked down on by the group.

What does this mean? It means that the formal structure of an organization is simply spelling out in the table of organization what takes place in all informal work groups. If the formal structure always matched the informal structure, most organizations would be highly productive, highly cohesive, and enjoy considerably more communication efficiency than they now do.

Our problem comes from the fact that the informal structure is changing, fluctuating, and dynamic whereas the formal structure is static. Too often the formal structure no longer describes what is in fact going on in the dynamics of an organization. Trying to understand the dynamics of such an organization by reading the table of organization or the names on the office doors is like trying to find your way in a town by using a map that is 20 years out of date.

To understand the communication patterns in an organization one must understand the small work groups that actually do the job. We must begin, therefore, with an analysis of the process that governs the small work group.

Group Members Are Specialists. In the test tube of the leaderless group discussion, the first important reaction to take place is the specialization of the members. When it becomes clear to a person in a leaderless group that she is specializing and when the group discovers that she is doing more of certain things than the others, she takes a place in the group. That is, while she may do a number of things to help the group reach its goal the group expects that she will concentrate on certain things. She too expects to do these tasks. When these expectations are clear and shared by both the member and the other people in the group, she has taken a *role*. We will define *role* as the part a person expects to play and the part that the other members expect her to play in the group. It includes the duties that she specializes in and the way she socializes with the others. The latter is often called her personality.

One extremely important and interesting finding from basic research is that an individual's personality changes to some extent from group to group. The receptionist who has such a sparkling personality at the office and kids around with the others may be very quiet and reserved when she meets with the young people at her church. She may be ill-tempered and bossy with her family. You may take different *roles* in different groups. In one group you are the "take-charge" member who gets things rolling. In another you are likable and fun-loving. In still another, you are a quiet, steady, and responsible worker. Which is the *real* you? This may seem to be an easy question to answer, but in reality it is not. You bring to every work group certain skills that you have developed in school or in working with other groups at other jobs. You also bring certain inherited capacities for work, for intellectual activity, and for socializing. But what you do for a given work group is dependent upon the skills and potentialities of the other members of the group as well as your own talents. To ask whether a person is more real using his abilities to play the role of parent in his family or whether he is more real assuming the role of manager at work is not very helpful. It is also too simple. If we think of people as having a certain set personality and abilities, we can often explain away our problems by placing the blame for them on individuals whom we consider innately bad people. We then attribute to them such traits as stubbornness, bossiness, and unreasonableness. They are causing all the trouble in the organization; if they just changed their ways or if the group could get rid of them, the problems would disappear. The role a person plays is partly a result of talent and skill but it is also partly a result of the role the group gives the person. This brings us to the first important principle relating to role development:

Roles Are Worked Out by Members and Group.

This principle has an important corollary that is too often overlooked in the operation of the modern organization:

Group Is Responsible for Members' Behavior.

When a person understands this principle and its corollary he or she experiences a complete change of viewpoint about the people in the organization and how best to work with them.

Once every member has found his or her place and the duties that make up the role, a second important reaction takes place in the test tube of the leaderless group discussion. The members evaluate the relative worth *to the group* of each role. They give the highest status to the roles they judge to be most valuable.

After several hours of meeting, the group begins to *look up* to some members. Groups with stable role structures generally agree on the status ladder that characterizes their group. Again it might seem that peers working together without any formal structure (no leader or supervisor or manager assigned) could function as equals, and all share in all the tasks. We have not observed any groups that worked in this way. There is an innate drive to establish status relationships and a "pecking order" in the leaderless discussion group.

An observer can classify the roles in order of importance by watching the way the members act toward one another. For example, the members will talk directly and at greater length to the people they consider important in the group. The high status person tends to talk more to the entire group. The high status member receives more consideration from the others. They listen to what he or she says. Indeed, they often stop what they are doing in order to listen more carefully. The others often ignore or cut off the comments of the low status individuals. The members spend more time and thought on the ideas and opinions suggested by people with high status.

The group decides which members they will look up to on the basis of their notion as to who is most important to the group. This decision is influenced by their goals. Some groups clearly succeed or fail. A basketball team for example either wins or loses. In addition, a given player's contribution can sometimes be measured in terms of how many points he contributed to victory. In such a situation the player who makes the most points may have high status. In organizations where success or failure is not so easily measured, such as in administering a university or a governmental service department, the best liked person in the group may have higher status than the task experts. For many organizations the member who organizes the work is thought of as the *leader* and often has the highest status.

No pattern of role and status arrangements will fit all groups. Even similar groups will differ on these matters. Some people may be so skillful at the jobs they do that they have a higher status than others playing a role that usually is more important. Some work groups may give the task expert a higher status because she is particularly skillful and less status to the leader because she is not as skillful in her role.

Satisfaction Depends on Status. The social and esteem satisfactions that members receive come largely from their status. High status roles are pleasant and rewarding. The group makes a high status member feel important and influential. They show her deference, they listen to her, ask her advice and often take it. When she expresses an opinion they give it careful consideration. In formal organizations the high status member often gets a greater share of the group's goods than the lower status member. She gets a bigger office, more secretaries, better furniture, more salary. One of the most powerful forces drawing members into the organization and making them cohesive and dedicated members willing to work more than is required is the reward of high status.

The member filling a high status role in an organization has many of her social and esteem needs filled and she thus works hard for the good of the group. Too often the low status member does not get these rewards so she simply puts in her time and draws her salary. However, highly cohesive groups developed in our laboratory have worked out ways to fulfill the esteem and social needs of low status members as well as those of the high status members.

Struggle for Higher Status Is Natural. Since the role is closely associated with the standing in the organization and a great deal of reward goes to the "leader" and the other high status members, several of them typically struggle for the top positions. This struggle creates a conflict and disagreements between the competing members. The group's energy is directed to the question of who will win out and a good bit of its attention is directed away from the job. If these struggles are prolonged and heated, the group may be torn with internal dissension to the point that their work suffers. Most of us have been associated with or heard about an organization in which the fight for control, the backbiting, and infighting have reached the point that the organization's effectiveness and sometimes its very existence are threatened. Several years ago one of the authors invested a small amount of money in the stock of a newly formed company that had an unusually bright future. The company had a patent on an easy to build almost foolproof outboard motor that worked on a jet principle. They floated a successful bond issue and went into production. For a time the stock held up and then it began to drop. Shortly, a bitter proxy fight broke out between the engineer in charge of production and the sales manager. The company was in danger of failing. A desperate reorganization was attempted. The stock continued to decline and finally it was no longer listed in the local market.

Later a long letter outlining the problems of mismanagement and the struggle for control of the young company was sent to all stockholders. There may have been other contributing factors, but certainly the primary reason for this firm's failure was the internal struggle for leadership.

How Roles Emerge. The most intriguing question we have investigated has been, How do roles emerge? How does the process of specialization take place? In concrete terms, what makes the small work group tick? We will spell out the answer to this vital question in terms of an idealized group that serves us as a model of the basic process. Although any given group will vary to some degree from this model, basically this is the way it works.

Five members have been assigned to a work group. They have not been given any role assignments. They do not know one another but they do have a clear goal and comprehension of the specific jobs that must be done to reach that goal. Some members, however, can do some of the things better than others. Some are trained and talented in mechanical matters and are capable of thinking through technical problems and are clever at building things. Others are more adept at making plans, still others are good at testing ideas. To get this work done and to reach their goal, the members must depend upon the resources of skill and talent that each of them brings to the job.

If a chemist mixes the proper proportion of chemical substances in a test tube and starts a chemical reaction, it usually takes some time before the process is completed. When the reaction comes to an end he will have a different substance. Should he halt the reaction before it is finished he would find that the test tube contained some of the original substances as well as some of the new ones. Our test tube of group process operates in an analogous way. Into the group we place members with abilities to perform with varying degrees of skill the tasks required, and when the process is completed each member of the group has a role that describes his specialized function. We will begin with one of the first social tasks required when people first meet. They all feel tense and ill at ease. Anyone who has been at a dinner where ̱ is unacquainted knows how stiff and formal and uncomfabᶫ social climate can be. Every group that meets for the first time experiences a similar feeling of social stiffness. The insecurity of the situation causes the social tension. We define this early tension in a group as members get acquainted as *primary tension.*

Precisely because the members do not have roles, they do not know what to expect. They may be laughed at, ignored, ridiculed, admired, respected, or liked. When the group first meets it provides a social climate that deprives the members of social and esteem needs. Not only that, but it holds out the promise of satisfying those needs. No wonder the members feel tense and nervous. The first important task facing the group is the release of this primary tension. They have to get to know one another and feel at ease before they can get down to business.

Primary tensions can be broken by a member poking fun, making small talk, being friendly and gracious, or appearing to be at ease. This task can be called the *release of tension function.*

Although there are tensions to be released early in the first meeting, it is found that social tensions build up at other times as well, so that the need to release tensions remains. For example, the group experiences a short period of tension at the beginning of every meeting and tension continues to crop up at the start of each work session even though its nature is usually much less severe.

Typically, each work day (work session) begins with some chit-chat or joking of a social nature to reestablish in everyone's minds that the roles are pretty much the same as they were when they left the work group and that they can continue on in the same way.

In our model group there are two members, Bill and Joe, who have previously released tensions in other groups and who have some talent in this direction. In addition, they enjoy the rewards it offers— laughter, social approval, and being well liked by the other members. They know that the person who performs the tension-release function is often the most popular member. They are both, thus, alert to any signs of social tension. They both must try to "break the ice."

Bill has developed a characteristic way of doing this. He begins to make small talk about anything that comes into his head. The sillier the better, and when he sees someone respond in a friendly way he makes a mildly insulting personal comment about that person and then laughs to indicate that it is all in fun. Joe has his own style of humor. He is clever at impersonations and has an expressive face. He is a good pantomimist and actor.

Bill begins by making small talk and then insults Harry. He then waits for the reaction. Normally he does not get a big belly laugh. The first response of the group is tentative, and often Bill cannot tell whether they liked it or not.

Joe is encouraged to give it a try and he does a little pantomime routine about how cold it is in the room. Can't they get a little more heat, he wonders. Bill watches to see the result of this ploy. Again the response is not clear. So Joe tries once more and then Bill gets another chance. The other group members watch Joe and Bill demonstrate their wares and then they decide whether this job should be primarily Joe's or Bill's or whether they might share it. In the latter case they would "clown" around together.

All of this takes place subconsciously. The group members are often not aware of what is going on. They simply notice that Bill is tactless and smart-alecky and that Joe is really rather funny. When they come to this conclusion they begin to laugh at Joe and ignore Bill's attempts at humor. If he continues to try to be funny, they may start to groan and grimace and in other ways let him know that they do not appreciate it. After some time Joe will do more and more of the joking because he gets positive rewards for doing so, and Bill will gradually stop his attempts. At this point part of Joe's role will be set. He will begin to specialize. He will expect to be funny and the group will expect him to step in when things get tense and inject humor to relax the atmosphere.

But what will happen should Joe fail to live up to expectations? If he appears at work one day with a long face and is quiet and glum, the group resents his change. They say he is not himself today. They ask if he is sick. Should Joe begin to take on a different role, such as making a serious suggestion about an important decision, the group may not take him seriously at all.

Once the social tensions are broken the group will get down to business. To do so someone must take the initiative. The "take-charge" function is much like the tension-release function, and several members will be competent in this area. Mary and Dick have done this task for groups in the past and they enjoy the rewards of being the "take-charge" person.

As soon as Mary feels that the social tensions have been eased she says, "All right. Let's get going. I suggest we start by . . ." She does not get immediate acceptance. The other group members do not say, "That's a good idea. Let's do that." They say and do little one way or another; this encourages Dick to step forward. "I don't quite understand what you mean. Would you run through that again?" Mary patiently explains her plan of action, thinking that Dick is not very bright.

Dick now sees what Mary is driving at but he says, "I'm not sure that we have to do it that way. How about this? Wouldn't this be better?" Dick now makes a suggestion about how the group can best accomplish its task. Gradually the others begin to follow Dick's directions more than they follow Mary's suggestions. When most of them follow Dick, he takes charge and organizes work and gives assignments and directions; he will be thought of by the group as their "leader."

In the same way each member is gradually accepted as the person who performs most or part of a given task. Each member is thus led to specialize by the group's encouragement. He or she does not have a complete monopoly on a given task, but does most of it. Thus, Mary may be witty on occasion, and although the group appreciates her wit, the members think of Joe as their "tension releaser." Similarly, Joan may take charge of getting the group work done from time to time even though Dick is the member who does this for the group most of the time.

Although some roles are established easily and quickly, the role of "leader" is often among the last roles to emerge in the leaderless discussion groups and sometimes no leader emerges at all. The groups in which a leader failed to emerge are uniformly unsuccessful and socially punishing to their members. They are often torn with strife, wasted time, and frustration. Much of the energy of the members goes into the contention for high status positions and little is left over for getting the job done. These groups suffer from absenteeism and low levels of cohesiveness.

The most highly cohesive and successful groups, on the other hand, are those in which leaders emerge quite early and in which the other members assume stable roles. In addition, every individual is happy with his or her role, even those with low status positions. In these groups the members' security needs are fulfilled. They know what to expect when they come to work. They know what they are supposed to do and how the others will react when they do so. They can relax and "be themselves."

Typically, the test-tube groups experienced a dramatic increase in cohesiveness when role structure stabilized. As a result they were more productive. They began to help one another get the job done for the good of the group. They also experienced an improvement in the *communication efficiency* of the group.

Role Struggle Takes Time. The group undergoing the "shake-down cruise" that is associated with the role struggle experiences a number of communication problems. In the first place, during this stage people do not *listen*. Chapter 7 will indicate in detail the importance of the proper attitude in the development of listening skill. Even experienced listeners seldom have the patience to listen during the periods of role struggle. When it is important to be listening, people are eager to get the floor and make a showing. They want to demonstrate their abilities and make a good impression.

When they are not talking they do not listen carefully to another person but rather they are thinking of things that they might say next, and how they might best say them. Very little questioning goes on during this period. When a member does make a comment he often moves from one topic to another because he wants to get as much into the speech as he can while he has the floor. He is, in a sense, showing off his abilities rather than working together with the other members to get the job done. As a result, the group involved in a role struggle often wanders from topic to topic with little plan.

In addition, a good many disagreements arise that are not disagreements at all but simply a result of not listening carefully. Bill catches just a phrase about "production standards programs" in something Joan says and immediately launches a speech on the failure of previous plans to set rates of production. Had he listened more carefully and given Joan a chance to finish her comments, he would have discovered that Joan was not advocating a new plan of any sort. Joan, however, perceives Bill's speech as an attack on her intelligence so she makes some general philosophical comments to the effect that just because previous plans have failed is no sign that the group should not try to improve things.

Second, the groups struggling over roles have some pseudo-misunderstandings. A member has no desire to follow the directions of a contender for leadership. He does not say so directly, however. He simply does not do the job he was directed to do. When he is called to task about it, he answers that he did not understand that he was to do the job, or that he did not understand that the job was to be done at this time, or that he did not understand what the person was talking about at all.

When Mary made her first leadership move by taking charge and suggesting that the group go to work in a certain way, Dick's first response was not to disagree but to pretend he did not understand. During the time it took Mary to explain her suggestion once more, Dick was thinking up his own course of action. In short, he understood all right but he did not want to follow Mary's lead and so he pretended not to understand.

Finally, people in the midst of a role struggle are often more interested in the outcome of battle than they are in their job. They have a "hidden agenda" that is more important than the matter they are talking about. Some of the test-tube groups have quibbled for an hour or more over the wording of a report during this phase of their work. To an observer who did not understand the hidden agenda, the whole argument was ridiculous. The changes in wording were relatively unimportant, but when at the conclusion of the quibble the woman whose wording was accepted was also clearly perceived as the leader, an important item on the hidden agenda had been settled. The meeting went a long way to stabilizing the roles in the group and although this meeting was very frustrating to many of the members and they felt they had wasted a lot of time, the next meeting was much more productive because the roles had stabilized.

This preoccupation with the role and status also keeps down the "feedback" within the group. The member who fails to ask for information often does so because of a desire not to lose status by admitting ignorance. A person who appears ignorant is unlikely to get a high status role in the group. The member often pretends to know more than he or she does, and as a result is confused and unable to do a proper share.

When the roles stabilize, the communication efficiency increases not only because of the increased cohesiveness, but because each member feels secure in his or her position. Members can afford to admit ignorance without losing status. They can now afford to disagree with ideas and point out shortcomings in plans of action.

During the period of role struggle such disagreements and testing of ideas are often perceived as a personal attack on the individual presenting the ideas. After roles have stabilized, the ideas themselves can be considered on their merit without undue attention to whose ideas they are because the members do not rise or fall on the basis of their ideas. Rather, ideas and plans are now tested in terms of their usefulness *to the group*. When this happens the members no longer need to take the floor and demonstrate their abilities and they are more willing to listen and to understand. A large part of the social structuring has been dealt with and they can concentrate on the task at hand.

The Role of Leader. The basic model of the test-tube group explains the way in which a "leader" naturally emerges during the course of a group's working on a task. The leader role is a high status role, normally the highest position in the group. People size up the potential leaders with great care before indicating a willingness to follow a particular one. Individuals are cautious about committing themselves, not only because of the high status of leadership and the fact that when a leader is selected the others lose their chance at the important role, but also because the leader relates directly to each member in a personal way. The task expert may have a high status but he does not give directions and orders to the others nor does he make decisions that so frequently and clearly affect the entire group as does the leader.

Our studies of test-tube groups reveal a definite pattern in the social interactions leading to the emergence of leaders. The group does not choose a leader at once. Rather, the group eliminates members from contention until all except one are removed. When all but one are eliminated, the person remaining has emerged as the leader.

Very early in their meetings the leaderless group discussion eliminates those who seem clearly unsuited for leadership. Members are searching for clues that will disqualify people rather than for evidence that will support a campaign for leadership. In our case studies the first to be eliminated were those whom the others perceived to be quiet, uninvolved, or uninformed. The inactive members were generally eliminated within the first hour. Roughly one-half of the members were ruled out of leadership in the early phase. The others were in active contention for leadership during the second phase of the process. Typically, in groups of five the pattern was to have two or three members still under consideration after the early rejection of those perceived as clearly unsuitable.

The second period was characterized by intensive competition among the remaining contenders. During the second phase the role of lieutenant for one of the potential leaders often appeared. A member, out of contention, began to give strong and overt support to the leadership moves of a candidate. The point at which one of the contenders wins a lieutenant is a crucial one for the structuring of the work group. If a member who wins the support of another is quite clearly the best of the remaining candidates, one strong supporter is often enough to swing the votes of uncommitted members.

A rather common pattern is to have three of five members

eliminated early in the work sessions. Member A might become the tension releaser and best-liked member and thus be removed from contention as a possible leader. Members C and D might be eliminated because they do not seem involved or informed. Members B and E are left to contend for the top position. If during this second phase member B is perceived by member A to be arbitrary and tactless, while member E seems more understanding and better organized, member A will begin to support actively and follow the directives and suggestions of member E. Members C and D will usually follow A's example and member E will emerge as leader.

The member who loses in the final clear-cut struggle for leadership is a potential source of trouble. As a rule he is one of the more capable people, otherwise he would not have remained in contention for so long. When he loses his bid for leadership he will be frustrated and upset—perhaps sufficiently so as to try to sabotage the group. He often believes the group to be unreasonable and disorganized. He thinks they have made many wrong decisions about the best way to proceed, and he usually considers the man or woman he has been contending with to be personally obnoxious. He finds himself involved in a *personality* conflict. He does not think that he can work with the leader. When possible, groups take the easy way out at this point and force the loser out or transfer him to another group. Sometimes he removes himself by dropping out or resigning.

This member can be knit back into the group and given a productive and useful role. The conversion is not an easy one, however. The newly emerged leader often has as much animosity toward the contender as the contender has for the leader. The leader finds her antagonist unreasonable and thinks of him as a source of trouble. The greatest mistake she can make is to exploit the power of her new leadership role to make life miserable for her antagonist. Indeed, in some of our case studies the newly emerged leader who proceeded to punish her opponent lost her position.

The wise leader, with support from her lieutenant and the others, always takes special pains at this crucial point in the group's development to encourage the last member eliminated in the shuffle for leadership to take a high status position commensurate with his capacities. Although the loser may never become completely reconciled to his role, he should be given a place in which he is committed to the group's goals and in which he can work for rather than against them.

The groups that follow the above pattern of emerging leadership (we will call it Pattern I) generally have a short and easy time of structuring and specializing the tasks that each member will perform.

Pattern II provides a more frustrating and difficult path to achieve roles and cohesiveness. In cases that followed this pattern the first phase was the same as in Pattern I. That is, if the group had five members, three would again be eliminated quickly. We will again call these three members A, C, and D.

The second phase would proceed in much the same way until the crucial moment when member A became member E's lieutenant. At that point in a group following Pattern II, member C would become member B's lieutenant. The group's work is now conducted in the following fashion. Member B suggests a course of action and member C supports it. However, member E disagrees and suggests a different way of proceeding and member A agrees with E. Member D thus is in the crucial position of determining almost every major decision.

Member D finds himself in this swing-vote position because he was tentative, quiet, and apparently uninvolved during the early meetings. He is the typical independent voter—not committed to either party and seemingly apathetic. He does not make clear-cut decisions and he does not come down strongly on the side of either faction. He tries to "stay out of it" and "above the battle."

In one case study the structure solidified for almost a week at this point. The person playing the role of member D was unusually tentative and uncomfortable with the responsibility of breaking all major deadlocks. Finally, after a particularly fruitless session in which the two factions had bickered for most of an hour, member A turned to him and challenged, "Where do you stand?" To which member D replied, "Right in the middle." Finally, after continued pressure of this type, member D did begin to support members E and A, and the role structure stabilized amidst much joking, release of tension, and general agreement that the meeting had been useful and "the best meeting so far."

In this case the group did succeed in finding a high status position for member B, and the leader, member E, exercised considerable tact and understanding in the process. The extended and acrimonious struggle resulting from this pattern made the accommodation of member B a crucial and extremely difficult one.

Pattern III is also a more complicated and often more difficult way to structure a group than is Pattern I. Groups that follow this pattern contain people whose actions for one reason or another are so impressive and fascinating to the other members that they become engrossed with their behavior and permit their attention to be distracted from the normal preoccupations with role structuring. We shall call these members *central persons*. They are central in that the group's attention is focused on them.

The central person may be a "star" in that her early behavior gives so much promise in helping the group at its task that she stands above the other members of the group. Perhaps she is a "star" because her efforts at creating a pleasant social climate are exceptionally pleasant, charming, and amusing.

Possibly the central person may be perceived as a great threat to the success of the group. If he is seen as extremely hostile to the organization and its purposes or seems unusually apathetic and uninvolved, his attitude can become a central concern. One case study following this pattern had a member called "Mr. Negative." Often the negative central person is an active and dominant personality.

One of the more common negative central persons is the "manipulator" who comes into the group with a conscious intention to exploit it *for his own ends.* He intends to take it over. He plans to get *his* ideas rammed through the group. He sees his task as one of carefully planning a strategy of take-over and then coercing the people to follow his way and achieve his purposes.

Manipulators tend to employ either a "hard" sell or a "soft" sell approach, but no matter what technique they use the members soon perceive these persons to be a central problem to the success of the group. The hard sell manipulator usually comes on strong. She talks a great deal and she takes charge almost immediately, with vigor. "Let's get down to business. Here's what I suggest we do." When the group rejects her attempt to take over she tries to argue them down. She grows louder and more voluble. When the group begins to support another leader-contender she attacks the ideas of this member. Often she stands alone against the rest, with everyone getting more excited, loud, and frustrated. Occasionally, she talks so vigorously that for a time no other member of the group wishes to challenge her. She is so certain of her positions and asserts herself so strongly that the group reluctantly appears to go along for a time.

Here, the manipulator thinks that she has achieved leadership. However, when she gives orders they are not followed. People continually misunderstand her and fail to follow through even when they admit they understand. The manipulator, typically, decides that she has not been doing a good job of leading and she must exercise more leadership. Her notion of more leadership is to do more of what got her in trouble in the first place. She now gives her orders very slowly and carefully in simple English as though she were talking to morons. When she finishes directives she says, "All right, now repeat it so that I am sure you understand." When this tactic results in even greater resentment and more "goldbricking" she bawls them out for being lazy and irresponsible.

Inevitably another contender emerges and the group gratefully supports her for the position of leader. The manipulator is now extremely frustrated. Her self-image is badly dented. She came into the group confident of her superiority and her ability to run things her way.

The group, however, had rejected her and foiled her attempts. She seldom examines where she has failed but she often turns on the group. They are ignorant and stupid. The group itself is unimportant. If she remains, she is likely to prove a troublemaker. Several of our test groups have managed to find a role in which the often considerable talents of a manipulator were useful to the group, but this is unusual.

The manipulator who employs the soft sell approach is often more successful in the early stages of the group's development. He may quickly emerge as group leader. This type of manipulator is more sophisticated than the first. He has greater awareness of the "tricks and formulas" of human relations. He is friendly and congenial. He seems less bossy and more democratic and shows a great deal of consideration for others. He asks their opinion, puts himself in their shoes, prefaces his disagreements with statements of understanding and agreement. He tries to size up the other members of the group and figures out which ones he can "con" and which will be troublesome for him. He does more work outside formal meetings by chatting with other members over coffee. When he begins to structure the group, he often asks the group's opinion. "How should we begin?" he asks.

If he is good at playing this part, the manipulator may fool the group for several days and they will give him their support as leader. After several weeks of working together, however, the others find him out. They discover that he is getting his way and that behind his congenial and democratic front he has been using the group for his own purposes. In over 100 cases studied only one manipulator succeeded in fooling his group for more than one month. When the smooth manipulator is found out the group must undergo another reshuffling of roles. His leadership is challenged, he is deposed, and the new leader emerges. All of this is painful to the group and reduces their cohesiveness and efficiency.

The groups that follow Pattern III to a successful conclusion all select leaders who demonstrate that they can handle the problems posed by the central person. Quite often the moment of leadership decision comes as the result of a dramatic crisis that the group attributes to the central person. Many times members testify that they supported a given individual for leadership because he was "strong" enough to handle a hard sell manipulator. Sometimes the leader-contender who can find a productive role for a "Mr. Negative" and can knit him into the group so that he no longer takes up so much of the group's time and attention will emerge as leader. Some groups never complete Pattern III. The struggle over leadership is never resolved. No member is strong enough to handle the manipulator. The negative central person establishes the group norms so that finally the group itself becomes apathetic or negative.

Pattern IV is a truncated pattern, and the groups that take this path seldom achieve role specialization and stability. They typically are fraught with social tensions and frustrations for their entire time together. People find these groups punishing; hence their general cohesiveness is low and they do not make efficient use of their human resources.

Quite often a group fails to stabilize roles when each of the contenders for leadership has substantial handicaps. A typical case of this variation of Pattern IV is furnished by the group that eliminated three of its five members as leaders in the first phase and was left with two potential leaders.

Member A was much more capable at developing a clear coherent course of action to facilitate the work, so she was clearly the best person to help the members do the job. Member D was much more adept at showing consideration for the group members and fulfilling their social and esteem needs. Since on balance the members perceived the two remaining contenders as roughly equal and both had severe handicaps, they did not follow either and the role structure never stabilized.

How Changing Membership Affects the Group. *New Members Join.* In some case studies we introduced a new member into the group after the role structure had stabilized. The addition of another member proved to be unsettling. He or she brought a complement of skills and talents to the organization, and a role had to be found for the newcomer. In a sense all of the roles had to be reshuffled to free enough duties to form a place for the new person.

The process of absorbing a new member proved extremely distressing. Often the members did not understand what was happening. For a brief period he was something of a central person and, on occasion, a popular one. That is, he was attended to and welcomed into the organization. The members talked to him and got acquainted with him and sometimes felt that he would be able to make a positive contribution to the work. Soon the members turned their attention back to the job and found that people were acting in unexpected ways. They were back in a painful period of role reorganization. When the old members did not grasp what was happening, they responded to the natural frustrations associated with this role struggle by blaming the new member for their problems. "If he weren't in the group, we would still be all right. Everything was fine until he joined us."

Old Members Leave. In some case studies we removed a member from highly cohesive groups with stable role structures. Here, too, a new role struggle resulted. The tasks that the former member had performed now had to be assumed by the remaining members of the organization. If she had performed important duties that had made her a highly regarded member, the members who had been doing low status tasks often tried to take over her role and gain the social and esteem rewards that went with it. The struggle was particularly intense in those instances where several members of the group stood to gain by *climbing* upward into the vacant role.

Again the members often were surprised by the change of events. They did not understand what went wrong. "A few weeks ago they were highly cohesive and successful," they would say. "Everybody pulled together and they had a good time. Now nothing seems to get done. Joe and Lucy have had a falling out and things are going badly. We need good old Harry. When he was here we were able to work together."

Old Member Is Replaced by a New One. When a member was removed from an organization with stable roles and another member added, a period of testing resulted. The new person did not take over the role of the member who left the organization. Rather, he or she went through a period of working out a suitable role, and in the process some of the remaining roles were reshuffled.

In short, the study of the effect of changing personnel in a work group, by adding, removing, or adding and removing members indicates that the entire role structure of the group is threatened and sometimes changed. Typically, changing personnel results in a period of role instability and struggle that surprises and frustrates the members. When the people in the organization are unaware of the necessity of such a period of reshuffling they often respond by blaming the new member for their problems. However, when the members of the test-tube groups are taught the principles of group process, they go through the process of reshuffling but they can tolerate the stresses and strains and are often able to speed up the acceptance of the new member.

Effect of Unsatisfactory Role Performance. Members of newly formed test-tube groups find the social indeterminacy hard to live with, and consequently they drive hard to establish roles. Sometimes in their eagerness to fit people into place they force a member into a role on scanty evidence, and as the group continues the members become dissatisfied with the way the person is performing. When the members become dissatisfied they act in accordance with their feelings. The most overt evidence of this attitude will be direct resistance to the role of the unsatisfactory member. This is almost the opposite mechanism by which they worked with the member to achieve a role in the beginning. Now, they extinguish the role by punishing the member when he plays the part.

If member E is being funny, the member who perceives that E is not playing the role to his satisfaction will stop laughing. He may even begin to groan and show his dissatisfaction openly. If this is not sufficient to stop E, he may become antagonistic and say to E, "Why don't you shut up? You aren't as funny as you think you are."

If the emerged leader begins to lose support, the first danger signals are manifested by decreasing compliance with his or her directions. In the army the dissatisfaction with the leadership resulted in the widespread practice of what was called "goldbricking," which meant not doing anything more than absolutely necessary to keep from being put on KP. In the experimental group, goldbricking is often followed by outright noncompliance. At this point the noncomplying member often pleads a communication "breakdown" to excuse his failure to follow directions. "I did not know *I* was supposed to do that," he asserts. A number of so-called communication breakdowns in the groups we studied turned out to be smoke screens to hide the resentment of members toward a bossy leader.

When other members of the group discover that a leader is being resisted, they often step forward to challenge his leadership; when they are supported in this attack, the leader may lose his role. No sooner is he deposed than the group repeats the pattern of role emergence once again until they settle upon a new leader. Meantime, the conflict involved in deposing the leader and finding a new one strains the social ties that bind the group together. The deposed leader and the person who led the attack upon his role may find themselves involved in a "personality conflict" with the result that they often grow to dislike one another.

If we understand the process by which roles develop in groups, we understand the roots of so-called personality conflicts. They do not stem from the way a member talks or combs his hair—although the deposed leader may suggest that her dislike of the person who led the charge on her role is based on such things. The real source of the conflict lies in her attempt to hold onto her high status role in the group. With the old leader eliminated it might seem that the person who led the group in removing her would be the new leader. This is not the case. The role of leader is now open; the leading remaining candidates must now contend for it.

Effect of Appointing a Leader. In some of the case studies the group was given some structure by the appointment of a leader. We designated one of the members as leader and then we gave the groups tasks to perform as we did the leaderless discussion groups. Appointing a leader did not keep the group from a period of testing. Indeed, *the appointed leaders often did not emerge as the natural leaders.* Even though a member was appointed leader, she still had to demonstrate her talents for the group, but they either reinforced or resisted her leadership moves in much the same way that they responded to members contending for leadership in the initially leaderless discussion group.

Appointing a leader did have several interesting effects on the basic patterns of leader emergence, however. First, the appointed leaders uniformly began the group sessions by acting as they thought leaders ought to act. They took charge and tried to structure the group's work. The same pattern appeared when the members found themselves in the midst of a difficult struggle over leadership; they evaded the problem by electing a person who was not in contention. Very often, after a particularly acrimonious session filled with role struggles, a group will decide that it needs a leader or a chairman to "give it direction." The members will then elect as leader a member previously eliminated as unsuitable for the role and will often choose a quiet, uninvolved, or withdrawn person. Usually they report that they picked this person because he was "neutral" or because he would not "take sides" with either of the leading contenders. When such a neutral and quiet member is elected leader he or she immediately *begins to act like a leader.* However, none of the contenders for the position supports the elected leader, and usually within a matter of minutes the person gives up any attempt to continue in the role.

The second effect of assigning a leader was to speed up the emergence of the natural leader when the members saw the assigned leader as the best person for the job. If she was the member who would have emerged during the natural course of events, assigning her the position hastened the process and eased the strains of the role struggle. In the case studies where this took place the group's cohesiveness and productivity were enhanced by assignment of the leader. The contenders for leadership who lost out to her did not lose much face in the process. The other members breathed a sigh of relief when they discovered that their leader was a person they could cheerfully follow. As a result the structure stabilized quickly.

A third effect of assigning a leader was to slow down the process of the emergence of a natural leader in those cases where the assigned leader proved unsatisfactory to the group. The assigned leader acted like a leader, was resisted, deposed, and then a new leadership struggle was initiated, which resulted in the emergence of another member as leader. The pattern here was quite analogous to the situation in which a member emerges as a leader in a leaderless discussion group and then is perceived as unsatisfactory. In these cases the group's cohesiveness and productivity were impaired by the assignment of a leader. The assigned leader who failed to emerge as the natural leader lost a great deal of face, and the group had to find a productive role for him or be plagued with a disgruntled member in a formal position of leadership.

SUMMARY

Every organization uses small group meetings for a variety of purposes. Some meetings are primarily rituals, others are briefing sessions, and still others serve instructional, creative, consultative, or decision-making purposes.

The leaderless zero-history small group is an important research tool in that it provides a test-tube situation in which the normal operations of everyday work groups are speeded up and basic patterns of group process are easy to observe and study.

In the test-tube groups the first important reaction that takes place is the role specialization of the members. A role is a set of shared expectations about what a person will and will not do or say in the group. The role a member takes in a group is worked out jointly by the member and the group.

After roles emerge, the members award to each role more or less internal status. An observer can estimate the status of each member's role by observing the direction, flow, and content of the communication during group meetings. The social and esteem rewards a member receives from group participation come largely from internal status.

The major role that is closely associated with high status is that of group leader. Several members typically contend for the position of leader. Leadership contention creates conflict, frustration for members, and group ineffectiveness. The emergence of natural leadership increases cohesion and efficiency.

During the "shakedown cruise" associated with role struggles, members of test-tube groups experience communication problems related to poor listening; these groups fail to provide adequate feedback to assure understanding.

The study of test-tube groups indicates that natural leadership emerges through a two-phase process of elimination. In the beginning the group members stereotype some participants as clearly unsuitable for leadership and eliminate them. In the second phase there is intensified competition and conflict among the remaining contenders.

The process of leadership contention falls into four basic patterns. In Pattern I a member begins to serve as a lieutenant for one of the contenders. After a period of time if no other contender gains a lieutenant, they are eliminated. A second pattern involves several contenders each of whom gains a lieutenant. The result is that the group has several power centers. Pattern II is typically longer and more difficult than Pattern I. Pattern III involves an internal crisis in which a contender gains leadership by handling a crisis such as that posed by a negative central person. Groups which never achieve leadership fall into Pattern IV.

Changes of membership such as adding new members, losing old members, or replacing members upset the group's role structure. Such changes bring about a period of readjustment similar to the original shakedown cruise as members jockey for new roles.

Appointing a leader in a zero-history group will facilitate the emergence of a leader if the appointed person turns out to be a natural leader. However, if the appointed leader proves poorly qualified for the role, the group will reject his or her leadership and return to ground zero. When the group rejects its appointed leader, the process of finding leadership is painful and time-consuming.

QUESTIONS FOR DISCUSSION AND REVIEW

1. In what ways are the informal and formal group meetings important to the communication of an organization?
2. What are some of the typical abuses of group meetings within organizations?
3. What are the typical types of group meetings in organizations?
4. List six essential points in planning a meeting.
5. What is the basic process of role emergence in a leaderless, zero-history, task-oriented small group?
6. How is status related to role?
7. What effect does the role struggle have on communication?
8. What is the process of leadership emergence in a leaderless, zero-history, task-oriented small group?
9. Describe the effects of three kinds of membership changes on role structure and communication.
10. What are the effects of appointing a formal leader on the basic process of leadership emergence?

REFERENCES AND SUGGESTED READINGS

Bormann, E. G. *Discussion and Group Methods: Theory and Practice,* 2nd ed. New York: Harper & Row, 1975.

Fear, R. A. *The Evaluation Interview.* New York: McGraw-Hill, 1973.

Goldhaber, G. M. *Organizational Communication,* 2nd ed. Dubuque, Iowa: Wm. C. Brown, 1979.

Levinson, D. J. "Growing Up With the Dream," *Psychology Today,* 11 (Jan. 1978), 20–31, 89.

Maier, N. R. F. *The Appraisal Interview.* New York: Wiley, 1958.

Stewart, C. J. and W. B. Cash. *Interviewing: Principles and Practices.* Dubuque, Iowa: Wm. C. Brown, 1974.

5

Learning the Symbolic World

—————————— **Laboratory Application** ——————————

In Chapter 2 we discussed the importance of learning the stories the members share about their common experiences in order to understand how they go about their business and how they get along with each other. We noted the need to find out the stories the participants in the subgroups, the larger communities, and the entire organization remember and retell about their common past.

Each identifiable small group, formal or informal, has a culture. By *culture* in the context of organizational communication we mean the sum total of ways of living, organizing, and communicating built up in a group of human beings and transmitted to newcomers by means of verbal and nonverbal communication. The culture consists of the shared norms, reminiscences, stories, rites, and rituals which provide the members with a unique symbolic common ground. Some of the members from several or more small groups in the organization may share cultural features and these people will thus form larger communities. Finally, members of the organization may share elements of common culture which tie them together even though the cultures of their primary small groups and communities have important differences.

Unless there are some strong common themes cutting across many or most small groups and communities within the organization, it will be difficult for people to feel a commitment to the organization itself. Without some common symbolic ground members of the various attractive and cohesive small groups may find it difficult to communicate across cultural boundaries to people in other groups and communities. The formal organizational context which may seem on the surface to encourage cooperative communicative behavior so all can pull together for the common good may, instead, be the background for many competitive and warring formal and informal small groups.

As a new member seeking to analyze the audience members for your communication it becomes important for you to learn the symbolic worlds, the cultures, of the salient groups and communities.

GATHERING MATERIAL

A good way to discover the symbolic world of a group is by collecting the dramatic messages, stories, histories, and anecdotes that they tell and retell. You can do this by individual interviews as we noted in Chapter 2. Several of the authors were preparing a training program for a division of a major corporation. As part of the preparation we visited the plant and the facilities and met the supervisor. We were then allowed to interview each member of the unit. One of the authors simply asked each interviewee for a typical story or anecdote which caught the spirit of what it was like to work in the division. Many of the anecdotes related to the theme of time. The stories were about time management, the lack of time, working overtime, the supervisor's preoccupation with deadlines, doing the job on time, and putting in the extra time needed to do a good job. After the first few interviews established this pattern, the interviewer kept a close watch on the clock and started and stopped each interview at exactly the scheduled time. Subsequent interviewees commented on how impressed they were that the interviewer was staying right on schedule.

The stories also revealed that the supervisor was a heroic figure in some of the stories and mentioned only in indirect ways in others. In many of the stories the competitive atmosphere in the unit was an important part of the scene. The supervisor was portrayed as a person who stressed the unit being competitive with other units in other corporations and being the "best" unit within the corporation.

In a short period of time a group of outsiders, by asking the right questions, learned a great deal about the communicative climate and group culture in a series of brief interviews. You can do the same if you are careful to remember to search for *common themes* and stories. (You may find a talkative member of your formal group who has a unique slant on things and is really a symbolic isolate in terms of the informal groups. While such stories may be interesting, they are of little use in analyzing group culture.)

Another good way to discover the shared stories is to watch during group meetings for those anecdotes which most or all of the members enjoy, get excited about, or respond to in a similar emotional way. Equally good evidence comes from brief mentions of people or events or from code words which spark a similar response but which make no sense to outsiders. These "inside jokes" provide strong clues that a story has been shared rather than just told without becoming an important part of the group's common culture. Member involvement is what you are looking for as you learn the symbolic world of the organization, its communities and groups.

You may also collect useful material by reading official written messages. Look for mission statements, outlines of organizational and unit goals and plans, and statements reporting what the organization or unit has accomplished in the last few months or over the years.

Unofficial written messages are another good source of material. Underground messages such as satirical poems, songs, jokes are important, particularly if they spread rapidly and are shared with approval. Jokes, cartoons, humorous messages on bulletin boards, or graffiti on rest room walls can be important, too.

Most of the material you are looking for is in the form of a mini play or TV drama. The dramatic form is illustrated by any good television show and consists of characters in action within a scene. For the purpose of finding out the organization's symbolic world you need to examine these dramatic messages to discover their meaning for the group's culture. The basic question is: How do these messages provide common ground for those who share them, enabling them to communicate more effectively among themselves and with members of other groups and communities?

To gain such an understanding, you should make a script analysis of the more important dramatic messages. We present here the basics of script analysis so you can get started in analyzing the way people in the organization portray themselves and their groups. We emphasize your role as a consumer and critic of the communication. You are still somewhat on the outside, working your way in. You are an active observer. You are learning your way in a new culture. In Chapter 14 we go into greater depth about these matters in terms of how you can create messages designed to bind members of the organization into productive and rewarding communities.

SCRIPT ANALYSIS

Hero and Villain Analysis. You can begin the study of a script by asking: Who are the good people and who are the bad? Sorting out the heroes and the villains is an important feature in finding out the group's culture. When we found that the supervisor of the unit discussed above was a "good guy" for a substantial group in the unit but a "bad guy" for another sizable group, we had learned some important information which had a bearing on the way the group worked and communicated together. To understand the basics of good versus bad people in the organizational stories we must first sketch the basic feature of most dramatic scripts.

The typical successful script focuses on a central character and the story is about what that character does and what happens as a result. The central character has a goal or objective and the script provides an account of the character's attempts to reach the goal. If the script is to work dramatically, however, the central character cannot get what he or she wants without some problems along the way. The old formula script for a Hollywood love story in the 1930s and 1940s was boy gets girl, boy loses girl, boy gets girl. If the boy gets the girl and they live happily ever after, there is no dramatic suspense and little audience interest. One legendary writer of popular short stories is supposed to have explained dramatic complication as follows: get your character up a tree and then throw rocks at him.

The central character tries to achieve the goal and runs into a major obstacle. The obstacle is often posed by people who symbolize unsavory groups or forces that are striving to keep the hero from getting the goal. This sets the stage for a battle of wills and for a test of strategy, values, and ethics. The human antagonists to the central character are the villains of the script.

Usually the central character gains our sympathy to some extent because the goal he or she is after is a good one such as achieving peace, justice, harmony, the welfare of the community, true love, and so forth. The skillful storyteller makes the goal concrete so the script is more believable but the concrete goal clearly symbolizes the larger good end. The hero might reveal corruption in city government or fight a plant that is polluting the water supply of the town.

One of the more graphic stories we heard when we were conducting the interviews with members of the corporate unit mentioned earlier involved a manager who was an avid sailor and devoted family man. His children were at an age where they enjoyed sailing and he liked to spend his weekends with them. The "boss" called the manager one Saturday morning to report that he was at the office going over some matters and asked for some relevant information. In the course of the telephone conversation the boss asked the manager about his plans and the manager told of his going sailing with his family. According to the person telling the story, a call from the boss on the weekend was a signal to drop everything and come to the office to help with whatever project the boss was working on. In this case, however, the manager went sailing. Shortly thereafter there was a reshuffling of offices and the manager was assigned an office in another building away from the center of things. As time went on it became clear that his career was coming to a dead end. The way the interviewee dramatized the script, the manager was a sympathetic character wanting to build a good family life and the boss was a bad guy who was unsympathetic and vindictive.

The central character may run into obstacles other than those posed by villains. The hero may have to battle natural problems such as bad weather, tall mountains, floods, and so forth to reach the objective. The hero may, on the other hand, face obstacles within herself such as fear of failure which keep her from achieving a management position in the organization.

The first step in script analysis is thus to look at who are the heroes and who are the villains. What do the heroes want? What do the villains want? Why are the heroes attractive? What values do they represent? What organizational forces do they personify? Does the hero write a song ridiculing a slogan the company uses to encourage productivity and sing it over an intercom system? Does the hero stand up to the boss, speaking out for the workers in the matter of break time? In a study of three organizations and their cultures relating to women in management, Dotlich found the following story. A woman recently promoted to a management position found herself working for a male supervisor who had a reputation as a sexist. When she was new on the job, as the two of them were walking down the hall, they met several other members of the unit. The supervisor introduced her to them as the new manager and then in front of them patted her in a familiar way on the bottom. She reached down and patted him as familiarly on his penis. According to the narrator, the sexist supervisor never tried anything like that with her again. In this script the hero is symbolic of forces for equal treatment of women in the organization and the villain is symbolic of male chauvinism and sexism.

Usually people get caught up in the script because they find the central character attractive and they pull for that person to succeed. In a sense the pull (effectiveness) of the script for the listeners or readers is equal to how much they are pulling for the heroes. One important question is how much pull does this script have for the people in the organization.

The Action Line. Scripts may concentrate on the characters and deemphasize action but they often have a strong action line. The action is essentially what the characters do to achieve their goals. Does the heroine want to increase productivity? Does she, therefore, adapt to the sexism she finds among some male colleagues and tackle the production bottleneck with technical know-how, hard work, and ingenuity to develop a better way to do it which improves production levels? Does the hero strive to set production goals at a level the group wants rather than at the level management sets and does he organize groups of workers to "talk to" rate busters and bring other group pressures on them to fall in line? Do a script analysis on some of the stories you hear regarding students who speak up in class, study a great deal, break the curve, and get straight As. Are they heroes? Laudable and admired? Are they derided and ridiculed? Do they evoke sympathy and identification? Resentment? Usually the actions of the heroes are those the group approves and applauds. The actions that pull the hardest on the members' sympathies are those they would tend to emulate or support. The actions often imply the values embedded in the group culture.

Scene Analysis. One final part of the script that deserves your attention is the scene in which the drama takes place. At the simplest level you should look at where the stories take place. Are they set in the office? The production line? On the golf course or softball field? In barrooms and discos? Often you can tell a good deal about the group's culture by noting how many stories about critical events stress various features of the organization's territory. An example from general North American culture can serve to illustrate the importance of setting. Very few people nowadays are fixing fences, going on round-ups, punching cattle, and shooting up cowtowns on their days off. Yet a good many television commercials show scenes of sparsely settled range country with he-men who wear big hats and ride horses while they herd cattle. The "Great American West" remains important sacred ground for many North Americans. It has helped sell a host of products from clothing to beverages. Although we have not seen it yet we may someday see cow country helping sell a male perfume called something like "horsehide."

At a deeper level, in making an analysis of the script, you should ask about the *locus of control* of the dramatic action. *Locus of control* refers to the place where the forces that cause things to happen reside. The settings may just be backdrops for active heroes (members of the group) who control their own fate, make things happen, and are responsible for the results. The locus of control, thus, is within them. The stories may imply that other people have fate control over group members and that the members themselves are without power to change events. The scene may be controlling events in the sense that the situation is such that things are destined to turn out in a certain way or as they did. The members of the group are thus at the mercy of fate or chance or accident. "If it hadn't been for the heavy snowstorm right then . . ." "The cards were stacked against us; we were up against a hopeless situation. No matter what we did it would have turned out that way anyway." An important part of the scene therefore may include supernatural forces, fate, providence, God, or chance. Human beings cannot change what will happen. To translate from Spanish the words of an old popular song, "What will be, will be."

ASSIGNMENT: A Script Analysis

Your instructor will assign you a project which involves gathering suitable material and making a script analysis of an organization, a subgroup, or a community within an organization. You will do a brief field study and write a short analysis paper. You may be assigned to do this as an individual, or your instructor may assign you to a task force group which will do the field study as a team, then write a group report. Task force groups can tie in this assignment with the assignment in Chapter 4. Working on the task force will also give you a chance to experience how your team builds a group culture during the course of working on the project.

─────────── **Theoretical Rationale** ───────────

The theory which relates and explains the use of script analysis to study the organizational symbolic world is called *symbolic convergence*. *Symbolic* refers to the human tendency to interpret objects and signs and give them meaning. This human tendency also carries over into the interpretation of the things people do and say and in the unfolding of events. People tend to make human movement into symbolic action by trying to figure out what it means. *Convergence* means the tendency of two or more private symbolic worlds of individuals to incline to each other, to come together, to meet. When two or more people communicate in such a way that their private views begin to converge they come to share a common symbolic ground. They interpret signs and human action in the same way. Some scholars have called the result of symbolic convergence a state of *coorientation*. If you are oriented toward an object you look at it from a certain angle. If several people share the same angle they are *cooriented*.

A number of investigators have pointed out the importance of coorientation to the process of communication but few have tried to explain how it comes about. The theory of symbolic convergence does provide an explanation of how people come to share a common orientation or symbolic world.

Group Fantasies. The basic communicative process by which people experience symbolic convergence is *the dynamic process of sharing group fantasies*. Investigators studying small groups first discovered the communicative process by which people share fantasies. Subsequent study of these moments in small group meetings revealed that they perform an important convergent function in building group culture.

If we watch the members of a group who are involved in a conversation, either an informal social group or a task-oriented group meeting, we may notice a moment when the discussion seems to drop off and people are not involved in the give-and-take. They may seem tense and not sure of what to say next. They may slump down in their chairs, look bored or disinterested. Then one of the people dramatizes characters in action at some other place and time than the here-and-now of the meeting. The script may deal with something that has happened to the person or something the person hopes will happen or it may have to do with something in the news or a movie or TV program. Another person sits up and responds to the story. Something about it has caught this person's interest and attention. Another person joins in. Others begin to be caught up in the story. Someone else may comment and dramatize another script similar to the first. They all begin talking. They may laugh or express fear or sadness. They may grow emotional. Then, as abruptly as it began, the moment is broken and the group goes back to a different topic.

We call these moments of dramatization which pull the members of the group into sympathetic participation *fantasy chains*. We do not mean to use the term *fantasy* in one of its common usages which is as something imaginary, not grounded in reality. What we have in mind is another common usage of the term which is the creative and imaginative interpretation of events that fulfill a psychological or rhetorical need. Fantasy includes fanciful and fictitious scripts of imagined characters as well as the interpretation of things that have actually happened to the members of the group or that are reported in authenticated works of history or the news media.

Studies of small group communication indicate that not every dramatized script in a group discussion will result in a fantasy chain. Many stories are told and get very little response. Scripts which do not pull people together and shape their interpretation of the world into a common symbolic form are not shared fantasies. Sometimes you will find it interesting and helpful to study the scripts which failed to result in symbolic convergence. Our emphasis here, however, is on the study of the common ground which people share.

The shared group fantasy works something like the dreams we have as an individual. When we daydream about people we admire doing things we like or when we imaginatively take a role in a dramatic setting and enact a script in which we are heroes, we reveal our values, our goals, and our motives. If a person learns our most intimate daydreams, that individual learns a good deal about us, and about how we are likely to behave.

Group fantasies serve to create common dreams, goals, and values for a group of people and thus make communication easier in some important respects. When group members share a number of fantasies over a long period of time they develop essential elements of their group culture. They come to share the same heroes and villains; they applaud the same actions, share the same values and ethical codes, and, most importantly, the same past.

No collection of individuals can become a group or community or organization until it has an identity. An important way to give a group an identity is to develop a common history. Scripts which feature all or some members of the group enacting the dramatic action from the past provide the common history. Members must dramatize these scripts in conversation at which some or all group members are present and they must trigger a fantasy chain if they are to work as a provider of group history and identity. When you first join your work group at the new organization you know nothing about "it" or what its past has been like. Once you hear some of the stories about what has happened to it and you come to share those stories, you begin to know its history. Then the group takes on an identity for you.

Fantasy Type. Often groups of people will tell a variety of stories but many of them will be similar in theme and action. They will essentially be the same story but with different characters and slightly different incidents. A *fantasy type* is a recurring script in the shared symbolic ground of the group.

Suppose a small new company is beginning to succeed in a highly competitive branch of computer applications of cable television. The top management group is composed of young, highly trained engineers and technicians and sales personnel, largely male. One of the founders of the company has emerged as leader of the group. Because they deal in large contracts each sale is vitally important to the company's success and the negotiations often take a period of months; the top management is heavily involved in the sales effort. The leader, also the president, takes an important role in the sales presentations. Often a delegation will come to visit the plant offices from firms that might buy the services of the company.

If you were to observe the group at work you would discover that they are on easy communication terms with one another and there is much kidding and joking and laughter. Soon you discover they have many in-jokes which they find highly amusing but which an outsider cannot understand. One day, you hear the group raucously sharing fantasies related to a script about how they entertained a delegation of visiting buyers the evening before. Over time you discover much sharing of such scripts. While the names change and the details of the escapades vary from evening to evening, the basic story remains the same. In each story, they have shown the visitors a hard-drinking, exciting time on the town, hitting the best night spots, investigating the weirdest night life. They have been hard-drinking hosts and the boss has once again proven to be the hardest drinker of the bunch as they have once again, as a team, drunk the visitors under the table. Once again they have tumbled into bed at 3 a.m., caught a couple of hours of sleep, shaved and showered, and been at their desks at 8 a.m., ready and able to put in a hard day of outstanding work on the newest project.

The basic story line is a fantasy type. When you discover a fantasy type as we did with the division whose fantasies about the importance of time clustered into types, you have found a script which is likely to be widely shared and well worth careful script analysis.

When you have found the main fantasy themes and fantasy types which are shared by members of a group you can go on to make an analysis of the scripts. This procedure will provide you with a basic understanding of the culture of a formal or informal group within the organization. As a new member of the organization you will soon find several groups of primary importance to your place in the work setting. You will want to analyze carefully the symbolic ground of these primary groups as soon as possible.

The dynamic process of sharing group fantasies is not confined to small group communication and two-person conferences. Speakers and commentators also dramatize events on the mass media and in the messages that flow through an organization's communication channels and networks. Communicators within the organization may comment on the relationship of the organization to the local community, the national scene, and international events. They may also dramatize internal happenings relating to upper management decisions, interdepartmental feuds, realignment of priorities, decisions about moving into new product lines or areas, striking personalities and the internal politics of moving up or down or out of the management structure.

Usually the important scripts for larger organizational communities are linked to two-person and small group communications. Often a small group will participate in a fantasy chain and, excited about their shared interpretation of an event, the group or its members will tell the story to other people either in a formal statement or in informal conversations. Others may share the fantasy as well and often do so in another small group setting where the story is dramatized by someone who has read or heard about it through the formal or informal communication channels of the organization or even from mass media or other outside sources.

We suggest you analyze the way people come to share fantasies in an organizational setting by viewing the communication as a system.

Scholars in many fields have taken the systems perspective to study events on the assumption that what they are studying is a complex process which has interrelated subparts and that important features emerge from the complex give-and-take of elements of the system. Basically the notion is that the whole is greater than the sum of its parts.

When you look at the organization as a communication system in terms of the sharing of fantasies you can divide up the total system into subsystems for the purposes of understanding certain events. One possible way to divide up the total is to examine who has control of a subsystem of messages. For example, some formal communications are controlled by upper management. Only those scripts which upper management approves are formally dramatized in such messages as quarterly reports, mission statements, and official policy statements. Indeed, larger organizations often have professional communicators such as public relations or media specialists who develop press releases and speak for the organization at press conferences or to inquiring reporters.

Upper management may also use these communication specialists for internal persuasive campaigns aimed at increasing "motivation" or productivity or compliance with safety regulations. The campaign may include a variety of messages and many dramatizations in slogans, posters, company newsletters, individual letters, or memos attributed to various officials. The professionals may also write speeches, letters and announcements that are attributed to the president of the company or to other highly placed people.

Some formal communication may be controlled by middle management and some by workers and technicians. These latter may include such things as letters to the company newspaper, recommendations placed in a suggestion box, formal complaints to an ombudsman or placed through grievance procedures or legal channels.

Informal communication tends to be an open marketplace for script competition, which is beyond the control of any special interest group, formal organizational unit or management level. Within this informal system the carefully orchestrated campaign developed and planned by management may include scripts which become shared fantasies. On the other hand, people may reject, ridicule or ignore the dramatizations. New and much different fantasies may chain through these informal systems and create a community of people which cuts across organizational structures, management levels, and primary group memberships.

Another way you can divide up the subsystems as a participant is in terms of the subsystem of communication of which you are a part as compared to the subsystem to which a fellow worker, or your supervisor, or a middle manager, or the chief executive officer is a part. You may never hear some fantasies because you are not part of the communication subsystem in which they are chaining. The chief executive officer has access to a different subsystem than you do. He or she will share quite different fantasies than you will.

There are a number of forces that restrict the flow of messages to limited subgroups or communities within the organization and thus make it unlikely that all members will have access to all scripts which could form the basis for common symbolic ground. Since information is often power in the organizational context, there are many pressures for secrecy. Departments and divisions may not want other units of the organization to know what they are up to because they compete with them for resources and other rewards. Upper management may feel that certain key information should not be made generally available to everyone. People committed to various informal and formal groups may not want to tell relative strangers about gossip, rumors, or interpersonal relations within these primary groupings.

Rhetorical Vision. When a number of people within a communication subsystem, no matter what their official position or what division or unit they are part of, come to share a number of fantasies and fantasy types, they may come to share a rhetorical vision.

A *rhetorical vision* is a unified putting-together of the various shared scripts which gives a participant a broader view of the organization and its relationship to the external environment, of the various subdivisions and units of the organization, and of their place in the scheme of things. The rhetorical vision is often integrated by a master analogy which pulls the various elements together. Usually a rhetorical vision is indexed by a slogan or label.

For example, the analogy which integrated the rhetorical vision of a substantial number of students at one community college was that "X community college is a high school with ash trays." In another example, the analogy which integrated a rhetorical vision for upper management in a large manufacturing company was that the employees comprised one big happy family. This company had started out as a small partnership and the chief executive officer still ran things the same way. When we discovered the master analogy, we had a better understanding of the strange phenomenon which saw the company continuing a traditional holiday meal for all employees. Over the years the employees had grown so numerous that a convention hall of large proportions was rented to stage the event and employees were required to attend.

Rhetorical Community. A *rhetorical community* consists of the people who participate in a rhetorical vision. Members of a rhetorical community share "inside jokes" and tend to appreciate the same cartoons about company matters. They share a common symbolic ground and can be counted on to respond to messages in ways which are in tune with their rhetorical vision. Since rhetorical communities are formed on the basis of the dynamic flow of messages through formal and *informal* channels, their boundaries are seldom the same as the formal boundaries set up by the table of organization. You cannot decide what the rhetorical landscape looks like by looking at the formal map, nor can you tell by looking at the obvious cues to status and position such as location of office, number of secretaries, or possession of the key to the executive washroom.

Organizational Saga. A *saga* is a detailed narrative of the achievement and events in the life of a person, a group, or a community. We use the concept of *organizational saga* to include the shared group fantasies, the rhetorical visions, and the narratives of achievements, events, and the future vision of dreams of the entire organization.

The common symbolic ties which bind the participants to the organization and provide the symbolic aspects of the organizational culture and customs are furnished by the saga. To function, the saga, like a fantasy, must be shared. We only include in our definition of saga those narrative elements to which the members are committed. Given our definition, you can see that the organizational saga may relate to only a portion of the formal membership of the organization.

When there are substantial communities within an organization committed to different organizational sagas, you can anticipate many battles and conflicts over policy, mission, decisions relating to future commitments, budget allocations, hiring and firing of new people, and so forth. You can also anticipate many meetings to develop mission statements, future plans, ten-year projections, and to clarify the basic purposes and functions of units and divisions.

The organizational saga answers such questions as, What kind of an organization are we? What kind of people are members of our organization? What do we do? What is our purpose? What exploits of the past are we proud of? Why are we admirable? What great things do we plan to do in the future? Answers to these questions provide an explanation of our better natures and our strengths. They often are the aspect of our symbolic ground which we emphasize when we develop messages for outside consumption. For example, a good way to get some answers to questions such as the above about a community or liberal arts college or university is to look at the brochures and bulletins the institutions send to prospective students.

Here are some examples of college and university saga statements:

> ... X University is a unique experience. It is more than red tile roofs and sandstone buildings. It is a blend of opportunities, a combination of resources, a smorgasbord of events, lectures, discussions, buildings, and people. Especially people. ... The importance that X attaches to each

student and what that student thinks goes back to the Founders. . . . The Founding grant stresses the importance of developing individual leadership qualities.

. . . Y College, founded by immigrant pioneers in 18--, continues to thrive in the spirit and substance of which pioneers are made. . . . The worth of individuality is attested in a student-operated Free University, in an active student government, in a variety of student publications, in an on-campus coffee house, in independent research projects during Interim. . . .

. . . Z College is a small Christian liberal arts college in an urban setting. Dedicated to a liberal education and to preparing Christian young people for making a contribution to society, Z College is composed of a student and faculty community where Christian living becomes a reality in the pursuit of truth.

The organizational saga will also contain material that is primarily aimed at insiders but that emphasizes the heroic exploits and glorious future of the organization. Thus, upper management may portray a department store as the innovator and leader in high fashion merchandising, unorthodox in method, ahead of the competition, and always among the top stores in the country in terms of earnings. The shared fantasies of the firm in computer applications of cable television that depicted the organization as a hard-driving, hard-drinking collection of super-people able to pull off miracles because they were inherently more creative and harder working than the competition represents another example of organizational sagas.

What we have been describing are the front parlor elements of the saga. The front parlor narratives are those that the members include when they want to put the best face on their organization either for public consumption or for their own needs, their self-images. Organizational sagas also include material relating to the back kitchen, the storage closet and the bathroom, but these insiders often keep from the public. They usually talk about such matters in informal settings and under circumstances of interpersonal trust and disclosure. Here is where members of the college who see themselves as a Christian community discuss some of the un-Christian things that characterize the operation of the school. Or where members of the hard-driving, hard-drinking firm admit that drunkenness and fatigue were responsible for the loss of a large contract or that some members were becoming alcoholics. Or where members of the University whose front-parlor saga affirms that the mission of the institution is threefold—teaching, research, and service to society—discuss scripts that portray the main mission of the faculty as being research and publication rather than teaching. Often the less savory scripts are shared in terms of "Yeah, yeah, I know that's what we say, but this is what is really going on around here."

As you learn the organizational saga relating to your new position you should gather elements relating to both the front parlor and the back kitchen. Sometimes newcomers are taken with the inside-dopester tone of the "this is what is really going on around here" communication and discount the more formal and best-foot-forward parts of the saga. You should not make that mistake. An organization, to survive, must have a saga that gives its members a feeling of significance and worth.

SUMMARY

Each small group, formal or informal, has a culture that consists of shared norms, reminiscences, stories, rites, and rituals. The group's culture provides the members with a unique symbolic common ground. Larger communities within the organization may share similar cultural features, and all or most members of the organization may participate in a shared culture.

A good way to discover the symbolic world of a group is by collecting the dramatic messages, stories, histories, and anecdotes that they enjoy telling and retelling. Inside jokes are a particularly rich source of information. Further information about the common culture can come from studying official and unofficial written messages.

Script analysis of the shared stories can provide an understanding of the group culture. In making a script analysis you can begin with a study of its heroes and villains, move on to an analysis of the dramatic action, and, finally, examine the scene in which the drama takes place. In looking at the entire script one important feature is the *locus of control* which refers to who or what causes things to happen.

The theory which explains organizational culture is called *symbolic convergence.* People come to symbolic convergence during the dynamic communicative process of sharing group fantasies. Fantasy chains are those moments within a communication episode when sympathetic participation in the dramatizations moves from member to member in a chain reaction. The stories which make up an important part of group fantasies are about what people in the group have done in the past or what they dream of doing in the future. Fantasies may also be about outsiders and external events. Usually only a small portion of the fantasies are about fictitious or fanciful characters.

A *fantasy type* is a recurring script, a stock scenario, a common narrative frame. A group or community with a strong consciousness of itself has a clear definition of "we" and "they." Such a group will have clusters of stories all with the same moral, the same general action line, and the same scene. The common spine of such clusters is a fantasy type.

The dynamic process of sharing group fantasies also takes place in larger communities within the organization as dramatized messages flow through the organization's formal and informal channels.

When a number of people within a communication subsystem share a group of fantasies and fantasy types they may be cooriented toward important features of the organization, of its external environment, and of life in general. When such a coherent and organized collective consciousness emerges with a community of people involved in it the result is a *rhetorical vision.* A *rhetorical community* consists of the people who participate in the rhetorical vision and share the common consciousness.

The organizational saga is a detailed narrative of the achievements and events in the life of an organization. To function as an organizational saga the elements must be shared by all or by a substantial number of the members.

QUESTIONS FOR DISCUSSION AND REVIEW

1. What is a group or organizational culture?
2. How might a person gather material to examine the symbolic world of groups and communities within an organization?
3. How would you gather material to examine an organization's saga?
4. How would you go about making a script analysis of an important organizational fantasy?
5. How is the symbolic convergence theory related to the coorientation of communicators within an organization?
6. What is the dynamic process of sharing group fantasies?
7. What is the content of messages involved in the communicative process of sharing fantasies?
8. What is a fantasy type?
9. How is a rhetorical vision related to a rhetorical community?
10. What is an organizational saga?

REFERENCES AND SUGGESTED READINGS

Baldridge, J. V. "Organizational Change: Institutional Sagas, External Challenges, and Internal Politics," in J. V. Baldridge and T. Deal, eds. *Managing Changes in Educational Organizations.* Berkeley: McCutcheon, 1972, pp. 123–44.

Bormann, E. G. "Fantasy and Rhetorical Vision: The Rhetorical Criticism of Social Reality." *Quarterly Journal of Speech.* 58 (1972), 396–407.

Bormann, E. G., L. L. Putnam, and J. M. Pratt. "Power, Authority, and Sex: Male Response to Female Dominance." *Communication Monographs.* 45 (1978), 119–55.

Clark, B. "The Organizational Saga in Higher Education." *Administrative Science Quarterly.* 17 (1972), 178–84.

Dotlich, D. L. "Worlds Apart: Perceptions of Opposite Sex Managers in Three Modern Organizations," Ph. D. Dissertation, University of Minnesota, 1980.

Part Two

Learning to Communicate as a Subordinate

6

Dealing With Communication Opportunities and Problems

Laboratory Application

In previous chapters we have laid the groundwork for your development as a skilled communicator as you settle into your new position.
We have described the formal organizational structure and communication channels, the informal channels, and the ways in which the
dynamics of two-person and small group communication function in
the organizing of collectives of people into a goal-directed, structured
entity.

We have stayed away from formulas to apply to stock situations
because of the complexity of the communication process and the
influence of the specific context and situation on the event. We see a
difference between training and education in that training provides
you with recipes to meet standard opportunities and problems and
education equips you to make wise choices after careful analysis of
each unique situation. Training is useful when you are drilling on how
to improve skills such as the ability to gesture effectively or to use your
voice in a more expressive way. Knowledge, on the other hand, is what
is needed for the typical communication opportunities and problems in
an organization whether you are performing an entry-level job or
assuming the position of chief executive officer.

You have now gained enough knowledge to try your hand at
analyzing and working out strategies for dealing with individual
situations. Law schools and graduate schools of business administration often use the case study as a teaching device to allow students to

apply their knowledge to a specific instance in which they have enough information to make an analysis and discuss solutions. We present here the case study of the Fable of Invention Incorporated, a mythical company which goes through communicative processes which we have observed in a number of "real life" organizations. After reading the rest of the chapter you should review Part One. Examine the study questions that follow the case study and be prepared for class discussion of the case.

CASE STUDY ASSIGNMENT: Invention Incorporated

One evening in the late 1960s five neighbors on Girard Street are playing poker in the basement recreation room of an advertising executive. In addition to the host there is a lawyer, a psychiatrist, a stockbroker, and a pediatrician. During a break in the game someone observes that there is an unusual combination of training and talent gathered around the table.

The group begins to expand along the lines suggested by that observation, and the advertising man remarks that with this much talent combined they ought to be able to dream up a number of successful money-making schemes. The brainstorming session is on. The lawyer immediately falls in with the suggestion and starts to plan the formation of a corporation. The next morning it hits the stockbroker that the castle-building at the poker table the night before has significant potential. He phones the others and all of them meet for lunch. The plan still sounds good to the advertising executive and the lawyer, although the doctors are skeptical. Nonetheless they all agree to meet for lunch several times a month to discuss possible ways to make money. They also think up the name Invention Incorporated. For several months they meet and propose a number of ideas but none of them seems sufficiently practical. Then one day the doctors, who have gradually become enthusiastic about the potential of Invention Incorporated, hit upon the notion of developing a line of toys "scientifically" designed to improve the emotional health of the child. The psychiatrist and pediatrician team up to work out a series of such toys. The advertising executive sees a campaign aimed at parents and grandparents that stresses the emotional and mental health angle. He thinks that promoting the theme that by the age of six the child's personality is formed will sell such a line of toys.

The doctors develop two toys. One is Sadie the Sibling Rival. Sadie is a large child-sized doll suitable for hitting and kicking. She is equipped with a loud crying and wailing mechanism and designed fondest hopes. The entire inventory is sold out, and still inquiries from buyers around the country continue to come in.

Invention Incorporated shows an incredible profit for its first two years of operation. After their big success at the first Christmas season, the board of directors has a meeting in which it faces some difficult decisions. The advertising executive agrees to resign his job at the agency to assume full-time duties as president, bringing his colleague with him as full-time sales manager. They expand their office and promotion force, and the stockbroker resigns his position to assume full-time duties as production manager. The next year sees a continued expansion of sales and they rent a plant and begin producing their own toys. The production manager now becomes plant manager and hires three assistants, a line supervisor, a procurement officer, and a supervisor of research and development.

The line supervisor has two foremen, each supervising a work group of ten people who assemble the toys. The procurement officer has an assistant and a secretary and two office workers; the supervisor of research and development has two assistants. The ideas still come largely from the original five-man group. Figure 9 indicates the formal organization of Invention Incorporated as the firm has evolved. Of course the organization keeps changing and the informal organization does not fit so neatly into the boxes of the table of organization as one might think. Small work groups are evolving and interacting and stabilizing (or failing to stabilize) roles in the way (described in Chapter 4) new people do when they are brought together to work on specific jobs. The office force that the president sets up soon becomes a small task-oriented work group. The workers and supervisors who are placed in the plant to assemble the toys soon become small groups with an informal role structure. To be sure, a worker on the assembly line will not be able to emerge as a leader in the production division because of the rigidity in the formal structure that makes it difficult for her or him to establish the necessary lines of communication with the supervisors and the production manager. Within such formal restrictions, however, the work of Invention Incorporated is done by a number of small task-oriented work groups that function in the same way as the basic model developed in Chapter 4.

In a sense the table of organization of Invention Incorporated reflects the role structure that emerged first in the small group that formed the company and then in each group of the company that was added to the founding group. The formal structure is the fossilized remains of the first living informal structures of the organization.

During the 1970s the demands of Invention Incorporated upon the time of the board of directors continue to grow with the success of the company. The psychiatrist finally decides that he can no longer be an active member of the board. He feels his first duty is to his profession

expressly for the child who needs to express hostility in a healthy way
The second toy is Randy the Robot. Randy is an electrically operate
lifelike toy. If the child barks orders and at the same time pushes th
proper button, Randy will walk, stop, turn around, run, and fall dow
at command. Randy is designed especially for the youngest child in a
family and can be ordered about to relieve the child's frustration
because as the youngest he often has no one to "boss."

The stockbroker contacts a local toy manufacturer about producing
several prototypes, and the lawyer patents the two toys. After several
tries the manufacturer produces models that seem attractive, sturdy
and functional. The local manufacturer is willing to contract to
produce the toys, and the advertising man prepares an attractive
brochure promoting the stock. The broker takes care of getting the
stock marketed, and the lawyer makes legal arrangements for incor-
poration. The group must now decide on the formal corporate structure.
They must pick a president, vice-presidents, a treasurer, and other
officers. The problem is an easy one however, for during the course of
their poker games and luncheon meetings a clear and stable role
structure had emerged in their work group. When they select the
advertising executive as president, the two doctors as vice-presidents
in charge of research and development, the lawyer as vice-president in
charge of production, and the stockbroker as treasurer, they are simply
formalizing their informal role structure.

Invention Incorporated now has both a *formal* and *informal* role
structure. At this point in the development of the organization these
two structures are the same. The name of the formal position is also the
name of the informal role.

Invention Incorporated offers its stock on the local market and it
sells moderately well. They now have working capital and they borrow
enough additional money to go into production. For the time being the
officers plan to run the corporation as a part-time hobby. However, the
advertising man hires a colleague at the agency to be a part-time sales
manager. They sell the first order of the toys to department and toy
stores in the local area and, using the modest profit, they borrow more
money and take a flier. They place a much larger order for the two
proven sellers and develop three more toys. They now hire a full-time
secretary and clerk-typist (two new formal positions) and open a
office in a downtown office building. The job of selling the line is too b
for the part-time sales manager and he hires two full-time salesme

The time of decision is the pre-Christmas period. Invention Inco
porated is operating on a razor-thin margin. They have all their capi
and a considerable amount of borrowed money tied up in a hu
inventory of toys. The result of the pre-Christmas sales surpasses th

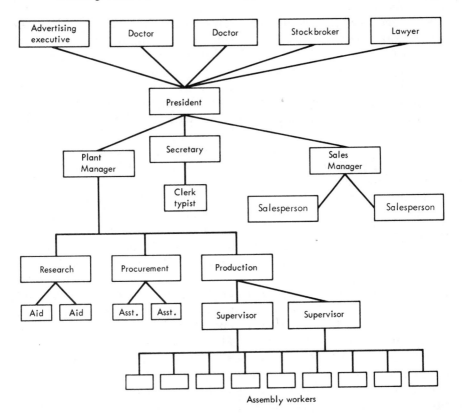

Figure 9. Table of Organization for Invention Incorporated

and so he withdraws from active participation. The research and development section is crippled when he leaves, for his role has largely been in the area of providing new ideas for toys. Two new people are hired to "beef up" this section. Under the pressure of affirmative action and the changes in societal attitudes toward women, one of the new people is a woman. In a short while the remaining four members of the board elect the sales manager to fill the vacancy on the board of directors. The board undergoes a rather severe role struggle to reshuffle positions, and the other doctor decides to withdraw from active participation also. Before he leaves, however, he and the sales manager have a falling out, and the sales manager, who has an excellent offer from another bigger toy company, accepts it and resigns. The research and development section bogs down and the president decides that they are no longer pulling their weight despite the two additional members.

Invention Incorporated has added salespeople until at the time of the sales manager's resignation they have a force of five, three men and two women. They search for several months to find a suitable replacement and in the meantime they appoint their top salesman as acting sales manager. Finally, they hire a highly recommended woman from another toy company. Within two months the salesman who has been acting sales manager comes to the president with a list of grievances from the three men and threatens that all three will resign if something is not done about the new sales manager.

An expert in organizational communication is hired to examine the possible causes of the difficulties that have recently developed within Invention Incorporated. She makes an intensive study for several months and finds the following communication problems within the organization.

Communication Problem 1. After the psychiatrist left the firm, the head of the research and development section could not find out what was expected of him. He tried to get some guidelines from the president, but the president did not give him adequate directions. He tried to talk informally to the pediatrician, but to no avail. He was given two new people but he did not know how they were to fit into his unit or how they were to be used. He had enjoyed good lines of communication to the psychiatrist and they had always worked out new projects together. Without the psychiatrist to turn to he felt lost.

Communication Problem 2. The two new people in the research and development section were disillusioned with Invention Incorporated. They were sorry they had joined this new, rapidly expanding firm. One of them was particularly disturbed by a feeling of disorganization that he thought dominated the research and development section. He had a number of ideas on how the section should be reorganized and the work improved. However, when he developed a report outlining his suggestions—on his own time—and submitted it to the section manager the report was buried. He never did get a satisfactory response. In fact, he reported that the section manager refused to discuss it. The woman felt that the company was dominated by male chauvinists. She decided that she was a token female. She also felt that the two men in the research and development section who had been hired prior to her joining the organization were cold and surly. She could not talk with them. She felt frozen out of the informal communication channels, although she was glad that the new sales manager was a woman. The two women had become friends and she was becoming a part of an informal group composed of the three women in sales and a woman supervisor in production.

Communication Problem 3. The leader of the disgruntled salesmen was disturbed because he had not been able to talk with, or understand the directives of, the new sales manager. The men simply did not know what to expect next. Since the new manager came, the women on the sales force seemed preoccupied with women's rights. A man never knew when they would take something the wrong way. He thought that the entire corporation was going to pieces, that the lines of communication were down throughout the organization. His former boss started to have trouble from the moment he joined the board of directors. When the ringleader was acting sales manager he had some trouble getting through to the president, but after several weeks things had gone along more smoothly. However, with the appointment of the new sales manager he simply was not informed about what was going on or what the company was planning to do.

Communication Problem 4. Originally assembly workers had usually been female while supervisors were male. Recently, however, managers had promoted several women workers to supervisory positions. There was greater turnover now and morale among the assembly workers had dropped. They complained of boredom, routine, lack of involvement. They maintained they never knew how well they were doing. They never got straightforward information from management about what was expected of them or about what was happening to the company.

The grapevine carried constant rumors and reports of battles on the board of directors and among upper management. Rumors about trouble in the sales department were particularly graphic. Assembly workers shared fantasies about the new woman sales manager which split into two types. In one set of fantasies the persona of the sales manager was that of a heroic person fighting entrenched sexism and demonstrating outstanding competence. In the other set of fantasies, she was dramatized as a "woman's libber" who was so preoccupied with women's rights she was jeopardizing the sales effectiveness of the unit.

One recent rumor the workers spread through the grapevine was that the board of directors was thinking of closing the company and liquidating its assets. A possible factor in the widespread morale problem was a growing fear that they might lose their jobs.

QUESTIONS FOR CASE ANALYSIS

1. What problems can be traced to the role reshuffling that followed when the psychiatrist left the firm?
2. What problems are related to the addition of new personnel?
3. What problems have been created by replacing a formal leader with a new person from outside the work group?
4. What problems can be traced to inadequate transmission of information downward from upper management?
5. What problems can be related to the shared fantasies and the organizational saga?
6. If you were an assembly-line worker in Invention, Incorporated, what could you do to improve your communication situation?

——————————————**Theoretical Rationale**——————————————

Over a period of years at the University of Minnesota we have conducted a series of studies of zero-history simulated organizations. Each simulation ran for approximately three months and we made a careful study of all aspects of the communicating and organizing behavior. We used the simulated organization as a research tool much as we used the test-tube groups in Chapter 4 to study groups. A major finding of our study of zero-history organizations was that we could no more impose a formal structure on a larger group of people than we could on a small group.

In our case study above, Invention Incorporated grew without much planning at first, then gradually the informal role structure became formalized. As time went on the changing structure began to depart from the formal map. In our study of organizational simulations, we began by imposing a formal structure. Within a short period of time these formal descriptions of how communication and behavior should be organized were reinforced, discounted, and changed by the informal groupings, communications, and interactions of the members as they worked together.

Often when we join an organization we are impressed by the imposing and clearly visible features of the formal structure. It seems solid, permanent, and all-important. As our studies continued we became more and more impressed with how *unimportant* the formal structure was in terms of the actual flow of messages and the real assignment of power, status, and esteem. People did not make decisions, integrate their efforts, or do their work as the formal descriptions of these matters suggested they did.

After our early studies we hypothesized that the formal structure was unimportant and that students of organizational communication should not pay much attention to it. Rather, they should emphasize the informal organizing and communicating behavior of the people involved. However, we examined that hypothesis with more case studies and now feel that the formal structure is, indeed, important, but not in the way conventional wisdom suggests. The formal organization description turned out to be important symbolically in terms of territory, shared fantasies, and organizational sagas.

In only one of the simulations did the members have a revolution and overthrow the formal structure. In the others, the formal titles, divisional lines, and personnel assignments continued to play a vital symbolic role. Sometimes the formal leaders emerged as the natural leaders and the formal and informal communicative channels were similar. In such instances the informal structure did not depart widely from the formal. Members were happier and integrated their work more smoothly when their formal structures and informal behaviors were similar than when they were different. They seemed to prefer to have their symbolic world and behavioral world in harmony. When the formal organization was much different from the informal, a number of trouble spots arose. The formal leader who failed to emerge as the natural leader was usually disturbed by developments. Such a leader often tried to use the sanctions provided by the formal structure to enforce compliance. The figurehead leader communicated in ways typical of a person who feels inadequate in a position. That is, the figurehead was faced with crisis after crisis. He or she responded with ultimatums and supervised details closely to be sure not to have any more crises. The result was that the figurehead created a communicative environment that assured turmoil and further crises.

On the other hand, persons who emerged as natural leaders or task specialists, but who did not have the formal position to go along with the roles, were often upset because they did not get credit for their efforts. Such people often grumbled about the fact that the figureheads had the offices, and big salaries and the public acclaim when, in fact, those who knew what was going on realized that "we are doing the work."

In any case, we decided that whether or not the informal structure fits the formal, the latter is symbolically important in the social reality of the organization. The formal structure provides rhetorical lines which divide unit from unit, division from division. These lines provide the basis for territorial disputes and jurisdictional problems. They also define insiders from outsiders and give members symbols to praise or blame. If we can assign the blame for organizational failure to another unit we can escape responsibility for the troubles, conflicts, and problems. Accepting responsibility evokes guilt and guilt is unpleasant.

Formal positions provide the members with persons (characters) for shared fantasies about events. Ordinary mortals become president of the United States but THE PRESIDENCY becomes a sacred symbol somehow larger and more important and more enduring than any mortal. Most presidents therefore spend much communicative effort in defending, enlarging, and utilizing the symbol of the presidency. Indeed, one important duty of a chief executive officer is managing the organizational saga and, specifically, the portrayal of the persona in the position of the CEO.

FORMAL COMMUNICATION NETWORKS

In Chapter 1 we charted the formal communication channels and indicated that organizations tend to have the direction and flow of official messages spelled out in understandable fashion for their members. The members of an organization exchange formal messages through communication networks. A communication network may include as few as two people or the entire personnel of the organization. For a firm such as Invention Incorporated there are, therefore, a number of formal communication networks of varying size. Different networks are used for different message types and various communicative functions.

We will refer to the people whose formal communication is primarily with each other as a *formal communication group*. In addition to job descriptions or supervisory responsibilities there are communication network functions that are part of the duties of formal positions. Often a member of a *formal communication group* will have formal access to members of other groups. We define a *formal communication bridge* as the position that allows the member of a group to communicate in official fashion with members of other formal communication groups. Some formal positions stipulate that the job requires that communication be spread among several groups and not concentrated in any one. We define such positions as *formal communication liaisons*. Finally, the formal structure may be such that some individuals are seldom able to communicate officially with any formal group. We define these positions as *formal communication isolates*.

As you settle into your job at the organization you should make an analysis of the formal communication networks and your position within them. Is your position part of a formal grouping? What other positions are part of your group? Is your position a formal bridge? With what other positions in what other groups? Is your position a formal liaison? With what other positions in what groups? Is your position formally isolated in terms of official communication?

Isolates are in a difficult position and must rely on informal messages for most of their communication. If you are in an isolated position, that fact may be the result of unplanned growth and development. Perhaps you can bring your position's isolation to the attention of your supervisor and a minor restructuring of channels can bring you into a formal group to the benefit of both you and the organization.

If you are in a position that is part of an official group but not a bridge you are in a better place than an isolate but you will be dependent on the quality of communication within your subsystem. If you find the official communication inadequate you might seek to improve the communicative effectiveness of the people who occupy bridge and liaison positions for your group.

People who occupy bridge and liaison positions tend to be at a communicative advantage and will have access to more official information than isolates and group members. Of course if people who occupy these key communicative positions do not perceive the importance of their communication function, or do not have the necessary communication skills, they may not keep the formal channels open or they may filter and distort the contents of the messages as they pass them along. Such failure will encourage the development of informal communication channels. Organizations where the people in formal positions such as gatekeepers, liaisons, or bridges fail to function, provide fertile ground for informal communication specialists (information magnets) to grow and prosper.

FORMAL COMMUNICATION FLOW

Direction of Flow. Formal messages may flow upward or downward, either in diagonals or straight lines on the organizational charts; they may flow sideways across the organizational chart.

In your job as a subordinate you will be primarily a receiver of downward communication. Downward communication deals with the nature of your job. It includes material about job objectives and performance. From downward official communication you also learn about working conditions and employee rights. It includes material on salary matters, fringe benefits, vacations, sick leaves, and safety procedures. Your official messages from management and your supervisor should evaluate your performance in terms of how well you are doing your job and how you can further improve. Finally, important elements of the organizational saga come downward in official messages.

Often investigators of organizational communication are management oriented and study downward communication in terms of its effectiveness in achieving the intent of the message sources, usually upper or middle managers. These studies frequently find that official downward communication tends to be ineffective. Much information is lost on the way down from upper management to you. You may well find that you are not getting enough of the sort of information you want.

Upward communication flows from subordinates to superiors and usually involves your trying to give relevant information or providing feedback for your supervisors to indicate what you have decoded from their messages or making suggestions for improvement of work conditions, procedures, or morale. Often the study of an organization reveals much more official information flows downward than upward. Adequate upward flow is important in that it encourages commitment to the organization, provides for innovation and useful change, and keeps up morale.

Lateral communication flows across the organization at the same status levels. When you talk with other people who are subordinate to your supervisor you are participating in lateral communication. When your supervisor talks officially with the supervisor of another unit at the same level of management, the communication is also lateral. Lateral communication can aid various units in coordinating efforts, and in solving task-related problems.

Some years ago a young man went to a speech professor at a large state university and said that he would like to secure a Ph.D. degree. The professor replied: "Well, your credentials look good enough; but instead of working on a Ph.D. in the speech area, I would like you to do it in the field of listening. I have a project in mind. Take a notebook; go to this firm in New Orleans and interview all the management people you can get in to see during one week. Ask them these questions." Then he gave the young man a list of questions he was to raise with each manager.

A week later the young man returned. His little notebook was full of testimony that he had acquired from these management personnel. The gist of it was that they worked for a tremendous organization, that they had a great future, that they felt they had one of the finest communication systems ever devised in any business or industry.

They said, "Our workers know what we are trying to do. They understand our program. We have the most loyal group of employees to be found anywhere. The morale in our outfit is tremendous. The future looks good."

"OK," said the speech communication professor. "Put on a pair of overalls. Go down to that same firm and see Joe Walker, head of the trucking department for that industry. You are to work for him for one year. Every day carry a notebook in your inside pocket, and whenever you hear the employees say anything about their management—write it down."

Twelve months later the student came back with a great stack of notebooks. The professor spent several weeks poring over the testimony in them, and when he got through announced that it was one of the most vicious, malicious denunciations of one group by another that he had ever laid eyes on in his life.

After examining what employees really knew of their firm's policies, procedures, and philosophy, he concluded that the workers understood less than 25 percent of what their managers thought they understood.

One might doubt such a generalization if it were not constantly being verified. One of the best such verifications comes from the Pidgeon Savage Lewis Corporation of Minneapolis, an advertising and communications firm. This company made a very careful study of the communicative efficiency of 100 representative industrial manage-ments. In order to understand their figures, one should recognize that typically in these 100 industries there were five levels of management above the worker pool at the bottom. Up at the top always was some kind of board of directors. Right below, a vice-presidential level; then came the general supervisory level; the plant manager level; the foreman level; and then the manual workers at the bottom, sometimes unionized, sometimes not.

Early in their study they found that one director talks very well with another director. Sometimes the directors achieve 90 percent efficiency in transmitting messages from one to the other. Sometimes first line supervisors do as well. Horizontal or lateral communication with our own peers seems to be no great problem to us in our organizations. But vertical communication downward reveals an entirely different picture. If the chairman of the board calls in a vice-president and tells her something, on the average only 63 percent of the message is assimilated by the latter.

If the vice-president relays the same message to a general super-visor, 56 percent of it arrives. If the supervisor gives it to a plant man-ager, 40 percent arrives. If the plant manager passes it along to a super-visor, 30 percent is received. And if the supervisor gives it to the squad of workers who are *her* or *his* responsibility, only 20 percent of the original message will have passed down through five levels of authority to reach its ultimate receivers.

Studies have dug deeper. What kind of people are the employees who understand only 20 percent of what their management hopefully believes they understand? The 20 percent informed individual is usually negative-minded. He believes that he is being exploited by the managers at the top who hog most of the profits and do not give him a proper share. He may be inclined to commit theft in order to get even—and the easiest thing to steal is time. One can check in late and pretend he got there early. Or he can leave early and report he left late. It is always easy to slow down at the desk, on the assembly line, or wherever one is working. Some malcontents have gone even further and have stolen tools or equipment.

Communicative efficiency down through the levels of management is extremely poor. But *upward* communication through the levels of management may be even more important. It seems probable that downward communication is likely to improve significantly only when top management comes to a better understanding of the attitudes, the opinions, the ideas, and the suggestions of the people at the bottom of the whole structure.

Most forward-looking American companies have become deeply concerned about upward communication. They have apparently accepted the premise that the efficiency of their operation is closely related to how well management understands its employee group. The result is that these companies are making repeated efforts to discover the worries, problems, fears, and ideas of their hourly workers. Many techniques have been tried in an attempt to establish a regular system of upward communication.

The first attempt was for the boss to try to get acquainted with everyone. Many a president took great pride in the fact that he knew everybody on his payroll. Many of them liked to spend half a day walking through the shop or plant, shaking hands with all the workers. The system worked fairly well in the smaller companies. But mergers were taking place everywhere; companies were growing in size. So other systems were devised.

We tried labor-management meetings in which labor was supposed to "speak out." We had elected representatives of labor meet with selected management people. We tried hiring a chaplain as a special counselor, with all personnel encouraged to confer with him at any time. We tried labor reporters for the house publication, suggestion and complaint boxes, father confessors, opinion and attitude surveys; and we found that even though each device carries certain elements of merit, in every case it has a built-in weakness.

Their failing is that they *are* merely devices or techniques; they do not get at the heart of the problem, which is sympathetic listening by one person to another.

Speed of Flow. While communication flow is much more complex than the transmission of electricity, we can use the analogy to start our explanation of the concept of *communication load*. In electrical transmissions systems the lines have a capacity to carry a certain load. At a given time a line may be underloaded, carrying its capacity, or overloaded. Often an electrical system will have a safety mechanism such as a fuse which breaks the circuit to stop the current when the system becomes overloaded.

We will define *communication load* in terms of how fast you receive messages and how difficult the messages are to decode, interpret, and evaluate. While we emphasize your personal communication load in our definition you could substitute a formal unit of the organization for an individual and examine the communication load of formal groupings.

If you receive few messages and these are relatively simple and you feel that you want to know more in-depth information you can be said to suffer from *communication underload*. If you receive many messages and they come so rapidly that you cannot process them you can be said to suffer from *communication overload*. If we pushed our analogy a bit further we might say that you have a message capacity which is the limit at which you can comfortably process them in terms of their rate and complexity. For our analysis of organizational communication it is probably better to think of overload and underload in terms of your desired amount of communication flow. Are you receiving enough communication about the organization, about your job, about how you are doing, about benefits, salary, working conditions, and so forth? Enough in terms of what you want and need?

As a subordinate you are much more likely to suffer from underload (information starvation) than from overload. Some organizations practice official *overpublication,* however. Overpublication consists of official bulletins, memos, letters, announcements, public statements, safety campaigns, posters—all of which are distributed in a depersonalized fashion to all organizational members regardless of interest or status. Overload of such material is an irritation and most subordinates simply throw the material away without reading it. Sometimes they throw away important messages in the process but often such overload is easy to deal with.

Overpublication does illustrate the fact that in analyzing your communication load you need to separate the different kinds of messages that reach you in the downward flow of official communication. You may find the communication flow just right for some types of messages but feel a need for more messages of another type. That is, you may get sufficient information about what you are to do on the job, and how you are to do it, but you may not get enough communication related to your identity as a person and your successes and failures on the job.

If you suffer from underload you may experience symptoms such as boredom, apathy, and the feeling that you have no control over your fate. One response to underload is to search each message you perceive as important for hidden meanings and implications. Your supervisor probably has a number of subordinates with whom he or she communicates. Middle and upper managers have even larger numbers of people in subordinate positions to whom they send official messages. You, however, have only one immediate supervisor and since that person has fate control over job-related matters you will have a tendency to view much of your supervisor's communication as significant.

If you are not careful you will read into the message much more than the supervisor thought he or she was putting into it. The supervisor may intend to tell you about some minor matter you should keep in mind as you work on the Abbott account. You, on the other hand, may search the message for underlying deep meanings such as that you are doing poorly on the Abbott account and in danger of losing it or that you have done well and may be under consideration for a move to a better assignment. Often the supervisor will select a word or phrase hurriedly and it will strike you as so full of meaning that it dominates your thinking for several days. Important misunderstandings between you and your managers often result from this common response to communication underload.

You can guard against overinterpretation of messages by reminding yourself of the tendency. You can also ask for more official information. If the supervisor is suffering from communication overload you may get a number of nonverbal messages that time is short and communication opportunities difficult to arrange, but for important matters you have a right to seek official information and, in the long run, such clarification will help the manager as well as yourself. Official information need not always come directly from your supervisor. You can ask that more official messages of certain sorts be provided for you and your fellow workers. You can seek to have bridge and liaison functions added to the formal job description of yourself or of members of your communication group. Of course you can always seek out informal communication networks and informal communication magnets to get general organizational information.

SUMMARY

Usually the informal structure of an organization will more or less depart from the formal. Whether or not the informal departs widely from the formal, the latter is symbolically important in the culture of the organization in terms of territorial disputes, shared fantasies, and organizational sagas.

Members of an organization who exchange formal messages primarily with each other make up a *formal communication group*. A *formal communication bridge* position allows a member of one unit to communicate in official fashion with members of other units. A person holding a position that is a *formal communication liaison* is required to communicate with several groups. *Formal communication isolates* are positions that do not provide the people who occupy them much opportunity to receive official communication.

Formal messages may flow upward, downward, or sideways on the organizational chart. Subordinates are primarily receivers of downward communication relating to task matters, working conditions, and employee rights. Upward communication flows from subordinates to higher levels of management and usually consists of messages about improvement of working conditions, task procedures, and morale. Often much more official communication flows downward than upward. Lateral communication flows across the organization at the same status level. Lateral communication usually poses fewer problems than vertical.

Communication load involves the speed at which the individual receives messages and the difficulty he or she has in decoding the information. *Communication underload* is a condition in which an individual receives few relatively simple messages in a given period of time and perceives a need for more in-depth information. *Communication overload* results when people perceive they are receiving too many messages too rapidly and that many of the messages are hard to absorb.

People who suffer from underload may experience boredom, apathy, and a feeling of no control over their fate. One response to underload is to search each message for important hidden meanings or implications.

QUESTIONS FOR DISCUSSION AND REVIEW

1. What was a major finding of the case studies of zero-history simulated organizations?
2. What is a formal communication bridge?
3. What is a formal communication liaison?
4. What is a formal communication isolate?
5. Describe some major problems relating to upward communication flow in organizations.
6. Describe some major problems relating to downward flow of communication in organizations.
7. What is lateral flow of communication in an organization?
8. What is communication load?
9. What is communication overload?
10. What is communication underload?

REFERENCES AND SUGGESTED READINGS

Baird, J. E., Jr. *The Dynamics of Organizational Communication.* New York: Harper & Row, 1977.

Bormann, E. G. *Discussion and Group Methods: Theory and Practice,* 2nd ed. New York: Harper & Row, 1975.

"Communicative Efficiency in American Industry." An unpublished study of the Pidgeon Savage Lewis Corporation of Minneapolis, Minnesota, 1958.

Farace, R. V., P. R. Monge, and H. M. Russell. *Communicating and Organizing.* Reading, Massachusetts: Addison-Wesley, 1977.

Rosenblatt, S. B., T. R. Cheatham, and J. T. Watt. *Communication in Business.* Englewood Cliffs, N.J.: Prentice-Hall, 1977.

7

Listening

―――――――――――――― **Laboratory Application** ――――――――――――――

One outcome of the formal communicative structure of most organizations is that subordinates do a lot of listening. The formal channels and status arrangements assure that supervisors tell subordinates what to do, how to do it, and when to do it. In many organizations, supervisors and other managers also tell subordinates how well they have done their work. In such situations supervisors are expected to be sources and subordinates are receivers, listening and providing feedback. In addition, subordinates listen to formal communication from official spokespersons about changes in organizational structure and procedures, about maintenance, and about the organizational saga.

In Chapter 6 we pointed out the general research findings that organizations are often ineffective in both their upward and downward communication and that workers often get only a small portion of the messages sent downward through channels from upper management. Some of this inefficiency stems from source incompetence. Many supervisors are lacking in understanding of communication processes and do not have the basic skills required to communicate clearly. Many of the communication problems also come from receiver incompetence. In this chapter we stress the point that people with poor listening habits and skills are often responsible for communication problems.

To be sure, a skillful listener might choose not to listen, and therefore the problem would result from attitude and motivation rather than lack of skill. The communication climate within the organization has much to do with the willingness of people to play the role of receiver and try to be good listeners. Ideally, the organization should provide a cooperative communication climate since the participants can create value by working together and helping one another do a better job. When members can share in the value they create by working together, the resulting communication climate should encourage cohesiveness and teamwork. Organizations are the keystone of our corporate society; they allow people to cooperate to perform large-scale tasks by breaking them up into smaller parts and then providing them with a way to put them back together again.

A simple example of the teamwork principle is provided by a football club. In planning a given play, the coaches divide the necessary tasks among the eleven players. Each player has an assignment and the success of the effort depends upon each doing that particular job at the right place and time. In order for a given player to know what to do he must listen carefully to the coaches during the period when they explain the play. During a game he must listen carefully in the huddle to hear what the next play is to be. He must listen as the quarterback shouts out the signals in order to know when to begin his task. If a player fails to listen and understand instructions at any place along the way, the play is less likely to be successful than if he knows what the team is planning to do.

Some communication climates are competitive. In these settings the participants are contending for a set amount of value which is to be distributed unequally. A simple example is provided by the game of poker where the same amount of money comes out of the game as was contributed by the players. The only point of playing the game is to redistribute the wealth. In such settings the climate puts a premium on bluffing, jamming the channels to confuse the others, providing little or misleading feedback, and in other ways making it difficult for the others in the game to figure out what cards you have in your hand. A more complex example of a competitive communication climate is provided by a courtroom trial where the lawyers for plaintiff and defendant each try to attack the other side, defending their own, withholding information, throwing up smoke screens, seeking technicalities to claim an advantage, and so forth.

A number of motives come into play in all complex communication situations. We have been discussing two of the most important: (1) the motive to work for the good of the team and help create common value, and (2) the motive to work for personal gain at the expense of others. Some communication situations encourage a mixing of the two motives. If we are part of a political organization running a campaign to elect a president of the student body, we must work together as a team in order to achieve the goal and the value which results in something we can all share. If we are selecting the candidate for the election, however, we may have a personal choice and those backing other candidates will lose out if we succeed. Under such circumstances we sometimes communicate as though in a value-added context and sometimes as though in a zero-sum game like poker. In many organizations the ideal of cooperative communication is seldom approximated and people communicate from mixed motives.

In a mixed-motive climate you may find yourself in situations where you do not want to listen. You may be more interested in getting the floor and having your own say. You may not like the person who is speaking and may not want to hear what he or she has to say. You may not like to take orders from a supervisor because that person has a nonverbal component in the message that you interpret as putting you down, or "lording it over you."

Recognizing the problems of motive and attitude, in this chapter we assume that you are trying to work cooperatively, that you are trying to listen carefully to understand the other person. Our emphasis is upon developing the skill to listen when you decide that you need and want to do so.

ASSIGNMENT: Developing Listening Skills

Depending on the time available, your instructor will provide you with exercises in class to help you improve your listening skills. If time is available you may be given a standardized listening test to diagnose your present level of ability.

───────────────Theoretical Rationale───────────────

Continuous, purposeful listening in face-to-face communication can help us solve basic problems in human relations. Their identity and nature deserve special attention.

THERAPEUTIC LISTENING

The primary function of listening is to secure information; but it is only one function of many. Another enormously important reason for listening is that of providing an aroused speaker with significant emotional relief.

Nondirective counseling, now widely practiced, depends upon persons trained to listen quietly and objectively. The counselor is instructed never to argue with a client; rather, his or her central function is to provide a sympathetic and open ear—an ear that serves as a kind of sounding board enabling the speaker to judge more accurately the seriousness of her own problems. At times, the client merely needs human companionship; in addition, she may urgently need to rid herself of anger or some other pent-up emotion; or finally, she may need to modify some idea or project she has in mind—to understand more clearly her own previous thoughts. When she voices her thoughts to an attentive hearer, her ends are often realized.

Actually, therapeutic listening is by no means a new idea. Some 4400 years ago, Ptahhopet, one of the pharaohs, instructed the viziers and officers of his staff as follows: "An official who must listen to the pleas of clients should listen patiently and without rancor, because a petitioner wants attention to what he says even more than the accomplishing of that for which he came." These words were early suggestions, perhaps, of how to attain those healing effects now sought by so many of our current experts in human relations. Today, nondirective counseling—which essentially means noneval-uative listening—is common practice in both hiring and exit in-terviews, in handling workers' grievances, and even in collective bargaining sessions.

If we are to have listeners when we ourselves need them, we must learn to be kindly and attentive when someone wishes to talk to us. The whole matter seems a rather clear-cut application of the Golden Rule. Listening and speaking are the two things people do most frequently and constantly throughout their lives. Because we are basically and inherently social beings, our problems and concerns are inextricably involved with those of our associates. For these reasons the following admonitions may well be worth observing by those of us engaged in daily communication in an organization.

Be quick to spot a troubled associate. Whenever we sense that someone is about to "blow his stack," our first thought should be to provide him with an open and sympathetic ear.

Be attentive. If a violent tirade is launched, our best contribution will be to let it flow uninterrupted until it is exhausted. If a pause occurs en route, certain assists by the listener can be made.

Employ three kinds of reactions only. Three listener responses may at various times prove useful during helpful listening. First, the listener may employ what someone has called a series of "eloquent and encouraging grunts"—"Hum," "Uh-huh," "Oh," or "I see." Second, if the speaker pauses momentarily, the listener may remain silent but continue to nod her head thoughtfully until speech starts again. Third, if the speaker becomes wild and unreasonable in his declarations, the listener may restate what the speaker has just said, putting it in question form. Examples of such restatements might be: "You really think, then, that all middlemen are dishonest?" or, "You believe your mother-in-law is deliberately trying to ruin your marriage?"

Never probe for additional facts. There is a distinct difference between willingness to listen and curious inquisitiveness designed to elicit extra information. The latter must be avoided.

Never evaluate what has been said. The therapeutic listener must refrain completely from passing any moral judgments upon what she has heard. In no case should she give the speaker any advice, even if advice is requested.

Never lose faith in the ability of the speaker to solve his own problem. The whole key to helpful listening is to maintain faith that each person is a rational being who will eventually work out her or his own salvation.

Throughout supportive communication the listener must continue to think of the other person as he will be when his problem has been solved and all has returned to normal. In return for her kindness and sympathy, and for her restraint in keeping out of the center of the stage, the listener is often herself rewarded. She may experience as much relief from tension and worry as does the speaker.

LISTENING SPEED VS. TALKING SPEED

Research workers are continually polling various groups of people to determine what they deem to be their chief problems. Among white-collar workers the most consistently reported problem reported is "inability to concentrate." At one large midwestern university 82 percent of the students queried reported "inability to concentrate" as their central problem in school. These students did not get much help from educational literature. "How-to-study" books seem much given to offering advice, most of it rather silly. A typical list of admonitions offered would include: "Be interested," "Suppress distractions by sheer will power," "Pay attention," "Keep as quiet as possible," "Plunge right in," "Be dynamic, be constructive, be concerned." One might as well be advised to "Be intelligent!"

To advise someone to "pay attention" does not make much sense. We are attentive to *something* during all our waking hours; it is impossible to be anything else. True, we may be inattentive to the topic under discussion while we consider a growling stomach, but always we are attentive to one item or another in our environment. In one sense living itself is learning. As long as we are alive and awake we are almost certain to be learning something, perhaps at a very slow pace and very inefficiently. The important thing is *what* we are learning; at what rate; when, where, and how much of it we are going to absorb.

Giving sustained attention to a lengthy speech is particularly difficult. Such discourse demands a focusing of the listener's higher mental faculties for prolonged intervals. Moreover, much of our learning is in carefully organized sessions in school or on the job where inattention becomes very costly. Grade-school teachers, for instance, have been found to talk 57 percent of all class periods. (They themselves estimate that they talk only 25 percent of class time.) High school teachers talk 68 percent, and college professors 80 percent, of all class periods. White-collar workers and management personnel in industry are in face-to-face communication nearly 40 percent of every eight-hour workday, although not all of this takes place in organized group situations. One is forced to wonder what is going on at the other end of all this talk. How can our listening efficiency be most quickly improved?

Rapid listening is our best answer. The faster we listen, the better we listen. If speech could be produced articulately and normally at 400 or 500 words per minute, many of our problems in listening to sustained discourse would disappear. Just as the rapid reader comprehends more than the slow reader, listening comprehension increases with increased speech speed. A whole new technology of "compressed speech" has developed and has been employed at a number of professional meetings. Major concurrent sessions at these conventions are recorded, "compressed," and played back at "listening posts." Registrants are thus able to hear program elements otherwise missed in a fraction of the time required in the original, live delivery.

FACTORS IN POOR LISTENING

Inefficient listening runs through many of our organizations. Is there anything we can do about it? Yes, if we understand the things which hamper our ability to listen.

Some of the more important factors in poor listening were identified by one of the authors at the University of Minnesota a number of years ago. The study concerned 100 of the best and 100 of the worst listeners drawn from our freshman students.

They were two widely contrasting groups. The investigator gave the subjects 20 different tests and measures. Each subject took tests of reading, writing, speaking and listening abilities; of mechanical, mathematical, and scientific aptitudes; of intelligence; and of personality characteristics. All subjects filled out a long questionnaire and were interviewed at length about their communication.

After nine months of study into the differences between the good and the bad performers, the ten most important factors in bad listening became clear. Subsequent studies in Colorado and Michigan corroborated their character and the damage they do.

Disinterest. The first characteristic that separated the good performer from the bad was disinterest. Many bad listeners tend to decide that the speaker's topic is dull as soon as the chair announces it. Often it seems unrelated to our central interests; distinctly less pleasant to think about than our golf game, our sports car, or our plans for vacation.

The first key to good listening is the three-letter word, *use*. The good listener is a sifter, a screener, a winnower of the wheat from the chaff. He or she is always trying to find something practical or worthwhile to store away in the back part of the brain and put to work for his or her own selfish benefit in the months to come.

We should acknowledge the selfish character of it. Whenever we hear sustained speech, we have every right to be selfish; to hunt for the worthwhile, and to store up these things for personal gain in the years ahead. This was well put by G. K. Chesterton some years ago when he said, "In all this world there is no such thing as an uninteresting subject. There are only uninterested people."

Over-critical. The second bad-listening habit is to criticize the speaker's person or delivery. This gets to be a tension release for most bad listeners. No sooner does the man start to talk than the bad listener says, "Look at that fellow, would you? Didn't anybody ever tell him to keep his hands out of his pockets when he is giving a speech? And his voice! Nobody could get anything from such a terrible speaker." Then the bad listener feels justified in going off on a mental tangent.

Again the good listener starts at the same point but gets to a different conclusion. When the man starts to talk he says, "Gee, this guy is inept. He is perhaps as awkward and graceless a speaker as I have ever heard. But he has information I need. So I will concentrate on his content and forget his mannerisms."

An amazing thing happens. Not many moments go by before the listener who is trying to get the message grows oblivious to all the delivery faults of the poor, fumbling speaker. The point is this: The message is many times more important than the clothing in which it comes dressed. As soon as we recognize this simple truth we are all on the way to becoming better listeners, because we then begin to assume at least half the obligation for completing each communication we hear.

Argumentative. Many listeners are combative by nature. A speaker seldom talks more than a minute or two before such listeners feel impelled to do verbal battle. Their impulses are disastrous to effective listening. The first desire may be to challenge the speaker on the spot, interrupting her to do so. A second impulse may be to compose a loaded question to hurl at the speaker at the earliest opportunity. Still a third may be to marshal a bit of evidence that contradicts something the speaker has just reported and to mentally build around it a whole rebuttal speech.

Too many times at the end of a good speech such overstimulated listeners have leaped to their feet, hurled their questions at the speaker, or have made their great rebuttal efforts. Usually they have found the speaker looking at them in complete astonishment, and saying, "But, sir. Didn't you hear what I went on to say later, that so and so was also true?" The listener had not heard. His listening efficiency had dropped to zero as he composed his critical commentary.

Fact-Hunting. The fourth bad listening habit is to listen only for facts. The 100 worst listeners were asked what they concentrated on when they listened. Every one of them said, "We listen for the facts." The truth was that they got a few facts, garbled a shocking number, and completely lost the bulk of them.

The 100 best listeners were also asked what they concentrated on when they listened. Very timidly, 97 said, "Well, we try to get the main ideas out of it. Usually, a person giving a speech is developing some kind of a generalization, a principle, or a concept. We try to understand these central ideas as best we can." We pursued this facet of good listening. Soon we became convinced that the good listener is always the idea listener. She or he understands the central ideas fairly well and uses them to give sense and system to the whole discourse. And after two days have passed such a listener has more facts appended to the connecting threads than the spongers and catalogers of facts are able to retain. Even if it is facts we want, the best way to get them is to get first the principle that limits and controls them. Then we have a chance to retain and make use of those facts.

Voluminous Notes. Many people discharge their real or imagined obligation to a speaker by taking voluminous notes. They carry the notes home, store them away, and perhaps never look at them again. What nonsense! The *taking* of notes pays no dividends; it is the *later use* of the notes that may be of some value. Actually, there is a negative correlation between the volume of notes taken and the quality of the listening performance.

The 100 worst listeners were asked their method for note-taking. They said immediately, "We make an outline, of course." They thought note-taking and outlining were synonymous! There is nothing wrong with outlining a speech, if the speaker is following an outlined pattern of organization himself, as perhaps he should. However, no more than half the talks we hear are going to be given by speakers carefully following a previously prepared outline. One of the most frustrating things is to try to outline the unoutlinable. Students who do this become deeply engrossed in symmetry. They get the borders around the four sides beautifully spaced; the content nicely centered. After each of their outline symbols they painfully inscribe a few words of meaningless jargon.

Two months later, reviewing their collection in an attempt to prepare for the final examination, they spend almost the entire review period trying to figure out, "What was I thinking about when I wrote that in my notebook?" What a futile business.

For half a century we have assumed that because big notebooks and good students travel together, the former must create the latter. No such cause-and-effect relationship has ever been established. However, it may well be the other way around. Perhaps the voluminous note-taker and paper-storer is merely a victim of a very conventional and not very beneficial practice. Certainly the contributions people make in this world are more dependent upon what they have in their heads than upon what they have in their notebooks.

Half Listening. A pitfall into which almost all of us tumble frequently is that of half listening, giving the speaker partial attention. The practice is ruinous to listening efficiency. There are only two possible outcomes: We succeed in our faking of attention, or we fail. In either case, disaster is near. If the faking is successful, the speaker assumes she has given us messages which actually we have not received. Sooner or later real blunders and breakdowns result. If the faking fails, the communicator sees through our shallow deceit and is insulted. She may become hostile and retaliatory about it.

Students practice half listening. Often they stare at the professor, chins in hand, and after this overt display of courtesy feel free to drift off in any direction appealing to them.

Good listening is not relaxed and passive at all. In plain words, it is hard work. Attention to speaking can be defined as a collection of tensions inside the listener that can be resolved only by getting some facts or ideas the speaker is trying to convey.

Noisy Audience. Occasionally a listener at the back in a large audience finds herself surrounded by a noisy clique making such a clatter that the speaker up front cannot be heard. Should such a listener conclude that it would be rude to speak up either to interrupt the speaker by demanding greater volume or to quiet her neighbors? Never! Such reasoning is based upon false logic and false courtesy. She ought to immediately wave an arm violently at the speaker, and in her loudest roar bellow at him, "Mister, can't hear you back here. Mind if we wave whenever you get inaudible?"

There is only one answer the speaker can make. He has to thank the person for her interest and turn on some decibels of intensity. One absolute obligation every speaker carries is the obligation of audibility. If he doesn't know this, he should be made aware of it.

If our listener does not like the first option, a second is available. Let her glower fiercely around her and suddenly scream at her neighbors, "QUIET"; and then look up intently at the speaker.

Lack of Effort. Many of us seem ever to seek the simple, the pleasant, the easy, and the recreational. Such practice may lead to "no pain—no strain," but it is ruinous to effective listening.

The 100 worst listeners were asked about their radio and television experiences. Not one of them had listened regularly to serious public affairs programs such as "Meet the Press." Instead, they had become authorities on comedy, variety, and action programs. The 100 best listeners knew who the popular comedians were, of course, but they often watched the more challenging kinds of programs.

Controversial Topic. It is curious, but true, that a single emotion-laden word often has the power to cause a listener to tune out the speaker.

One of the authors discovered this truth accidentally some years ago. In giving a talk to a large group of freshmen about the nature of speech, he found himself saying something like this to the group: "You know, man was never born to be a speaking animal in the first place. We have 26 organs in the midline of our bodies that we use to talk with, and every one was put inside us for a more primitive, biological purpose—such as breathing, chewing, swallowing, and the like. Probably by plain accident some Stone Age man made a grunt of some kind, and with it initiated, through a long period of evolution, the development of the code we now call speech."

Some frozen looks appeared. The speaker happened to have an objective test covering that particular lecture. Upon scoring the papers, he found that many of his freshmen had missed a cluster of items right after the one that dealt with the evolutionary character of speech. Curious, he had interviews with them, trying to find out why. To his astonishment, he discovered that 40 percent of his freshmen had been warned by their parents before being allowed to enroll in "that big university" that among the faculty members the students were certain to encounter a lot of atheistic professors; that these professors might try to undermine their students' religious faith; and that one way they could identify an atheist was when he started talking about evolution. His students had simply identified him as an atheist because he had used the word "evolution" in a lecture. Since their assumption was totally erroneous, he was furious. But he learned one thing: An easy way to lose 40 percent of an audience is to use the word "evolution" when talking to a group of freshmen. To avoid the loss, one needs only to say, "Speech is a long developmental process." The word *developmental* is acceptable!

The word is not the thing. It is merely a symbol for it. Yet on and on we go through our lives letting symbols stand between us and self-growth. If we but knew the 100 worst word barriers in the English language, we could rank order them according to their difficulty, discuss them in the classrooms of the nation, and put these silly barriers behind us.

Inattention. On the average, Americans talk 125 words a minute conversationally. Put a person in front of an audience, however, and ask her to talk informatively, and she will slow down to 100 words a minute. How many words a minute can people think as they listen, if all of their thoughts are measurable in words per minute? A variety of research all points to the same conclusion: Easy cruising speed of thought is always at least 400 words a minute.

Now the differential between 100 and 400 breeds false security; and this false security constitutes the worst listening pitfall we ever face. *Almost everyone wastes the differential between speech speed and thought speed.* This differential stimulates all kinds of mental tangents. We tune a speaker in, and in 10 seconds are usually able to identify what she is talking about. We then feel free to exit for a 50-second mental holiday. Then, because we have invested some energy getting to the meeting, we check in again, in 10 seconds find out what is being said, and treat ourselves to another 50-second holiday. We are in for 10, out for 50, in for 10, out for 50. Really, it is not so bad if we always come back to the ten. But sooner or later, on one of these mental excursions of ours, we may hit upon a topic too engrossing to drop.

At some age levels we cannot be certain just what that mental topic would be. But it is easy to follow in the case of the typical male college student. He goes to his engineering class, and the professor begins his lecture as follows: "Well, you think you are going to make engineers. Some of you will, but some of you will not make a passing mark. Be that as it may, if you make a success in your chosen career, it is going to be possible only if you have learned one fundamental thing on this campus; and that is that the most precious item an engineer ever owns, the thing with which you must learn to eat, sleep, live, and die at your side, is your slide rule. Thus, this morning I am going to review with you all the mathematic computations possible with this instrument."

The student is thinking, "Is he really going to spend another 50 minutes on that stupid thing? We've been around it 16 times in other classes. Got it first in junior high school." Tuning the professor in, he finds that sure enough the professor is multiplying one-digit numbers on the big slide rule. Immediately the young man begins to think about his car and its flat tire and what he can do about it after class. Fifty seconds later he checks in on the professor, who is now multiplying two-digit numbers on the big slide rule. Immediately the student begins worrying about his chemistry test scheduled for Thursday morning. Fifty seconds later he checks in on the professor again, who is now dividing one-digit numbers on the big slide rule.

The young man tunes in and out about six times. Then on one of the "outs" a very important subject comes to his attention: women.

The next thing he hears is the bell for the end of the hour. Just then the professor says, "Remember when you take cube root . . ."

"Cube root on a slide rule!" In panic, the boy grabs one of his classmates, just leaving, and says, "What's with this guy? How do you take cube root on a slide rule?" The friend does not know either; she has been out on some other mental tangent.

We listen with only 25 percent efficiency because we are hopping from one island of attention to another. While we are on the speaker's island we do very well, but most of the time we are in transit or in another port and do not even hear what is being said. Our basic problem is one of false security. Our thought speed is so great that we overrely upon it, and get into deep trouble.

IMPORTANT LISTENING ABILITIES

As listeners, we can avoid many of the pitfalls besetting us by developing three important listening abilities. These abilities will greatly increase our cognition from aural messages. All three demand an increased expenditure of energy, and require the listener to capitalize upon the differential between the speaker's speech speed and the listener's thought speed. We can greatly profit by making their practice habitual.

Overpowering Distractions. Inevitably, scores of distracting stimuli turn up in every listening situation. To escape them we should be isolated in some specially built, soundproof room. Some of our most frequent distractions are uncomfortable temperatures, annoying speaking mannerisms, apparently dull topics, fatigue, bad acoustics, noisy air conditioners, restless audiences, and myriad unexpected noises occurring during the speech. We either adjust to these stimuli, or we are defeated by them.

To overpower distractions we must keep our minds operating at high speed and be continually concerned with the speaker's topic. This can be accomplished by making automatic the practice of the following three mental activities, repeating them again and again whenever we listen to sustained discourse.

Anticipate what the speaker is going to say next. One of the best things we can do is to anticipate her and try to guess what her next main point is likely to be. If we guess it is going to be point A and it turns out to be point A, learning is reinforced, for that point comes twice into our consciousness instead of once. If we guess wrong, what then? If we guess it is going to be point Z, we are still the winner. Out of curiosity alone most of us begin to compare Z with A. If we do, we are then applying one of the soundest of all laws of learning—which is that we learn best by contrast and comparison with something else. To anticipate—to "guess ahead"—is one wager in life we cannot lose. Whether we guess right or wrong, we win.

Identify what the speaker has for evidence. No longer can a person go through life just asserting points. She has to build them. We must be able to identify the bricks, the mortar, the steel, and the wood with which the speaker supports each point she makes. To do so will capitalize upon the built-in advantage of thought speed over speech speed, and will give us a much safer foundation upon which to accept or reject her proposition.

Recapitulate periodically as we listen. The good listener will listen hard for four or five minutes, and then take a quick mental time out. In that time he will hastily summarize in his mind the best points made in the preceding segment of discourse. In ten seconds, with that enormous thought speed of ours, we can rephrase in our minds the best points made in five minutes of talk. Half a dozen of these mental summaries interspersed throughout a 45- or 50-minute lecture will double our retention and understanding.

These three accomplishments pay big dividends. We ought to cash them in and make them work for us. To do so will take more energy, but it will be a profitable investment. To automatically anticipate, identify, and recapitulate are our best hopes for "flattening the forgetting curve" and for greatly improving our overall listening performance.

Structuring Content. When we listen to connected discourse, it is almost always possible to detect a pattern of some kind in it. Even in informal conversation the participants usually go through the same three steps of verifying each other's health ("How are you?"), of verifying each other's progress ("How's it going?"), and of wishing each other well ("Take care of yourself")!

Ninety percent of all organized talks fall into one of four basic patterns. The most common arrangement is one of a variety of sequence relationships. For example, the speaker may discuss the past, present, and future of some problem or program. The chronological structure of his talk is readily apparent. A second pattern involves a spatial relationship. In this instance the speaker might discuss the application of his ideas on the Atlantic Seaboard, in the Midwest, and upon the Pacific Coast. A third pattern is also extremely common and has but two points in it: presentation of a problem and discussion of a possible solution for it. Indeed, this procedure has become almost universally labeled the problem-solution structure for speech making. The fourth arrangement is climactic, and is usually formed by asking and answering several questions of increasing significance. For example, a speaker might build her discussion of a general sales tax around these four questions: Does our state need more revenue? Would an increase in sales tax provide this revenue? Is the sales tax fair and equitable? Is there an alternative way to meet our needs? Climax and suspense grow with the answering of each successive question.

Visual imagery greatly enhances learning. To perceive the *structure* of the communications we receive substantially increases our comprehension of them; and the sooner we can identify the pattern the better. Structuralizing message content tends to help us separate fact from principle, argument from evidence, idea from illustration, assertion from reasoned conclusion. It tends to increase our interest in the content and makes it possible for us to remember longer both the facts and ideas we hear.

It is quite possible that a message to which we are listening may not contain a discernible organizational pattern. In this case we should start to take notes in a "fact-versus-principle" fashion. This requires two parallel columns on the notepaper, with the word *facts* written at the top of one column, and the word *principles* written at the top of the other. Whenever either one of these items is produced by the speaker, it should be listed in the appropriate column. As our lists grow, we can try to visualize an outline we ourselves might have used had we been giving the speech. We may want to sketch in such an outline at the bottom of the page as we listen; or, if the speech content has deep significance for us, compose the outline after the talk is completed.

Maintaining Emotional Control. All too often we become ineffective listeners or nonlisteners because of an emotional condition. The most common causes of our loss of control are personal dislikes: for the speaker, his central proposition, his language, or his line of argument.

How can we develop an ability to control our own emotions? Our central purpose in listening is not to develop ulcers, but to assimilate as many important facts and ideas as possible. Often useful facts and ideas come from obnoxious sources. The almost universal game of brainpicking can be played with hostile characters as well as with friends. If we do not listen to an opponent, we have little chance to understand or to influence her. In a large sense we are at the mercy of any person who understands us better than we do him or her; and the best way to increase understanding is to listen carefully to his or her message. Our listening is most effective when we succeed in establishing some *psychic distance* between us and the speaker; then comprehending the argument can be kept uppermost in our minds.

Two other factors contribute to emotional control: First, try to understand the other person's point before we judge it. We can and should make habitual the practice of withholding evaluation until we are certain our comprehension is complete. Second, make a conscious plan to report, accurately, the hostile message. The intended reporting may be to spouse, friend, or associate; but we ought always to identify in our mind to whom we will report. Our intention to report will, in itself, more closely limit our emotional arousal.

SUMMARY

Ideally the organization should provide a cooperative communication climate since members can create value by working together as a team. Some communication climates are competitive—negotiations between labor and management groups, for example, where the participants may believe that if one side wins the other will lose. Some communication climates encourage a mixing of the motive to work for the good of the group and create common value for all to share and the motive to work for personal gain at the expense of others. In the mixed-motive and competitive situations a person may decide not to listen, but cooperative climates should encourage listening. Even though organizations should provide a climate which encourages listening many in fact have a mixed-motive quality and some listening problems actually result when people consciously decide not to listen.

Even when people want to listen, however, they are often inefficient because of lack of proper attitudes and skills. Studies of good and bad listeners indicate that poor listeners are disinterested, overcritical, argumentative, listen only for facts, take voluminous notes, only half attend to what is said, take the easy way, are distracted by emotion-laden words, and are inattentive.

Good listeners have the ability to overpower distractions and concentrate on the message by anticipating what the speaker is going to say next, by identifying what the speaker has for evidence, and by summarizing periodically as they listen. Good listeners try to find the organizational pattern in a message or if it has no clear pattern they provide one. They also maintain emotional control despite the fact that a speaker may use loaded language.

QUESTIONS FOR DISCUSSION AND REVIEW

1. How can the formal channels of an organization influence the listening needs of a subordinate?
2. Why should an organization provide a cooperative communication climate for subordinates?
3. Give an example of mixed-motives on the part of a listener.
4. What are two important functions of listening?
5. What are six dos and don'ts of therapeutic listening?

6. What are the leading factors in poor listening?
7. How can a person overcome distractions while listening?
8. How can listening for structure aid comprehension and retention of information?

REFERENCES AND SUGGESTED READINGS

Barker, L. L. *Listening Behavior.* Englewood Cliffs, N.J.: Prentice-Hall, 1971.

Brown, J. I. and G. R. Carlsen. *Brown-Carlsen Listening Comprehension Test.* New York: Harcourt, Brace and World, 1955.

Jones, J. E. and L. Mohr. *The Jones-Mohr Listening Test.* La Jolla, California: University Associates, 1976.

Nichols, R. G. "Factors in Listening Comprehension." *Speech Monographs.* 15 (1948), 154–63.

Nichols, R. G. and L. Stevens. *Are You Listening?* New York: McGraw-Hill, 1957.

Weaver, C. H. *Human Listening: Processes and Behavior.* Indianapolis: Bobbs-Merrill, 1972.

8

Being Evaluated

─────────────── **Laboratory Application** ───────────────

A good organization can provide its members with many rewards. Of basic importance is the monetary reward that provides for our material needs. But money can also work as a message about our worth as members of the organization. If we are told by the organization's reward system that we are worthy, that we are good and respected as persons, and that we have done a good job, these message rewards are even more important than the material things money can buy.

Our informal relationships with other people in the work setting and the roles we assume in the important formal and informal groups that carry on the organizing behavior provide us with social and esteem satisfactions. If we make friends, if we earn respect and esteem for ourselves as people, we find the organization more rewarding than if we have few friends and little recognition as a person. Nonetheless we are part of a task-oriented collection of people striving to achieve common goals, and task rewards are important.

Within the overall framework of the organization we are part of several small task-oriented groups. We may be able to specialize in a profession or a craft because the organizational context provides an opportunity for such concentrated effort. You cannot practice a profession as a chef without the surrounding organization of a restaurant. You cannot be a law enforcement officer without a department of police. You cannot be a computer systems analyst without the support both in terms of people and capital resources of an organization.

One of the most rewarding aspects of a good organization can be the opportunity and resources to do work that you enjoy. If you end up with a career you find boring and unchallenging you might still enjoy the organization because of the fact that you like working with the people. However, a satisfying job is an important part of your quality of life and even if the social rewards are high, achievement rewards add an important part to your work.

One primary source of satisfaction for most of us is the feeling that we have done our job particularly well. Many people have crafts and hobbies that involve creating or building something. They write poems and songs, build kites and model airplanes, refinish furniture, weave, sew, paint. Much of the joy in such activity comes from completing a project with the feeling that this time everything worked together and the result is a good poem, a beautiful pot, a handsome chair. Few people, however, get maximum reward from looking at the completed task and enjoying it in private. Immediately, most of us want to show what we have done to someone we care about—family, friends, so those we value can appreciate our product, too. We wait, often, with considerable anxiety to see what people whose opinion we respect say about our work.

The greatest achievement satisfaction comes when our inner feeling that we have done well is publicly confirmed by people whose judgment we respect. Such rewards come from appraisal in a systematic, formal way. Playwrights anxiously await the reviews that appear in newspapers and magazines. Students anxiously await the instructor's evaluation of their tests and papers and oral reports. If you are spending eight hours a day working at organizational tasks you are naturally curious as to how others feel you are doing. The appraisal interview is one important opportunity to find out how good your work is in the eyes of others who should know.

THE APPRAISAL INTERVIEW

Usually you will receive some information prior to the appraisal interview. If you do not, you should ask for it. If the information you receive does not contain material you would like to know about, you should ask for it. If you ask, you probably will get the information. Even if you do not get it beforehand, your supervisor will know what you are interested in and will likely arrange to talk about it during the interview itself.

Planning the Appraisal Interview. You should do some planning before you go for the interview. You might want to review the material on preparing for a job interview in Chapter 1 for much of what we say there can be applied to the appraisal interview.

You should plan to help fulfill the needs of the supervisor. The supervisor may have many bottlenecks, personnel problems, and trouble integrating with other units and middle management, all claiming his or her attention. On the other hand, your supervisor's self image and feeling of worthiness as a "good" supervisor are closely tied to how you and your peers respond to her or his leadership. Just as you want to know how well you are doing, so your supervisor wants to know how well you and others think he or she functions as a supervisor; in turn, the supervisor needs to know what management thinks of his or her work. If your supervisor is likely to dread the duty of making an appraisal interview and defending the assessments in it, can you help make the interview less unpleasant? In what ways?

Most supervisors have a reasonably well-thought-out "theory" of management. Often the organization will have provided them with management training in which they will have learned approaches to good management. A supervisor's theory of management will be reflected in the way he or she conducts the appraisal interviews.

One popular theory is called "management by objectives." Management by objectives involves the supervisor working out with your help a set of personal objectives for you and a time table by which you are to reach them. The plan also includes checkpoints at which you meet with your supervisor to see how well you are doing. Under such a system the manager will meet with you to discuss the content of your job and the things that you are expected to do. You then are to develop target dates for specific accomplishments. You meet with your supervisor to discuss and agree on targets. The appraisal interview comes at the end of such a procedure and concentrates on a discussion of your successes and failures in meeting your personal objectives. If your supervisor is trying to manage by objectives you can anticipate an appraisal interview or interviews in which you are supposed to have an important part in establishing targets and checkpoints.

Another popular approach is management which calls for employee participation in decisions that affect them and their working conditions. Participative management assumes that people who help make decisions are more strongly committed to their success and will work harder to implement them. This approach also seeks to encourage initiative and ingenuity in problem-solving on the part of the people who are directly involved in the work. If your supervisor is seeking to establish a climate of participative management you can anticipate an attempt to frame a somewhat nondirective appraisal interview, to have you discuss your own solutions to problems that have come up.

Some supervisors will have a theory of management that sees the manager making decisions and evaluations of work and then "selling" or persuading the subordinates to go along with the manager's conclusions. Managers who subscribe to this approach will be concerned with "motivating" subordinates and with ways to win cooperation with their plans and goals. If your supervisor subscribes to such a theory of management, you can anticipate an appraisal interview resembling to some extent a sales pitch.

Of course there may be some managers without formal training in popular theories of management who work from a set of assumptions, usually not well-thought-out, that include simply that they know what should be done, how it should be done, and a view that subordinates tend to be troublesome. They may view the typical subordinate as somewhat lazy, disinterested in the job, in need of direction, control, and coercion if production is to be maintained. In an evaluation interview they are likely to be argumentative, given to making flat statements, laying down the law. They may be defensive and quick to argue on behalf of their interpretation of events.

We have not spelled out in detail all of the possible approaches to management that supervisors may adopt in the modern organization. Our point is that as you plan for your appraisal interview, you should analyze your manager's theory of management and make some plans as to how you can fulfill the needs of the appraiser.

In preparation for your appraisal interview you should analyze your supervisor as a communicator. How well does she handle the daily appraisal opportunities that her position provides? Do you get continuous useful appraisal from her about your work throughout the week? How skillful is your supervisor in communicating? How sensitive to the complexities of communicating from a status (or one-up) position? How much education in organizational communication does your supervisor appear to have?

You should also plan ways to fulfill your own needs. You should get the best evaluation you can of your work. This is important to your sense of achievement and reward, and it will help you make sensible career decisions. If the career you have chosen or the particular organization do not suit you, you should discover this as soon as possible. You also need to know what sort of future you can expect in the organization. What career paths are open to you and how can you prepare yourself for them?

Good evaluation interviews should provide you with guidelines for improvement, either by further education in the organization's training programs or by adult education classes elsewhere in the community, or by individual programs of study and reading.

TAKING PART IN THE APPRAISAL INTERVIEW

While counseling interviews are often nondirective in that the interviewer will encourage the client to decide what to talk about and will not take charge of the channels of communication, the appraisal interview tends to be directive. The supervisor often decides on the place, time, and agenda. The supervisor also will often decide what information you will receive prior to the interview. Most importantly, the supervisor has formal organizational status and being in a one-up position will tend to control the channels of communication. Whenever the supervisor wants to take a turn he or she will tend to take the floor and cut you off. It is very difficult to assert yourself and keep the floor or interrupt your supervisor to take a turn during an appraisal interview. In many of the appraisal interviews we have observed the supervisors have done most of the talking.

You may be fortunate and have a supervisor who has developed some skills in communication and has had training in how to conduct an appraisal interview. If so, your supervisor will be alert to the temptation to dominate the conversation and will make a real effort to give you a chance to speak up and discuss the things you want to talk about. Such a supervisor will be frank and thorough in pointing out weaknesses but will try to do so in a helpful way and with a problem-solving attitude.

As difficult as it may be in some interviews, you need to assert yourself and bring your most important questions to the surface. When the open-ended questions come that give you a chance, you should take the opportunity to control the agenda and the channels of communication. Many managers will be willing to relinquish both at certain points in the meeting. When it is your turn to be message source, you should have both a tentative plan of the topics you want to talk about and an order in which you want to talk about them.

When the supervisor is message source and evaluates your work, your role in the groups, and your interpersonal relationships, you must try to implement our recommendations in Chapter 7 on listening. Be sure you understand what the supervisor is saying before you defend yourself, argue for your position, or attack the evaluation. Be particularly alert to emotion-causing loaded language and its effect on your ability to decode the message. An inept manager may be trying to say you have done very well the last six months and are a prime target for promotion to a better job and, indeed, with a bit of work on some basic skills related to the new job you may well get it. However, the manager may begin by commenting on your "almost total lack of experience" in the new area and so upset you with that unfortunate phrase that you fail to get the gist of the total message.

Once you clearly understand what the supervisor is saying you should disagree with those portions of the message you feel are unjustified; make your position known clearly and forcibly. Oftentimes subordinates feel supervisors will be much more vindictive than they would prove to be if the subordinates expressed themselves fully and sensibly. Supervisors are usually committed to the unit and to its success. They are aware when there are problems even if the problems are not discussed and confronted directly and they have a high stake in the successful resolution of conflicts.

ASSIGNMENT: The Appraisal Interview

Your instructor will assign you a task of interviewing some supervisors or personnel officers in various organizations in your community. You will collect whatever evaluation forms supervisors use in performance appraisals and gather information about the organization's appraisal program and the theory of management involved in its purposes and plan. There will be a general class discussion in which you pool your information and discuss the various forms and approaches to the appraisal interview. Your instructor may ask you also to discuss the information interview (done to get the material) and compare and contrast that with the job interview and the evaluation interview since you have now had the experience of interviewing to gather information.

As an alternative to the above assignment, if a number of your classmates have had experience with appraisal interviews, your instructor may assign a role-playing exercise of such an interview.

————————Theoretical Rationale————————

Inevitably you get nonverbal communication cueing you in to how your fellow-workers view your work and you may read into the behavior of your supervisors other guesses as to how they see your efforts. If your supervisor does not mention your work either to point out improvements or to praise it, you may interpret such silence as disapproval or as a message saying your work (and you) are unimportant in the scheme of things. Often you will get informal verbal comments as well about how you are doing. Not all organizations provide direct formal messages of evaluation.

Good organizations, however, have established formal channels that carry messages that evaluate your work in the organization. While such messages often concentrate on task matters, they usually include ratings of your ability to get along with fellow workers, your teamwork skills, and your future in the organization.

Indeed, systematic appraisal of people is so important many organizations have carefully worked out appraisal procedures. Some have written forms the supervisors must fill out periodically, say at the end of every six months, or every year. Many have regular appraisal interviews.

Few communication situations in the organization provide more difficulties and problems than official employee appraisal. In our experience as consultants in organizational communication we have discovered again and again that no matter how elaborate the formal appraisal procedures, the actual communication about how well people are doing is ineffective and inadequate.

Why do supervisors do such a poor job of worker evaluation? As a general principle when someone in a one-up position evaluates some-one in a one-down position, the general communicative climate encourages defensiveness, lack of trust, tension, frustration, anger, irritation, and hidden agendas. Think of the last time you had an instructor evaluate some classwork and grade it as a C when you thought it was certainly of B quality and had a hope it might even be an A. You might decide the instructor is wrong because he is inept or biased against you or that while he is able, he did not take enough time to look at your work closely. Suppose you ask for an interview to discuss your work with him. You want to try out all your hunches and check to see if he is inept; you may even want to charge him with being a poor teacher. You might want to see if he is biased against you as a person, and whether he read your paper carefully.

The instructor in such an interview is one-up. He has final control over your grade. You may believe that if you are honest he will get angry and punish you further. You thus find it difficult to raise the topics directly. Instead, you find yourself talking all around the topic. The instructor, however, gets the nonverbal message that you believe he did not do a good job of grading and begins to defend himself. He makes a long argument about the faults of your paper. The inter-view ends unsatisfactorily. The instructor is irritated because the inter-view was unpleasant. You are angry because you got no satisfaction from the meeting. Whatever relationship there was between you has deteriorated.

The same pressures you feel when talking to an instructor about your work are present and stronger in the typical organizational setting where not just your work in a class which will earn you a grade and which is important for a term, but your daily efforts for months are being evaluated.

In many organizations the periodic appraisal interviews become ritual meetings in which neither supervisor nor subordinate want to have them function as an honest evaluation of employee worth. Usually such rituals develop after some honest efforts that result in unpleasant and unrewarding communications. We have noted in

Chapter 2 that self-disclosure of significant information comes only in a climate of trust and that communication that is evaluative and comes from a "superior" source, that seems manipulative, will result in defensive communication. Evaluative communication often irritates the receiver to such an extent that the listener stops trying to understand the message.

When a supervisor evaluates your work in a negative way it is very difficult to keep from defending yourself or explaining away your difficulties. "I was not told about that." "That was not my fault." "That was when I had that virus and missed some days." When the person who can recommend a raise in salary, give you attractive assignments, provide you with resources and equipment, and recommend you for promotion, asks you to unburden yourself about your innermost hopes and fears it is difficult to keep the fact of fate control out of your communication. What if you do disclose important information? How can the supervisor keep from using that information to your disadvantage—particularly if you want to discuss some weakness or desire for self-improvement?

However negative some of the evaluations of parts of your performance must be in the mind of your supervisor, if he or she knows anything about defensive communication and values you as a person and as an ongoing member of the organization, he or she should reinforce these values clearly during the appraisal interview. This is not hypocrisy; it is quite possible to value a person and be unhappy with something that person is doing, or is failing to do. If you, as the target of critical appraisal, worry about what value the supervisor places on you as a person, *ask*.

In poor appraisal interviews the supervisors typically schedule them for the last thing in the day. Often they have a written evaluation form, a sort of report card they have filled in as required, before them. The report will usually be placed in the employee's personnel file. They "run down" the written form essentially restating what it says. Then they "do the right thing," asking some open-ended questions of the employee such as, "Do you have any questions about any part of this evaluation?" The employee may have a host of questions but often finds it hard to get started on the most important of them and so asks about some less important feature. The manager answers the question with an argument to support the evaluation. A couple of argumentative defenses from the person in the one-up position usually results in the employee looking at the clock and realizing it is almost quitting time, using that as an excuse to stop asking questions and get out of there.

If the supervisor gives the employees regular systematic evaluations of work as it happens on the job, the ritualization of the formal appraisal interview is not important. You need, and have a right as an employee, to find out how you are doing, what your strengths are, and where you need to try to improve in the judgment of people who evaluate a number of others and see your work in relation to the larger whole. Research into appraisal communication indicates that positive evaluations are rewarding (if they are perceived as authentic), but more surprising is that employees prefer even negative appraisals to no formal appraisals at all. If the supervisor provides continuous authentic evaluations, both positive and negative, then the likelihood is that the appraisal interviews *can* function as they should. The bleak picture of the ineffective appraisal interview we painted above is usually found in those units where the supervisor seldom comments on the quality of work either positively or negatively unless there is an obvious crisis, at which point the manager makes a critical event of the negative evaluation of subordinates.

When a supervisor does a good job of appraising subordinates at the periodic checkpoints in terms of communication content, part of the authentication of that appraisal comes in the form of messages about increases or decreases in salary. In theory, the organization communicates to its employees the official evaluation of their worth in terms of money messages. The general idea is that you are paid what you are worth. If your supervisor praises your work and gives you a lot of positive "strokes" for being a top-notch employee in the appraisal interview and then raises your salary a dollar a week, you may begin to wonder about how much weight you should give to the appraisal interview. If you discover that all your peers had their salaries cut, you will probably be reassured, but if you find that all others were given larger raises and some much greater increases, then you will tend to believe that "money talks" in terms of how the organization appraises your worth. You will not be inclined to put much stock in the next appraisal after such an experience.

In the absence of communication you may have to rely on the monetary messages related to your salary and bonuses to interpret how well you are doing. In many organizations where appraisal communication is rare and ineffective there is much talk and concern about who is paid what. People with large salaries may be very dissatisfied because some person in a similar job receives $500 or $600 more per year. They are not upset because they need the additional $500 so much as they are by the implication that their positions and their efforts are considered less worthy than those of the person making more money. Much discussion of how unfair it is that certain people are being paid a given salary and that these people are "doing absolutely nothing" or that people who are doing the real work are underpaid is a clue that the major messages about the worth of employees may be coming in the symbolic form of the amount of money earned.

The irony involved in an organization relying on monetary messages for communicating worth is that without good formal and informal communication related to appraisal by both supervisors and subordinates, the organization has very little sound evidence upon which to base salary adjustments. In the absence of good evidence, salary increments are often given across-the-board, or on a schedule relating to seniority. Such devices usually assure that the salary messages thus fail to relate in any meaningful way with the contribution individuals make to the organization.

STATUS AND SUBORDINATE COMMUNICATION

In a sense the appraisal interview simply throws into sharp relief some of the important characteristics of your communication with people who have higher formal status in the organization than you. Subordinates can interpret every message from a supervisor as having an element of evaluation in it—even silence can communicate an evaluation that the low status person is not worth consideration. You can interpret your manager's explanations of how to do a job as the evaluation that you do not know what you are doing. The supervisor's directions can sound to you like you do not have a mind of your own and need to be told everything. Orders are particularly irksome. They suggest you are a child who must allow the supervisor to tell you what to do and when to do it.

In the United States we share a number of fantasy types in which individualism is stressed and that imply the values that everyone is equal, no one better than anyone else, and that equal opportunity must be guaranteed for all. Many people are also caught up in the drama of the importance of "the people" as the ultimate source of power and control—the majority rules. My opinion is just as good as yours. Such dramas encourage an "I'm-as-good-as-you-are" attitude in many social and work situations. Many of our organizations, on the other hand, establish cultures in which status is important and much of the communication flow and content emphasizes that high status members are in a one-up position when they communicate with low status members. Such a clash of interpretative scripts often puts the subordinate in a symbolic double-bind. "If I am as good as anybody, why does he have the right to boss me around?" "How come she can lord it over me just because she is the manager?"

Some common responses on the part of subordinates in their communication with supervisors and higher status members of the organization include frustration, irritation, anger, and resentment. If you feel such emotions you may play them out in your communication by pretending to be cooperative, open, and forthcoming when you are in fact hiding important information, putting the best face possible on situations, and generally making it difficult for your supervisor. Another strategy is to communicate as though you wholeheartedly accepted the one-down position. People who adopt this strategy show deference, listen respectfully, allow the supervisor to have the floor, seldom question what the supervisor says, use much verbal and nonverbal agreement when the supervisor is speaking, and generally tell the supervisor what they think the supervisor wishes to hear. Of course these are only two of a range of possible responses you can make to the formal status and its influence on the communication climate. Still, a number of studies of organizational communication indicate that these two strategies are common.

Generally subordinates tend to send upward messages that make them look good. They tell about successes, objectives reached, and generally report things are going well. They tend to filter out information that would make them look bad. They downplay problems, failures, mistakes, until the situation reaches crisis proportions and can no longer be kept from the boss. We can think of this problem as the "good news" filter through which upward communication tends to travel. Even if the bad news will not make you look bad personally, you may not tell your supervisor of troubles because of fear of the very human tendency to punish the bearer of bad news. One interesting research finding is that the more a subordinate is interested in moving upward in the organization, the more likely she or he is to filter out the bad news. Apparently people who feel they have already reached a settled place in the organization are more willing to run risks and tell about problems.

Some studies indicate that people who adopt the role of subordinate wholeheartedly may receive some satisfaction by identifying with higher status members of the organization. Thus they enjoy being friends with the boss, being able to talk with her informally. To some extent they enjoy the reflected glow of status and importance and by indicating their connection they gain some prestige rewards for themselves.

Since organizations assume cooperative effort to achieve common goals, and create value to be shared, they require high fidelity transmission of information and a commitment on the part of the members to the organization and to the various units that make it up. Obviously the communicative behavior of subordinates all too often takes on the quality of mixed-motive games. The supervisor whose subordinates filter information so he or she receives only the good news until problems escalate into crises is generally faced with a continual round of major problems and crises. People who work in a climate of constant crisis are seldom as effective or happy as they might be in a setting where problems are anticipated or identified in their early stages.

As long as you wish your unit and your organization well it would be a good idea to establish norms of communication with your supervisor that allow you to say what you think and to send the bad news as well as the good news upward. To be sure, the supervisor has a large responsibility in creating such possibilities. Still, you should not be over-impressed by the outward shows of formal status and adopt a stereotyped strategy such as the good news filter without making a strong effort at establishing good lines of communication. Remember the importance of the informal communicating and organizing in terms of the way the organization functions and do not take formal status at face value.

In general, our analysis of the impact of formal status must be modified and amended by the dynamics of the model of role emergence in leaderless zero-history groups. If a person emerges as leader through the give-and-take of working together with others, that individual will enjoy high status and the respect and esteem of the group members. While in one sense you may be in a one-down position in communication with a person who is the natural leader of your group, the symbolic impact of natural leadership is much different than that of formal leadership. The emergent leader has earned the right to give directions, structure work, and make the decisions the group asks that person to make. When you accept directions from the natural leader such followership does not mean that the leader is lording it over you, or personally ordering you around and therefore demeaning you as a person. Rather, the emergent leader is a symbol for the group and when that person gives directions it means that the group is asking you to do something for the common good. If the formal leader is the natural leader, then the problem of establishing trust and cohesiveness so lower status members feel free to criticize the leadership, report conflicts and problems, and confront and work them through to consensus, is eased.

CAREER PATHING

If you view your entry level job in the organization as a stepping stone to a better position you need to examine the possible opportunities available for better positions. *Career pathing* refers to the way you go about charting your future in order to achieve the position you want. It requires some thinking through of the kind of position you would like to have. Investigations into what separates successful from unsuccessful people are always tricky since they require careful definitions of success and the factors involved are so complex and interrelated. One interesting study looked at a large sample of people who had achieved success in terms of some tangible measurement, such as writers who had published several novels, and compared them with people who had not been successful in terms of typical societal norms of success. The investigators concluded that the successful people had three crucial elements in their careers that the unsuccessful did not have. First, the successful people had chosen a profession early. For example, they became interested in science in junior high and knew then that they wanted to be scientists. Second, they had a mentor. A *mentor* is someone who helps you in your profession and also provides a role model that you can try to follow. The mentor might be, for example, a teacher, or someone active in the profession who gives you help along the way and becomes a personal friend. A budding novelist might send a manuscript to an established writer who reads the manuscript and gives encouragement, provides contacts, gives constructive criticism, and generally encourages the beginner. Third, the successful people had a dream. That is, they had a personal rhetorical vision of what they eventually wanted to do. They dramatized themselves enacting the desired professional tasks. The key factor in regard to the dream was that the successful people believed their dream and continued to strive for it, whereas the unsuccessful, who also often had a dream, decided at an early point that it was "an impossible dream," and gave it up.

Your dream should provide you with a definition of success and a graphic portrayal of your career goals. The career path is designed to make your dream possible by charting the steps between where you are now and where you would like to be. The job interviewer who asks such things as, "Where would you like to be in terms of a career five years from now?" is trying to find out what sort of dream you have for your future and how much you have thought about the intervening steps. The interviewer often asks such questions because many organizations are committed to the development of their human resources. Part of their organizational saga is the drama that to be competitive and to succeed they need good people committed to the organization. Therefore, they develop management training programs, employee education opportunities, and other means to improve their employees' skills and education.

In your appraisal interview you should get information about possibilities for moving into a better position and find out from your supervisor the opportunities you might have for gaining additional skills and education. You can usually get additional information from the personnel office. You should also let your supervisor and other managers know of your desire to map out a career path and prepare yourself to move towards your ideal career.

Of course you may decide after a period of time and careful evaluation that you cannot reach your goal within this organization.

The career paths may be limited and the situation may seem unpromising. You may then decide on a career path which moves through several organizations on the way to your ideal position. In our mobile society moving upward by moving from one organization to another is not unusual. Such mobility exacts it price, of course. In each new organization you must go through the elaborate initiation or joining process we described in Part One. Your personal life is likewise uprooted and disrupted by moving. For our purposes in the remainder of the book, we will assume that you have decided on a career path that is feasible and exciting within your current organization.

Having learned your lessons well and become an excellent communicator at the level of joining the organization and being a subordinate, you have gained an education and a group of skills that are of central importance to being a good manager.

As might be expected, you are promoted to a position of management. You are ready now for Part Three of the book, which helps you learn management through communication.

SUMMARY

One of the most rewarding aspects of a good organization can be the opportunity and resources to do work that you enjoy. A primary source of satisfaction is the feeling one gets from having done a job well. The greatest feeling of achievement often comes when our inner conviction that we have done well is publicly confirmed by people whose judgment we respect. We may receive such confirmation informally but such rewards can come most powerfully from systematic formal appraisal of our work. The appraisal interview is one important opportunity to find out how good your work is in the eyes of others who should know.

The official appraisal interview poses many communication difficulties and problems. As a general principle, when someone in a one-up position evaluates someone in a one-down position the general communication climate encourages defensiveness, lack of trust, tension, and hidden agendas.

In many organizations the appraisal interviews become ritual meetings because neither subordinate nor supervisor wishes to face the unpleasant tensions that are likely to arise from direct, open, and honest evaluations.

Part of the authentication of the official appraisal comes in the form of messages about increases or decreases in salary. In theory the organization communicates to its employees the official evaluation of their worth in terms of money messages. In the absence of meaningful verbal and nonverbal messages employees often have to rely on the monetary messages related to their salaries and bonuses to interpret how well they are doing. The irony involved in organizations relying heavily on monetary messages is that without good formal and informal communication relating to appraisals the management has little sound evidence upon which to make salary decisions.

In the United States many people share fantasy types with the moral that

"I'm as good as you are, no matter what my social class or economic condition in relation to yours." Many organizations, on the other hand, establish cultures in which formal status is important and in which people of higher status are in a supposedly one-up position when communicating with lower status employees. The general cultural fantasies are thus often at odds with the organizational saga, causing subordinates to be torn between two portrayals of the proper way to communicate with authority figures.

Our analysis of formal status must be amended by the dynamics of the model of role emergence in the leaderless zero-history groups. If a person earns informal status through the give-and-take of working with and communicating with others, that individual will have earned the right to be in a leadership position in the eyes of the others. The willing acceptance of emergent leadership makes it much easier for all involved to communicate effectively.

Career pathing refers to the way people may go about charting their future in order to achieve the kind of position they want. In your appraisal interviews you should get information about possibilities for moving into a better position and your supervisor should point out the opportunities available to you for gaining skills and educational experience that will help you on your way.

QUESTIONS FOR DISCUSSION AND REVIEW

1. What are some things to keep in mind while planning for an appraisal interview?
2. How can the supervisor's theory of management influence the appraisal interview?
3. What are some things to keep in mind during the appraisal interview?
4. Why is the appraisal interview such a difficult communication situation for both supervisor and subordinate?
5. How does money function as an appraisal message?
6. How does the fact that a supervisor has a higher formal status affect the communication in an appraisal interview?
7. How does organizational status in general influence the way subordinates communicate upward?
8. How can a subordinate work against the status barrier in terms of upward communication?
9. How does the informal emergence of status affect the quality of upward and downward communication in an organization?
10. What are three steps to include in planning a successful career path?

REFERENCES AND SUGGESTED READINGS

Bormann, E. G. *Discussion and Group Methods: Theory and Practice,* 2nd ed. New York: Harper & Row, 1975.

Fear, R. A. *The Evaluation Interview.* New York: McGraw-Hill, 1973.

Goldhaber, G. M. *Organizational Communication,* 2nd ed. Dubuque, Iowa: Wm. C. Brown, 1979.

Levinson, D. J. "Growing Up With the Dream," *Psychology Today,* 11 (Jan. 1978), 20–31, 89.

Maier, N. R. F. *The Appraisal Interview.* New York: Wiley, 1958.

Stewart, C. J. and W. B. Cash. *Interviewing: Principles and Practices.* Dubuque, Iowa: Wm. C. Brown, 1974.

Part Three

Learning to Communicate as a Manager

9

Nonverbal Communication

Laboratory Application

Anyone who assumes a new position in management immediately begins to feel the rewards of organizational status. People congratulate you on your "promotion" and, at least publicly, communicate to you that you have won a victory, reached a milestone, and achieved a level of "success." Old acquaintances respond to you differently. In general, the communication suggests both verbally and nonverbally that you are more important than you were prior to your promotion.

You suddenly discover that you are called on to do more talking more often with people at your same level, as well as with members of upper and middle management. You begin to meet a number of higher-ups for the first time. Some of these people will be known to you only through the sharing of fantasies about them with your former colleagues; instead of stories about "them," you now need to form your own impressions of these people. You are asked to attend many more business conferences. You are required to write memos, letters, and reports about matters that were formerly out of your circle of responsibility. From a position of communication underload you have moved to a communication crossroads where you may soon reach your communication capacity and where you might soon suffer from communication overload.

You still find yourself playing the subordinate role in many of your meetings and conferences but even that role has become communicatively more complex. Managers of higher status are asking for your opinion and suggestions; they ask how your unit is doing, what it can do, and will be likely to do with regard to certain plans and programs.

153

They ask about your unit's morale, about its strengths and weaknesses. You feel considerable pressure from the communication context to be definitive, authoritative, and on-top-of-things. Much of the nonverbal communication suggests that now you are special and you had better measure up to the expectations of organizational status.

Even your informal communication becomes more task-oriented. Sometimes you get the impression that everybody is asking for your help, your advice, a decision, or a favor. Friends and acquaintances sometimes use their "connection" with you to seek direct access to communicate with you rather than go through formal channels. Some seem to expect favorable decisions because of their personal relationships with you. Your informal communication has become much more "political"; you begin forming your connections with the established communication networks. Even a social evening with colleagues or a game of tennis may have overtones of coming to an agreement or making a decision relating to power, office politics, or company resources. Luncheon meetings often establish relationships that serve to help managers of various units get things done among themselves. You find that if you have someone you can count on in personnel, who knows you and what you need and want, this helps with your job performance.

You are, to some extent, a new member of an established set of task-oriented groups with more or less role emergence and stability. As such, you are being tested, initiated, and evaluated. You will come to assume a role in these groups and your ability as a manager will be heavily dependent on what those roles become. In a much more complicated way you are involved in something like the "new kid on the block" dynamics of childhood. The first response to the new kid is generally gratifying interest, curiosity, and attention, but then comes the attempt by the newcomer to assume a role in the informal social groupings of the neighborhood. Recall our discussion of what happens when a new member joins a group in Chapter 4. The result of trying out for a role in the group is conflict and role confusion. Animosities develop and the newcomer quickly moves from the honeymoon period of interest and attention to a difficult period of adjustment and accommodation. You should anticipate a rocky time of it for the first months, not only as you assume a new role with your subordinates, but with your manager and other colleagues on the management team.

Suddenly you find yourself at a number of meetings in which the members share fantasies and rhetorical visions that are new to you. You become part of the communication network in which the organizational saga is enriched or, perhaps, merely different from the one you knew as a worker.

Your first months in the position are clearly an exciting and important time in your career. You get many messages, both verbal and nonverbal, that build your self-image. You are clearly an important person. People are communicating to you that you have real status in the organization. You get many messages that you are in a position to "do something" and "to make things happen." At the same time, you are often confused and disoriented. You do not know what role you ought to take in the established role structures. You are not sure about the work norms of the new groups or the routines of paper work. You do not feel confident about giving good definitive answers to many of the questions that flow upward from your subordinates as well as downward from upper management. You feel insecure. You often want to say that you do not know or that you are not sure or that you have not yet gotten to that particular message or made that decision. The nonverbal communication from others, however, suggests that a person in your position ought to be sure, secure, on top of things, and confident.

CASE STUDY ASSIGNMENT: The New Sales Manager

The top management of Invention Incorporated planned their search for a new sales manager very carefully. They decided that much of their success was a result of their outstanding sales force. When they lost Harry Wilson to one of the nation's biggest toy manufacturers they were troubled and upset. Wilson was outgoing and personable. Seldom serious, he had assumed a role of social facilitator in many meetings of top management. Wilson was also a slovenly administrator and tended to get bogged down in detail. Top management was unaware of Wilson's failings in the task dimension because Mary Harmon, his executive secretary, was a quiet, unobtrusive powerhouse.

Mary, who had worked ten years for the firm, had a deceptively quiet manner. She was pleasant, always there in the outer office, dependable, and would drop whatever she was doing whenever one of the members of the sales force had a difficulty. She handled much of Wilson's mail. She wrote drafts of his reports and memos after he mumbled some general thoughts and instructed her to "Fix up something along that line." In a sense, they were a team. He handled the public relations; she handled the sales department.

Top management decided that in addition to getting, as they put it, "the best person in the country" for the position, they should hire a woman. They were feeling considerable pressure from affirmative action and from the general business community because they had *no* women in upper management. Invention Incorporated had always used a high proportion of women for their production workers which made the lack of women in management even more embarrassing.

The search for a suitable person was long and difficult. Experienced women were in demand. When the Board of Directors brought some promising candidates for a visit and interviews they turned out to be what the all-male board referred to as "women libbers." In the shared fantasies of the board, a "woman libber" was an abrasive and destructive female; she would likely be more interested in women's rights than in doing her job. They were pleased, therefore, when Janet Perkins came for her interview and turned out to be a dynamic young woman who was not a "woman's libber." Perkins clearly knew business management and sales and she convinced the board members that she was interested in doing the job, not reforming the world.

Janet Perkins was a bright ambitious woman who had a dream of becoming president of a major corporation by the time she was forty. She had graduated from college with honors and had then done well in a prestigious Master of Business Administration program. Five years after earning her second degree she had risen from the management training program in a major manufacturing company to a position as regional sales manager. Janet Perkins looked just right to Invention Incorporated; she was hired as their new sales manager.

Janet was deep in second thoughts about the wisdom of her choice by the end of the first month. Clearly, Invention Incorporated had grown like a weed without any thought or planning. She saw quickly that the whole organization should be reorganized, lines of control rationalized, new theories of management implemented, and the latest approaches to production and sales put into effect.

Very quickly she discovered that her department was typical of the entire firm. The sales department seemed to reflect the happy-go-lucky personality of its former head, Harry Wilson. One of them, Jim Martin, in fact, seemed to be a carbon copy of her predecessor judging by the stories she kept hearing about Wilson. Martin had been acting as temporary manager after Wilson left and that, she thought, might account for the sad state of affairs she had inherited.

But Janet's first big difficulty with personnel came, to her surprise, from Mary Harmon. The two saleswomen in her department had approached her with some deference with an invitation to lunch. During the luncheon, she discovered that Mary Harmon and Jim Martin were still making most of the decisions and handling important details without consulting her.

The next day she called Mary Harmon in and clearly spelled out her job responsibilities. From now on, Janet would take over many of the things that Mary had been doing and—as for Mary's remaining duties—Janet was to be kept informed about them.

Within two weeks Mary and Janet were in the midst of an unpleasant "personality clash." Mary's resignation was particularly disturbing to all concerned. The loss of Mary Harmon was felt not only in sales but in many other departments as well. In her exit interview she was bitter and kept repeating she could not work "under the new sales manager who thought that having a master's degree in business administration made her far superior to somebody with ten years' actual working experience."

Janet hired a new person to take Mary's place. Billie was a bright woman who had dropped out of law school to take a job and earn some money before continuing her education. Janet changed the job title from "secretary" to "administrative assistant" since Billie refused to be a "secretary." Janet was surprised by the unexpected uproar that followed the simple change of title.

With Billie's support, Janet spent six weeks planning the reorganization of her department. Schooled in the latest human relations school of management, Janet was careful to try to communicate with all of her subordinates every step of the way. She found, however, that she could not communicate with Jim Martin. And because Martin was a ringleader for the other men, she could not seem to make her ideas clear to them either.

Janet was small and attractive and she dressed in becoming clothes. She read the latest books on women in management and, taking their advice, did not emphasize her sexuality but, on the other hand, she did not wear masculine styled suits and dull colors. She was on her guard against sexual overtones in her manner. Still, because she was nearsighted she had developed a habit of staring directly at people when she was concentrating on what they were saying, and Martin felt this was seductive. She also had a nervous mannerism of smiling and moving her shoulders that he perceived as flirtatious.

Whenever Janet tried to have a serious conference with Martin he kept kidding and joking and commenting about her physical attractiveness. When he complimented her on the way she did her hair she tried to be noncommittal but when he made some crack about her legs she found herself barely able to control her anger as she let him know in no uncertain terms that she would not tolerate such behavior. The unfortunate conference happened the same day she heard a whistle following her down the hall as she walked past some of the salesmen.

Shortly thereafter Jim Martin went to the President of Invention Incorporated to complain about the new sales manager and threatened the resignation of all the salesmen if something were not done about the "iron maiden" they had hired to run sales.

QUESTIONS FOR CASE ANALYSIS

1. What problems in the case of the new sales manager can be traced to the typical dynamics related to a new person taking on a new position of formal leadership?
2. What problems are a result of sexism in Invention Incorporated?

3. What problems are the result of the nonverbal dimension in the communication of the members of the sales division?
4. To what extent are the problems "personality conflicts" and to what extent are they a result of role instability and conflict?
5. What problems result from the fact that Janet is younger than most of her subordinates?

──────────── **Theoretical Rationale** ────────────

NONVERBAL COMMUNICATION IN THE ORGANIZATION CONTEXT

Basic Concepts. In recent years the study of nonverbal communication in general has grown a great deal over what it was 20 years ago. Scholars have developed some basic technical concepts for the most important parts of nonverbal communication. Scholars have often made up special terms for these technical concepts, basing them on Latin and Greek roots so they may seem to be "jawbreakers." We introduce you to the terms here primarily because you should know them as you read other books and articles about nonverbal communication. The terms are not as important as the concepts but these basic concepts about nonverbal communication are, indeed, useful.

Consider what happens when you write a letter and you want to emphasize certain ideas or words; you may CAPITALIZE the ideas you want to stand out; you may underline them. You can also use **punctuation marks to suggest possible interpretations of the same string of words.** In interpersonal communication, when you speak to others you can also emphasize and underline and punctuate ideas by the way you pause, vary the rate of speech, the pitch of your voice, and the loudness with which you speak. The technical term for the vocal melody and the punctuation you can use to change, emphasize, or reverse the meaning of the words you are using is *paralinguistics*.

You can add meaning to what you are saying by your facial expressions, eye movements, gestures, and other body motions. The technical term for the nonverbal communication of gesture is *kinesics*.

Scholars studying nonverbal communication have discovered that the way people arrange themselves in space in relation to one another as they speak is important to their interpretation of what the communication means. If two people are hugging one another as they speak, or standing nose-to-nose, or way apart, their physical relationship in space influences their communication. The technical term for spatial relationships among communicators is *proxemics*.

Clearly, you can communicate by the expressive use of voice, by effective and appropriate gestures, and by positioning yourself skillfully in relation to those with whom you are talking. If we are not careful, however, our enthusiasm for the importance of nonverbal dimensions in communication can get us carried away in terms of what we should include in our study of nonverbal communication. In one sense, every object made by human hands is symbolic and "says something" about the person who made it or uses it or about that person's culture.

We could, for example, say that your clothing communicates nonverbally. Or that your hairstyling and body shape communicates who you are. We could argue that the arrangement of the furniture in your office and the neatness or lack of it on your desk communicates nonverbally to the person who enters. Do you have a personally autographed picture of the Governor and your diploma from State College on your wall? Or do you have a dog-eared cartoon making fun of pretentious managers pasted to the wall with scotch tape? Certainly people will form an impression of you from your clothing, your personal appearance, and the appearance of your home and office. We could go on to argue that the arrangement of the offices within the building, such things as corner rooms or center rooms, top floor offices or bottom floor offices, all communicate status. Furnishings, rugs, desks, all sorts of other physical features of the company office building can be said to communicate status. The trouble with such endless considerations is that they are just that—endless. If we are not careful we will include almost everything in our analysis of nonverbal communication.

We prefer to draw a much narrower circle around what we call nonverbal communication and confine ourselves to the vocal intonations, the gestures, and the spatial relationships among those taking part in a communication episode. We define the other features, important as they are, as the nonverbal *context* for the communication.

In our model of communication in Chapter 3 we stressed the intentional nature of organizational communication. Janet Perkins had certain points she wanted to get across to Jim Martin when she had conferences with him. The message source in our model has a conscious intent, a meaning, a purpose that guides the encoding of the message and the use of feedback to bring the communication on target. We can use nonverbal communication, consciously, to enhance our effectiveness in communicating our intent. Conscious, intentional use of nonverbal factors to achieve the successful communication of meanings is an important feature of communication.

You may be unaware, however, that from time to time people are reading things into the context and your gestures, vocal intonations, and manner. Thus when Janet Perkins looked at Jim Martin with the expression she typically used when concentrating, listening carefully, he perceived that she was being flirtatious.

Just as troublesome as the person who gets an unintended message from the nonverbal cues is the individual who fails to get an intended message. When Jim Martin first tried his sexual innuendos and flirting with Janet, she tried to make her face expressionless and cold and ignore the comments. Martin was one of those who "wouldn't take the hint" and had to have it "spelled out" for him.

The nonverbal elements in a communication episode seldom have a dictionary feature like words have. To be sure, in a certain culture, a given gesture like a nod or shaking the head from side to side may have a meaning such as "yes" or "no," but these definite and commonly understood gestures are relatively few. Most nonverbal elements can be interpreted in several or more ways. Many may be interpreted as unintentional messages, and many may be overlooked. Because of the vagueness of nonverbal cues we may be more or less conscious that they are an important feature of the meeting. In addition, whether or not we are conscious that they are important, we may be more or less competent to use them intentionally or to find out what effect they are having.

In our work as consultants to various organizations we have observed people in a variety of communication contexts and episodes and talked with them about their problems and experiences. We have noted four levels of competence with regard to nonverbal communication.

Levels of Competence in Nonverbal Communication. The first level is unconscious incompetence. Every day people confront many problems in nonverbal communication and are not aware of the choices open to them. They do not recognize failures in nonverbal communication. They are unaware of the possibility of emphasizing the meaning in their words by skillful vocal changes, by meaningful gestures, and by proper arrangement of the participants. They do not know that the others are reading meanings into their unintentional actions or failing to get intended hints. They are unaware that the failure to get results is partly due to incompetence in terms of nonverbal communication. They often assume the failure is due to the inherent weakness of the others. ("Can I help it if they're so stupid?")

The second level is conscious incompetence. For example, people may know that their voices are giving the wrong impression. One of the authors worked closely with a member of upper management in a large corporation on skills in making oral presentations. After a time the manager disclosed a feeling of frustration because his vocal quality was harsh and he thought he had an image as a harsh, tough, unpleasant person largely because of how he sounded. Careful analysis of a tape recording of his voice revealed that it *was* raspy and unpleasant; vocally he did come across as rough and insensitive. He knew his paralinguistic communication was working against his intentions but he did not know what to do about it. He was consciously incompetent in nonverbal communication.

The third level is unconscious competence. Some people are communicating effectively from a nonverbal level without being aware of what they are doing and why it is succeeding. Others have consciously practiced skills until they are second nature. Both groups have reached a level of unconscious competence. Simply by trial and error a person may develop abilities to emphasize and modify ideas and express shades of meaning. Unconscious competence is not enough for certain communication problems faced by supervisors in the modern organization, however. Many of your communication problems will not be routine and past trial and error experiences will not help you in dealing with them.

The fourth level is conscious competence. A person who is consciously competent knows the resources he or she can draw on to achieve intent. Such people are alert to areas of context that result in communicating unintended messages and are aware that intended nonverbal messages may go astray. They are sensitive to unintentional meanings and alert to their potential damage. They also can arrange the context to provide a suitable climate for the verbal and nonverbal communication within the meeting.

Functions of Nonverbal Communication. Perhaps the most basic function of nonverbal communication is to carry the same message as the words. People who are competent in the use of nonverbal communication can emphasize and enhance the verbal part of the message by their vocal inflections, pauses, and gestures. People who speak in monotones and keep a poker face must rely very heavily on the words to carry their meanings.

Listeners will tend to believe the nonverbal component of the message when it differs from the verbal. People who are skillful in the use of nonverbal communication can detract from or reverse the meaning of the words by the way they say them. "What do you think of our new plan for work improvement?" asks the supervisor. "I'm very excited about it," the subordinate answers, but the way the subordinate says the words sounds as though the subordinate is thinking, "here we go again—another brainchild from top management that will amount to nothing and blow over in six months, but we'll have to go along and humor them."

When you use the nonverbal part of the message to reverse the verbal the result is often sarcasm or irony and this can backfire. The listener may miss the intent of your irony because your nonverbal message was not communicated effectively and thus get a meaning that is the opposite of what you had in mind. When you succeed in communicating irony or sarcasm, the listener may respond with considerable emotion. If the emotional response is favorable, you make your point much more strongly than if you simply said it directly, but if it is negative, the reaction against you will also be strong.

One of the more intriguing findings of investigators studying nonverbal communication is that people at the level of unconscious incompetence may be giving nonverbal cues that undercut their verbal messages without being aware they are doing so. "Don't," the parents say as they light up cigarettes, "make the same mistake we did and start smoking in junior high. Now we can't stop and it's such a filthy, expensive habit—it'll ruin your health, too." The parents communicate in a number of nonverbal ways that they do not really believe their own advice, and then they are unable to understand why the daughter starts smoking in junior high. "We told her and told her," the parents say, "but she just went ahead and did it anyway."

The incompetent communicators are unaware that they are sending double-edged messages and these can cause relationship problems. Janet Perkins was placed in a close status relationship with Mary Harmon by the formal structure of Invention Incorporated. They were immediately involved in a struggle over power within the relationship. If we were to study the written transcript of their communication we might conclude that Mary was accepting Janet's dominance and willingly cooperating with her directions and orders. If we would add the nonverbal dimension, however, we would find that while Mary's words said "Yes, all right, fine," her nonverbal communication said, "No, I don't like this, and I won't do it." Janet was therefore put in a difficult communicative bind. Was she to believe the words or the nonverbal components? Not only that, but if she were to challenge Mary about the situation, Mary could always fall back on the record of her words. "What have I said to make you think that?" she could ask. Janet would be left with some unsatisfactory answer such as, "I'm not sure it's anything you've said. I can't really put my finger on it. I just get a feeling that you're saying one thing but thinking another."

If a person keeps getting double-edged messages from a friend, relative, or co-worker, the relationship between them is likely to become punishing and unpleasant. If the relationship is difficult to break off, the person may well become emotionally upset.

In your new position as a supervisor you are in a one-up relationship with your subordinates and your unconscious nonverbal communication may contradict your well-meaning verbal assurances. Suppose you have taken to heart what we have stressed in earlier chapters about the status filter and its influence on communication flow both upward and downward. You want to assure that you establish formal communication networks in which status does not play an important filtering function. You send out memos, make announcements in staff meetings, and use other channels to get across your message. "I am always available to anyone in the department when you have something important you want to talk over with me. I have an open door policy." If someone tries to use your open door, however, your nonverbal messages may communicate that you are short of time, busy with more important matters. Without being aware that you have done so, you have succumbed to the pressures of your job. Unconscious of the actual effect, you may well believe that you have taken time from your busy schedule to implement your open door policy. You will likely be surprised when your open door policy does not work because nobody uses it.

Your nonverbal communication often carries the more "believed" messages about relationships. If you have a close personal relationship with the other person or if you have a good working relationship, the quality of that relationship can be communicated and checked non-verbally. Relationships are not static; like roles in small groups, they change and evolve. People constantly test to see if their expectations of one another still hold and much of this testing is done by touching, eye contact, general bodily posture, verbal intonations and other non-verbal cues.

One of the important ways nonverbal messages can comment on relationships is in terms of liking or disliking. Often the verbal expression of personal relationships is restricted by the organizational norms and customs of communication. The participants in a business meeting are often restricted by custom from actually saying to one another, "I really like you. You are such a good person." By the same token, the norms may keep people from saying, "I dislike you as a person." In many organizational situations the nonverbal dimension may get the meaning across nonetheless.

Nonverbal messages often reveal and sustain power relationships. Even in a group that has no formal leader, if a member has emerged in a power role, the nonverbal communication will reveal that fact to a knowledgeable observer of their meeting. Likewise if the formal manager who is supposedly leading a staff meeting is not the emergent leader of the group, that fact will also be communicated largely by nonverbal communication.

Nonverbal Communication and Territory. An important part of the context of nonverbal communication relates to the arrangement of space and the ways in which members of the organization define and defend territory both geographically and symbolically.

Human beings in general and within organizations specifically stake out various territories in which they live, work, and play. A student may sit in the same chair every time she attends a class and be disturbed if someone else sits in "her" chair. In addition, people act as though they had a bubble of personal space surrounding them that they like to keep free of others. The size of the bubble seems to grow larger or smaller depending on the context and the nature of the communication.

People talking with one another often stake out a small circle of turf and define its limits by nonverbal means. Members participating in a business conference will frame and outline the limits of their territory by the way they sit around the table and position themselves in relationship to one another. In the old western movies the pioneers under attack would draw up their wagons in a circle for safety. Similarly, the people taking part in a conference or meeting draw themselves up in a circle, thereby keeping out intruders who have no business or right to be part of the meeting.

When the meeting is over the members break up their circle and nonverbally say, "We have finished. Anything we now talk about is off the official record." They pull back their chairs, stand up, stretch, and in other ways indicate that the symbolic boundaries that defined the meeting no longer apply.

In the early years of settlement in the United States some people went into the frontier regions and began to live on and farm the land. They were referred to as "squatters" and their rights were "squatter's rights." Many, however, followed the legal requirements for ownership and had legal documents with which they claimed a legal right to their territory. People in organizations may take up some territory from time to time for conversations or informal meetings and define their turf by nonverbal means much as the squatters used to do. A small group may gather around the water cooler and informally stake out that territory while they talk. As you move into management, however, you often are given legal title, as it were, to some personal space within the facilities of the organization.

Indeed, one of the rewards of status is often a personal area which is now your turf. This may be a desk and the surrounding area in a large room where other managers of the same status also have desks. It may be a desk within a partial enclosure. Or, it may be a room which is your private office. The more clearly defined the boundaries of your personal territory, the more rewarding it tends to be. Managers who have a desk in a larger room with other desks tend to find their work environment less satisfactory than do those who have private offices.

You frequently get a "message" about how important the organization finds your position in terms of the amount and quality of space you are awarded when you take on your management position. Janet

Perkins immediately noted that the sales manager's office was smaller than the plant manager's when she toured the facilities of Invention Incorporated prior to accepting the position. One of the requirements she laid down for accepting the position was "better facilities" for the sales department.

Generally, the higher your organizational status, the greater the amount of personal space awarded to you. In addition, the people holding higher status positions can generally defend their turf more successfully than those in lower positions. You can keep your door closed to your subordinates if you choose. The president of the company, however, can probably walk into your office whenever he or she wants to. You can likewise invade the territory of your subordinates and observe the way they are working and initiate conversations with them whenever you want to. People with higher status tend to move around more; people with lower status in organizations are "expected" to remain at their desks or whatever specific territory contains their "job." (Except, as one student pointed out gleefully, for his particular job, usually considered low status; first he delivered the mail, then he delivered inter-office memos, and, after hours, he did some janitorial work at the company where he was a part-time working student.) Perhaps it would be good at this point, again, to state that there are no "rules" of nonverbal communication; that is, it can be said that certain nonverbal behaviors have been observed, in many cases, to be associated with certain intended messages. We feel strongly that any "reading" of nonverbal messages should be done very carefully. It is always wise to check out any assumptions you are making with more clues, verbal and nonverbal.

Throughout history, however, high status people within any community have tended to have visible possessions indicating that high status. In a modern organization, the chief executive officer may have an inner sanctum so heavily defended from outside invaders that only a few special members of the organization ever see it. The space occupied by the people of highest status is often quiet and sparsely populated. In contrast, the space occupied by entry-level workers is often noisy and continually invaded by visitors, supervisors, upper and middle managers.

Compare these two contexts for a two-person conference. In one you ask a worker on the assembly line to stop work for a minute to discuss something amidst the general noise and hubbub. In the other, you approach a gatekeeper's desk and announce you have permission (an appointment) to meet with the Chief Executive Officer. You are asked to wait a moment. Finally, there is a buzz on the intercom and the gatekeeper motions you to follow. You go through a room filled with assistants working quietly at a battery of desks and are handed over to a chief assistant. The chief assistant, treating you with the deference due someone who has been privileged to enter this space, takes you through several more doors into the thickly carpeted and lavishly furnished inner office.

Units within an organization also have territory awarded to them in terms of office space or production facilities. Members of these units tend to defend their territory from other units. Should another unit try to take over some of your space you will undoubtedly try to fight off the attempt. Groups in competition for status and prestige often fight it out over territory. At many universities and colleges the time and energy that go into battles for space may seem to an outsider to be far out of proportion to the space's usefulness to the teaching, research, and service purposes that the institution's saga portrays as basic. As part of the nonverbal context of communication, however, the battle over the amount and quality of space becomes understandable. The mixed motive features of communication come into strong play in the discussions over space allocation in many organizations.

Interestingly enough, people in organizations also draw symbolic lines defining their turf or territory. They defend these symbolic lines in much the same way they defend their actual turf.

Members often try to establish "empires" within the organization. The prestige of a given unit is enhanced by its growth in size and control. The status and prestige of the leader of the unit also grows with an increase in his or her empire. Not only do members of some groups seek to build an empire within the organization but they almost always defend their group when it comes under attack from other units within the system. Thus, when production blames Bill Johnson's group for delays in delivery, he tends to defend his unit and find some other explanation for the problems.

Group Competition and Change. If a complicated system of interconnected groups can reach a state of balance—that is, if the territorial boundaries of each group are clear and stable—and if the demands on the entire system are met without strain, then intergroup competition is minimized. The tendency in the modern organization, however, is to keep the system in a state of flux. Some of the change is planned. Most profit-making organizations contain a dynamic to improve the profit margin. Even when things are going well they have a drive to do even better. Other organizations, too, experience internal, planned and more or less continuous change to improve the effectiveness of the system.

Much change is unplanned. Pressures from other organizations create a need to adapt to a new challenge. Organizations typically grow or contract, and in a corporate culture where the size of the population and the complexity of the culture are on a rapid increase, the tendency is to grow or perish. A continual turnover of personnel, additional people, promotions, and resignations add uncertainty. Information Systems, a small data processing company, grew at a faster rate than most organizations because it was on the market with a product at the right moment. They rode the crest of a wave of technological improvements. The problems posed by the continual growth and addition of personnel for Information Systems, although perhaps more severe than for most organizations, are nonetheless typical.

Empire Building When the System Is in a State of Flux. When a system of interrelated groups finds itself in a state of flux, the normal jurisdictional boundaries are subject to change. Changing boundaries are an invitation to aggressive groups to enlarge their holdings, and they often develop plans to take on responsibilities and power. When a company experiences a rapid increase in size as did Information Systems it results in the opening up of new territory. New territory also invites the empire builder. Every organization has several groups eager to enlarge their jurisdiction and the result is a contest for the new area.

The reader may supply his or her own example of an empire builder in action. We will content ourselves with a resume of the career of the man who was once chief janitor at Information Systems, Inc., and who ended his career ensconced in one of the largest and best decorated offices in the building. His official title was Manager of the Department of Material Resource Development and Protection. The story of his rise within Information Systems reads like today's version of the classic American success story.

Jim Malone started at Information Systems as a watchman, janitor, and jack-of-all-trades when the firm consisted of little more than a receptionist, a secretary, and a few engineers and technicians building the prototype of the first computer. As the firm expanded he moved a desk into the basement beside the furnace and put up a sign that said "Custodial Services." He soon hired two janitors to clean up the building and concentrated on his duties as a night watchman.

Malone was able to do with little sleep so he started to come to the plant early in the afternoon and deliver coffee and doughnuts. Soon he initiated the installation of vending machines to sell candy, beverages, sandwiches, and fruit. By now the company had grown and Malone's group consisted of several watchmen, four janitors, and two cleaning women.

Malone next suggested a company cafeteria, and soon a division of food services became part of his department. He added a home economist to his staff, and when the executive offices were to be redecorated Malone offered her services to work with the decorating firm. Soon Malone added several painters, carpenters, and decorators to his department. He also developed a system of cross charges. When his department redecorated or remodeled any rooms or offices for another department, Malone would charge them for the labor. He thus had a relatively small budget for his department when compared to the actual funds at his disposal. He was able to get top management's approval for a scheme whereby all remodeling, redecorating, and carpentry work was to be done by his department, or at least his department's approval was required before outside contractors were allowed to do the job.

Since the firm had leased a large old four-story building to house its operations, Malone's services were in great demand so that his department grew in size and influence. One of the major problems for the growing firm was parking. The downtown parking situation was critical, and the employees and clients of the firm were irritated and inconvenienced by the lack of facilities. Malone stepped into the breach and expanding his division of protection added a "policeman" to take charge of parking in the company's lots, and his department assigned parking places for the company.

During the course of these developments, Malone's operation had moved from his desk in the furnace room to ever larger accommodations. By keeping a sharp eye for services that were not clearly related to the duties of established departments, he managed to increase his empire in many different directions. At first he was viewed with some amusement by the upper level managers, but as his department grew in size and influence, they changed their opinion of him. When Information Systems built a large new facility, Malone was one of the most powerful men in the company.

Nonverbal Communication and Time. The timing of messages and behaviors can have a symbolic meaning. Most cultural communities develop conventions regarding the meaning of making and keeping appointments, being "on time" or "ahead of time," or "tardy." In Chapter 5 we discussed the shared fantasies of one unit in a North American firm where time was an overriding preoccupation. Other cultural communities are less concerned with watching the clock or making the best use of time. Being pointedly on time and keeping an eye on the clock is considered extremely rude in some cultures, usually those not in continental North America. On the other hand, it has been said of some Native American cultures that the shortest unit of time is not a minute, or even an hour, but one day.

Usually you soon learn the symbolic meaning of time in your organization. Often unexpected trouble comes when people who are not conscious of the nonverbal dimension of communication try to communicate across cultures. When someone who comes from an organization where starting meetings fifteen or twenty minutes after they are called is the norm arrives twenty minutes late for a conference with someone from an organization where to be more than five minutes late is an insult, there can be misinterpretation and trouble.

The timing of messages is also important. If your subordinates usually receive information from you long after they have learned about it from other sources, they may cease to rely on you as a source. In some organizations upper management tends to be secretive and not reveal important information until they absolutely have to. The workers often receive messages so late that the usefulness of the information is greatly decreased. We have stressed the phenomenon of the good news filter for messages flowing upward in the organization, but for certain kinds of messages, there is a similar filter for the downward flow. If the company is having a bad quarter and needs to lay off workers or shut down a plant temporarily or cannot pay the annual Christmas bonus, the top management often withholds such information as long as possible.

Time is also an important feature in communication overload. One factor in communication overload is the rate of message flow. That is, how many messages must you encode and how many must you decode in a given time period. You may feel that you simply do not have enough time to give to two-person conferences, to reading written messages, to informal socializing, and to business meetings. If your telephone is ringing, your desk piled up with memos, and several people are waiting for a chance to talk with you, you may communicate nonverbally that you are a busy person whose communicative time is precious. The subordinate who comes to your office for a conference and finds you in such a flood of messages may well decide that he or she must apologize for taking your time and must rush through the conference as rapidly as possible in order to free you for other communications. You may respond to the overload by becoming more and more directive in your style of communicating in order to save time or to manage time more effectively.

Be careful about falling into the habit of trying to respond to communication overload by dealing with every message, helter-skelter, as it impinges upon you until you develop a hurried, talking-off-the-top-of-your-head directive way of communicating with your subordinates. If you feel this happening, take stock of your communication flow and revise your system.

One way to try to handle overload is by *queuing,* a term meaning to line up in an orderly fashion to gain entrance to a theatre or a bus. You can "line up" your communications in orderly queues and handle each in turn. A primitive way of using queuing is to simply accept each demand as it comes, first received, first served, as it were, no matter what type of communication it represents. Say that you read the morning mail, accept a subordinate through your "open door" for a conference, and take a telephone call in the middle of the informal conference. Another subordinate is calling, asking to see you, and you ask her to wait in the outer office. Thus the queuing begins. Usually, if for no other reason than that the organization itself requires you to do so, you will find that some communication takes precedence over others. "There has been a special meeting called by the vice-president. You are going to have to attend this afternoon at two o'clock." Generally, some selection of communication and some ordering of queues will help deal with communication flow. First thing in the morning, you tell yourself, I will go through my "in basket" and clear off my desk of written communication. After that I will make appointments with subordinates for conferences.

Another technique to help with communication flow is to set up a system of dividing messages into more or less important categories and then developing a queuing system to deal with the most important first, the next more important next, and so forth until time is no longer available. You can then ignore the less important communication, or at least postpone dealing with it, or perhaps assign it to a subordinate to handle.

Sometimes you can handle certain communication situations or messages more effectively by lumping them together rather than dealing with each in order as in queuing. This procedure is sometimes referred to as *chunking*. You may discover, for instance, that you get a number of letters each week that are the same in crucial respects and you can lump them all together and write essentially one letter in response to the lot of them. You can develop a series of standard messages (form letters of reply) that you can personalize by adding a few sentences and you can then chunk many messages into a short period of time.

Our point is that as a new manager, you need to develop communication skills related to message flow. If you are not knowledgeable and careful in your early days as a manager, you may become heavily overloaded and fall into unfortunate communication practices that will plague you for a long period of time even after you have "learned the ropes" and found a role for yourself. With some planning and management of communication flow, you may find that what at first seemed overload becomes a satisfactory level of communication and you can take adequate time to use nondirective communication strategies when they are indicated.

SUMMARY

The technical term for the vocal melody and the punctuation you can use to change, emphasize, or reverse the meaning of your words is *paralinguistics*. *Kinesics* refers to the nonverbal communication of gesture. *Proxemics* refers to the spatial relationships among communicators.

We can use nonverbal communication, consciously, to enhance our effectiveness in communicating our intent. People may, however, read unintended meanings into our paralinguistics or kinesics. Also troublesome in nonverbal communication are those who fail to decode an intended message correctly.

There are four levels of competence in using nonverbal communication: unconscious incompetence, conscious incompetence, unconscious competence, and conscious competence. The best nonverbal communicators tend to be those who have worked through conscious competence to make skills habitual, and those who raise their competence to the conscious level when they face the need to take difficult options or develop complicated communication strategies and tactics.

The most basic function of nonverbal communication is to support the message conveyed by the words. People who are skillful can also, intentionally, use nonverbal elements to detract from or reverse the meaning of the words. Listeners will tend to believe the nonverbal component as more authentic than the verbal when they are at odds. Incompetent communicators may be giving nonverbal cues that undercut their verbal messages. Those who are unconsciously incompetent may be sending double-edged messages which cause relationship problems.

One of the important ways nonverbal communication functions is in terms of creating, sustaining, and terminating personal relationships. Nonverbal messages often relate to liking, disliking, or power relationships.

Human beings tend to stake out various territories in which they work and socialize within the organization. Two-person and small group conversations are often defined by nonverbal means. Indeed, one of the rewards of organizational status is often a clearly defined area of personal turf. People get messages about how important the organization finds their position in terms of the amount and quality of office space they have.

Units within an organization also have territory awarded to them. Symbolic territory can include work responsibilities and jurisdictions over functions. Members often try to establish "empires" within the organization by taking over more symbolic or geographical turf than other units. Empire building tends to take place when the organizational system is unbalanced and in a state of flux. Growth or retrenchment tends to change internal boundaries and invite defense of turf in danger of retrenchment or attack for portions of new turf under conditions of growth.

The timing of messages and behavior often takes on a symbolic meaning. Time tends to mean different things in different cultures. Even within a dominant culture organizations will tend to share fantasies about time which result in establishing the way it is to be managed, viewed, and interpreted within the specific group. Timing is also important in communication overload and underload.

QUESTIONS FOR DISCUSSION AND REVIEW

1. What role do paralinguistics play in nonverbal communication?
2. What role do kinesics play in nonverbal communication?
3. What role do proxemics play in nonverbal communication?

4. What are the four levels of competence in nonverbal communication?
5. What are the major functions of nonverbal communication?
6. How does nonverbal communication relate to space and turf in an organization?
7. How does nonverbal communication relate to symbolic territory and to its defense?
8. What is the nature of "empire building" in organizations?
9. What is the relationship of time to nonverbal communication?
10. How does timing relate to communication load?

REFERENCES AND SUGGESTED READINGS

Birdwhistell, R. L. *Kinesics and Context: Essays on Body Motion Communication.* Philadelphia: University of Pennsylvania Press, 1970.

Eisenberg, A. and R. Smith. *Nonverbal Communication.* Indianapolis: Bobbs-Merrill, 1971.

Knapp, M. L. *Nonverbal Communication in Human Interaction,* 2nd ed. New York: Holt, Rinehart and Winston, 1978.

Leathers, D. *Nonverbal Communication Systems.* Boston: Allyn & Bacon, 1976.

Mehrabian, A. *Silent Messages.* Belmont, California: Wadsworth, 1971.

Sheflen, A. E. and A. Sheflen. *Body Language and Social Order: Communication as Behavioral Control.* Englewood Cliffs, N.J.: Prentice-Hall, 1972.

10

Taking the Lead

———————————— **Laboratory Application** ————————————

In Part One we introduced you to the typical communication situations in the modern organization. We discussed two-person conferences, informal conversations, and business meetings. We examined these episodes from the view of the subordinate and emphasized the influences of being in a one-down situation on your communication.

Now that you are a supervisor you find yourself in the same familiar communication situations but you are suddenly faced with a host of new communication problems within the old familiar contexts. You are now in a one-up position and are expected to take the lead in conferences and business meetings.

ASSIGNMENT: Leading a Conference or Meeting

Your instructor may divide the class into pairs and have you conduct a simulated two-person conference between manager and subordinate. These may be all of the same type, such as an appraisal interview, or various types of interviews may be distributed among the pairs so some do appraisal interviews, others do information-gathering interviews, others give job-related instructions from manager to subordinate, others do interviews in which the manager disciplines an employee, and still others do problem-solving interviews.

Or, your instructor may divide the class into groups composed of five or seven students. The instructor assigns a manager to each group to lead the meeting. Each group conducts an *ad hoc* business meeting. The topics may be related to something dealing with the course such as

173

grading procedures, organizing of projects, and so forth, in which case students play themselves. The meeting may be a simulation of some hypothetical business or professional meeting in which case students role play organizational positions.

The manager develops an agenda for the meeting and prepares whatever information is to be distributed to the participants prior to the session. Depending on the time available, the instructor may have the groups conduct their meetings in front of the class. If time is short, the groups may meet in separate rooms with tape recorders for the simulation and then listen to their tapes separately for analysis and discussion.

──────────────────── **Theoretical Rationale** ────────────────────

LEADING THE TWO-PERSON CONFERENCE

You already know a good deal about the communication dynamics of a two-person conference from your experience in the job interview and the appraisal interview. You understand the subordinate's position quite well. You have, therefore, personal experience to help you make a careful analysis of the person in the one-down position when you have a conference with a subordinate. You understand the pressures of status and being one-down and the distortions that can result from these pressures. If you are going to establish a relationship that encourages dealing with important topics and discourages a large hidden agenda and if you are to get at what is going on in accurate fashion, you will need to work hard to overcome the subordinate's tendency to filter out bad news and to tell you only what she or he thinks you want to be told.

As a person with status and the responsibility to decide whether or not to have a conference with a subordinate, when to have it, and how much time to give to it, you have a need for a new range of communication competence. Generally the organizational context provides a sanction, at least at the beginning of the conference, for you to lead the meeting. Certainly when you ask, tell, or order a subordinate to have a conference you are expected to set the time and place, and plan the agenda. Even when you grant a subordinate time for a requested conference you still have control of the meeting. Under such circumstances you might decide to turn it over to the subordinate, but such a decision is up to you. Should the subordinate have an agenda and begin discussing the topics on it, you will still have control of the channels of communication so you can take the floor and shift the topics should you want to do so.

As manager you need to develop skill in controlling the channels of communication in a two-person conference. In earlier chapters we have distinguished between the directive and the nondirective approaches to interviewing. In the directive two-person conference, you set the agenda, control the turn taking, and remain in charge of the procedures of the conference. In the nondirective, you give up control and allow the other person to speak when he or she wants to do so.

If your purpose in the conference is to gather specific and uncontroversial information from the subordinate, the directive strategy based upon a preplanned set of questions is a good approach. "When did you first notice the machine was acting up? How many hours this week has it been down? What was our rate of production on that machine this past month?" If your purpose is to give information to a subordinate about a team project, a directive strategy can save time. If your purpose is to counsel a subordinate who is having personal problems or difficulties with others in your unit, a nondirective approach may be best. Psychological counseling, however, is not a communication situation for amateurs, and if the person has serious problems relating to personality disorders, drug dependency, or family relationships, you ought to use the session to help the subordinate seek the aid of professionals. In an appraisal interview some mixture of directive and nondirective strategies is often indicated. If your purpose is to discipline or correct a subordinate, you may again want to be nondirective for much of the session in order to make sure you understand the other's position and view of the events and behaviors in question.

You contribute to either a directive or nondirective climate for your two-person conferences by the way you control the channels of communication. If you interrupt the subordinate and take a turn, if you leap in and speak whenever there is a pause, if you clearly indicate when the other is to take a turn and urge the subordinate to take it, you will create a directive climate. You may verbally assure your subordinates that they should feel free to air their grievances or speak their minds fully, but nonverbally, a directive manner about who should talk when, communicates control.

Most people can develop more skill in the way they control the channels of communication. Interrupting other persons in the middle of a comment and riding over what they are saying in a louder and more assertive voice usually gets you the floor, but the fallout may work against your basic purpose. Asking them to take a turn and speak up when it is clear they have little if anything to say is another evidence of lack of skill.

Another competence you need in leading interviews is the ability to ask good questions. You need to learn the types of questions and their various uses as you conduct meetings from a one-up position.

One important type of question implies a closed and focused

answer. The question restricts the respondent essentially to a "yes" or "no" response. "Have you graduated from college?" Another similar type of question is a bit more open than the yes-or-no query but it still restricts the respondent to an either-or forced choice. "Would you prefer to take your vacation in July or August?" The opposite of a closed question would be one that is open-ended, one that does not lead the respondent to select from a restricted list of answers. "I'm trying to plan a vacation schedule. Have you any thoughts about when you would like to take your vacation?"

In our examples above we have used questions, whether more or less closed, or open, that do not suggest or force an answer, even though the options are yes-or-no, either-or; you still have that choice in answering. All such questions could be called *permissive* in the sense that they allow or permit the subordinate to select a response without suggesting or leading the respondent to a particular answer.

Questions may also be *leading*. A leading question contains or implies the answer. "The foreman's report states that you were the one who dropped a tool into the machine. Is that true?" "Would you consider taking your vacation the first two weeks in July this year?"

Finally, a question can contain an argument or a charge against the respondent. We will call such questions *loaded*. Loaded questions nearly always build defensiveness in the respondent. "How can you justify staying on here when you appear at work with a hangover and carelessly drop a tool into an expensive machine costing the company thousands of dollars in lost production time?" Or, "When are you going to stop drinking on the job?" Or, "When are you going to start getting along with people around here?"

In general, when you use open-ended and permissive questions, you suggest a nondirective and open communication climate. If you select leading and loaded questions that stress yes-no or either-or responses, you emphasize your one-up position and discourage upward flow of information. Occasionally you may decide to use leading and loaded questions because, despite their costs, you feel that a crisis situation or a persuasive or disciplinary purpose can best be served by using such techniques. They are extremely dangerous, however, to a cooperative communication climate, particularly if you are trying to build cohesiveness, trust, and to encourage feedback.

Leading, closed, and loaded questions are the stock-in-trade of people in competitive communication games such as lawyers cross-examining hostile witnesses, or journalists questioning a political candidate. In such adversary communication they have their place, but in cooperative team communication they are to be used sparingly and only with understanding and skill.

You may provide a plan or an agenda to help organize the

conference. In some situations this "interview guide" may be a list of set questions that are to be answered in order. In other cases you may simply have a list of topics phrased in general terms that you hope to cover. How specific and set your plan seems to be and how closely you stick to it will also carry a nonverbal message about the extent to which the conference is directive or nondirective.

If you wish to adopt a nondirective strategy in order to encourage communication and the flow of upward communication which accurately reflects what is going on with your subordinates you can do so by turning over the channels of communication to the respondent and allowing the subordinate to control the turn-taking. You can also use permissive open-ended questions and allow the respondent to provide the agenda or plan for the meeting. If you wish to adopt a directive strategy to gather basic information quickly and save time you should control the channels of communication, use closed questions, and have a well-thought-out detailed plan for the conference.

THE MANAGER AS TEAM LEADER

In recent years there has been a significant change in the methods of managing the modern organization. Basic to that change is the view that modern managers must work with teams. They must not only manage individuals but they must also manage *work groups*. The new view does not mean that managers should ignore individual differences, but it does mean that in addition to employing their skills working with individuals (and developing their ability to communicate with individuals) they must also think of the people in their units as a team and supervise them as a group.

If managers fail to supervise their units as groups they will not keep informal groups from developing but they do run the risk of losing control of the groups that do form. Human nature is such that groups will be formed.

If supervisors concentrate on working with individuals, they abdicate their group leadership roles and others will step forward to become informal group leaders. The informal leaders may set up goals for groups different from the goals of the overall organization. For example, the informal leaders may establish different production goals for work groups than those that supervisors have set up.

Not until the 1950s did those making a study of organizational management come to a full understanding of the importance of the group as it relates to the problems of communication and leadership in the modern organization. As late as 1953 Rensis Likert could write from the Institute for Social Research at the University of Michigan that most books on management and administration dealt with the relationship between superiors and subordinates as individuals. Likert reported extensive studies at Michigan indicating that a supervisor's ability to manage his subordinates *as a group* was an important factor in his success.

IMPROVING COHESIVENESS IN THE WORK GROUP

Cohesiveness Defined. In small group communication *the more cohesive the group, the more efficient the communication within the group.* To fully explore the implications of the basic connection between group cohesiveness and communication, we must begin with an explanation of the nature of cohesiveness.

A highly cohesive group is one in which most of the members willingly work for the good of the group. They exhibit a great deal of team spirit. They recognize the group as an entity of importance to them personally. The members of a cohesive group reflect the spirit of the motto of the *Three Musketeers,* "All for one and one for all."

Highly cohesive production groups increase output by taking the initiative to help one another; they distribute the work load efficiently in times of stress. Workers who are supervised as individuals tend to stand around and wait for assignments. They feel they are only responsible for the work assigned directly to them. They are not concerned about the work of others in their unit. The members of groups with little cohesiveness tend to "keep their noses clean" and "look out for number one." Highly cohesive groups, on the other hand, have members who volunteer to help one another because they feel responsible for attaining the goals of their unit.

One of the manager's objectives in the modern organization is to help his or her group develop feelings of loyalty and direct the resultant cohesiveness toward the goals of the organization. The manager must always keep cohesiveness in mind as he or she goes about supervisory tasks. By concentrating on individuals within the unit, the manager may unwittingly destroy team spirit and encourage role struggles, tensions, and backbiting. For example, dealing with individuals may result in the appearance of playing favorites and create the problems associated with what we called in grade-school days "teacher's pets."

Cohesiveness and Feedback. Cohesiveness is directly related to the effectiveness of speech-communication within the group. Cohesiveness results in a greater desire among the members to communicate and it *creates a climate that encourages feedback.*

Group cohesiveness facilitates feedback by reducing the inhibitions of people that block full, free, and honest give-and-take. In one study of group communication at the University of Minnesota we established a standard for good communication. The criterion was that the person who knew the least about a central topic before the meeting should know as much as the most knowledgeable member after the topic was discussed. We then investigated the question: How many of the groups under study met the standard? Observers found that none of the groups even approximated the criterion. They also discovered that the main reason for the failure to communicate *basic information* (not complicated theoretical concepts or controversial positions) was that the person who did not know did not ask for further information. Individuals did not provide an opportunity for the knowledgeable member to share his information. They did not say, "I am sorry but I do not know about that. Could you fill me in?"

Next, we studied the reasons for the failure to ask for basic information. One big reason was that the person did not want to appear "ignorant" and lose standing. Often people would pretend to know more than they actually did rather than ask for information. Appearing ignorant is damaging to an individual striving for an influential role. Clearly, when the role structure of a group is unstable, the members will be reluctant to appear uninformed.

Another reason why so few questions were asked was that members were afraid that they would insult the person giving the information if they asked for further clarification. This factor is particularly important when a status difference separates the informed person from the one who needs to know. Thus, the subordinate often fails to ask for more explanation and information from a supervisor because he or she does not want to imply that the boss did not give a clear explanation.

In an organizational setting in the field we discovered one additional reason. The person who does not understand a message sometimes fails to ask for further information and clarification because of lack of interest. Sometimes members of an organization get into the habit of holding conferences and meetings whether the meetings are needed or not. If the members feel the sessions are simply "busy work," that is, time wasters, they often remain silent to hurry the meeting to adjournment.

Increasing the cohesiveness of a work group strikes at all these problems by creating a climate that encourages the person who needs more knowledge to ask for it. In the cohesive group all the persons know their roles and are secure in them. A person's position is not threatened by an admission of ignorance about a matter of concern to the unit. Indeed, the cohesive group rewards the individual who asks for the information needed to do a job. The knowledgeable member does not feel slighted, insulted, or threatened by a request for further clarification and information.

The highly cohesive football team rewards the guard who asks the quarterback to repeat information in the huddle because he must know his assignment if the play is to work. The quarterback, in turn, is not insulted by the question because he knows that without the help of the guard his job will be more difficult.

Finally, highly cohesive groups use their meetings to get things done. Their meetings tend to be noisy, full of joking, personal byplay, disagreement, and argument. They often run overtime. Few important decisions are made without thorough discussion with every member having a say. The highly cohesive group can afford disagreement because members know that any hard feelings caused by disagreements will be patched up after a decision is made.

Groups with little cohesiveness, on the other hand, often have meetings that are quiet, polite, and boring. The general attitude of the members is reflected in their posture, their sighs, and their yawns. They seem to say, "Let's get this meeting over with. I have more important things to do." The sessions contain little disagreement and hardly any interaction. Even important decisions are handled quickly.

Cohesiveness and the Comparison Group. Cohesiveness is a dynamic feature of group process. An organization that is highly cohesive this year—an effective, hard-hitting, well-regarded group—may suffer a series of reverses, lose personnel, and experience a drop in cohesiveness, so that within five years it is in serious trouble.

The work group is subject to constant pressures from other groups in the organization and from the parent organization itself. In addition, the work group feels the influence of other organizations. Some of the pressures increase cohesiveness and some reduce it. For example, if the group is competing with similar units, the element of competition may increase cohesiveness. Should the group win the competition, the result is often an increase in team spirit.

The supervisor examining her work group to estimate its cohesiveness should apply the principles of group process developed in Chapter 4 to examine the prestige, status, and esteem satisfactions that an individual receives from the interpersonal relationships in her unit. She must also look, however, at the other groups both within and without the parent organization that are competing for her people.

The attractiveness of a leader's unit is partly dependent on the *next best group* an individual could join. We will call the next best group the *comparison group*. The comparison group is important because a member may leave a job and join another organization if the comparison group becomes attractive enough. The case of Invention Incorporated presents several instances of a comparison group becoming sufficiently tempting to lure a person from one assignment to another. The advertising man, who joined the firm as its sales manager, is one example. The psychiatrist, who finally decided not to continue as a member of the board of directors because his clinical practice was more interesting to him, is another. Finally, the sales manager left Invention Incorporated because another firm seemed by comparison more inviting.

In summary, every member is constantly experiencing pushes and pulls to or from the group. Some of the pressures come from within the group, some from the parent organization, and some from comparison groups in other organizations.

Build a Positive Social Climate. When the members of your unit gather to have a meeting they begin to interact socially. They nod or talk to one another. They smile and frown and laugh. They may share fantasies or use "in" jokes which remind them of previously shared fantasies. These interactions contribute to the building of a social climate that is pleasant, congenial, and relaxing, on the one hand, or an atmosphere that is cool, businesslike, and tense, on the other. Among the important communications which contribute to the social climate are those that create and deal with tensions, with disagreements, and with conflicts.

Tension may manifest itself in several ways. One of these is by being quiet and giving the impression of being bored and uninterested. But no member is truly bored and indifferent when given an opportunity to speak up and be recognized as a person of ability and competence. However, she risks a great deal by plunging into the meeting and participating actively. The other participants may be irritated by her actions. She may appear uninformed or unintelligent. This gamble causes her to feel nervous and tense and she may take flight from the situation by pretending she is not interested in the meeting. Prior to it she states that she hopes it will not last too long because she has important things to attend to back at her desk. She seems restless and eager to leave. Everyone feels some of this tension at the start of any meeting.

At first the atmosphere is tense and cold. It has to be warmed up. Initially, people speak very softly, sigh a good bit, and are overly polite. If this tension is not released, the whole tenor of the session may be affected. This preliminary tension must be eliminated before the meeting can really get down to business.

Once the group does start to work, more social tensions are generated by role struggles and disagreements over ideas and suggestions. When these tensions reach a certain level they too must be released or the meeting will break down. A good participant is alert to these tensions and will attempt to release them herself or encourage another member who tries to do so. Of course, too much joking and socializing can interfere with the efficiency of the meeting. But after these tensions have been released, the group should get on with business.

Disagreements are socially punishing but absolutely essential to sound thinking. They are double-edged. When there is a high level of disagreement in the meeting, people grow more cautious and tense. It is difficult to keep the personal element out of disagreements, and the person who finds his or her ideas subjected to challenge feels, as one member of such a meeting put it, "shot down." At the same time, the ideas presented in a meeting need to be questioned and tested. If they are unsound, they must be rejected. Thus, disagreements pose a social problem to members of a meeting.

Some participants try to cushion the hurt by prefacing the disagreement with an agreement or a compliment. They say, "That's a good idea, Joe. I really think you have something there, but. . . ." Or they say, "That's right. I agree with you, Joe. There is an awful lot in what you say, BUT. . . ." This may be perceived as an agreement for a time and therefore does not hurt the person. Eventually in speech-communication, however, the other members of the meeting discover that these opening compliments are just preparing the way for the knife. They begin to cringe as the "BUT I do think we ought to look at the other side of it . . ." hits them. *A disagreement to do its job must be perceived as a disagreement.* After all, disagreements are the sieves that strain out undesirable ideas and they will not work unless they are understood to signify, "Stop! This will not do." When they are properly understood, however, no amount of preliminary agreement or complimenting will serve to sugarcoat them. In meetings where the standard procedure is to disagree very bluntly and in crude language a strongly worded "You meathead! Whatcha got for brains? That'll never work," may be no harder on the person who receives it than a more tactful disagreement in a meeting where the members traditionally use the "I agree with you, BUT . . ." form of disagreement. Of course, if the form of disagreements and the meetings were switched the results would be exciting.

What should the members of a meeting do about disagreements? They must develop ways to encourage and tolerate them. First, they should develop enough cohesiveness so that disagreements are offered freely. Second, they must develop ways to knit the group back together after a period of heavy disagreement. Quite often the number of disagreements as well as the amount of tension increases as the group moves to a decision. Good groups indulge in considerable positive interaction *after the decision.* They joke and laugh. They show solidarity toward the group. "It was a good meeting," they say. "It accomplished something. Let us all get behind this decision and make it work." They tell the members whose position was rejected that they had a good point, but now that the decision is made the organization needs their wholehearted support. The group cannot succeed without their help. Such apparent aimless socializing after the decision is vital to the health of the organization and must be encouraged if disagreements are to continue in future meetings.

Some successful groups concentrate the disagreements into one role. One member does most of the disagreeing and the group expects him to do so. Whenever they feel the need for disagreements they turn to him. They reward him by giving him a nickname or by kidding him about his penchant for disagreeing. If a new person attends the meeting and asks afterward about this member "who seems pretty disagreeable," the other members say, "Don't mind Joe. He's just that way. He tries to find the weak points in a proposal, and sometimes he's right." Since Joe plays this role, a member whose ideas are under attack is less hurt than if some other member disagreed. After all, Joe generally plays devil's advocate.

Confront Conflicts. Much of what we said about disagreements and their effect on group cohesiveness and productivity applies to conflicts. In a sense, disagreements and conflicts are similar in kind but they differ in degree. Conflicts do often require special attention and treatment that goes beyond the way good groups handle disagreements.

Conflicts are those disagreements that cause such high secondary tensions that they either render the group inoperative or severely reduce its productivity and employee morale. The conflicts are often a result of the dynamics of role structuring. Some group members grow in informal status and power and some become better liked than others. As the members strive for informal status and rewarding roles in the group, they are in a mixed motive situation and often come into conflict.

Groups find conflicts in the social dimension difficult to deal with. When interpersonal conflict erupts, secondary tensions rise. Members become extremely uncomfortable and groups usually take flight from dealing with the problems directly.

The most common and destructive way groups take flight from conflict is by ignoring it, acting as though it did not exist. When groups ignore conflict during formal meetings, the members often discuss their feelings about the conflict with one another outside the formal meetings, in subgroups. Such discussions away from the group seldom solve the difficulties. Generally as long as the conflict is an important item on the group's hidden agenda it remains a destructive force.

The best way to manage conflict is to confront it and work it out. You should put the conflict on the agenda and devote enough time to it to work it through. In some ways confronting conflict in a business meeting resembles relationship communication as we discussed it in Chapter 2. The group must develop a level of cohesiveness such that the group is important enough for them to tolerate the high levels of tension and unpleasantness that go along with conflict resolution. The members must have a climate in which they can honestly express their feelings, perceptions, and needs with regard to the issue. In one important way, however, working through conflicts differs from communication focusing on building a social relationship by getting to know others. In working through conflict the focus should be upon the *group* rather than upon the individuals within the group.

One common way for groups to take flight from conflict is to say it is all the fault of one troublemaker. Since scapegoating a member is a common neurotic tendency of a group in conflict, a good meeting for working through must not be allowed to degenerate into personal charges, name-calling, and blaming. Every member of the unit has a share of responsibility for the group's successes *and* failures and the conflict must be viewed as a group product.

As manager you should remind the group that cooperation in a task-oriented group is rewarding. The group that works like a team tends to be successful and fun to work with. If you can keep your common goals before the group and impress upon them the rewards of cooperative effort, the forces of cohesiveness can aid in conflict resolution.

Give Your Group an Identity. The supervisor who is preoccupied with managing individuals forgets frequently that he or she is in charge of a unit within the organization. If the supervisor ignores the group, the people who work in the unit will tend to ignore it as well. The informal groups that they join will seem to them to be separate from and perhaps antagonistic to the formal organizational structure.

To build cohesiveness in a work group the manager must think in terms of the unit as a group and talk about it as a group. The leader should refer to the machining division, or the buyers, or customer engineering when she talks to her subordinates. Highly cohesive groups always work out ways to confer identity on their units. Sometimes these are as obvious as insignia, mascots, or nicknames. For example, no swimming coach can afford to neglect the importance of thus identifying her team. Some typical names around the country are the Barracudas, the Dolfins, and the Sharks.

Members of highly cohesive teams are never allowed to forget that they are part of a group that is important to them and to the entire organization. Talking about "we," "our group," "our division," what "we hope to accomplish," and how "we can continue the excellent work we have done" is positive suggestion to the subordinates that they are part of a team and that the supervisor recognizes the group and is doing what she does for the good of the collective unit. Talk of "you," "me," "I," will suggest just the opposite to her subordinates. If the supervisor continually stresses that "I want this to be done and I'm asking you to do this as a personal favor for me," or "if you do not do this then I will find it necessary to do such and so" it will suggest that the formal group is unimportant.

Build a Group Tradition. An excellent way to strengthen the identity of the group and emphasize its importance and permanence is to build a group tradition. No sooner is the group clearly identified than things begin to happen to it. The group starts to have a history. Whether it faces a crisis and fails or a challenge and wins is an event that can be recalled later and thus becomes a factor in developing a tradition. Soldiers who go through hell together emerge as buddies and the informal groups of infantrymen that come through combat are highly cohesive. Quite often in the process of working together as a group unusual, exciting, or funny things happen; these too can become a part of the group's tradition. The group's supervisor finds the appropriate occasions to recall such past incidents. She builds cohesiveness by relating group experiences because they dramatize the permanence and importance of the group.

Highly cohesive work groups have traditional events or ceremonies that give the group added meaning and build loyalty. For instance, the group may have a party or a ceremony to celebrate the betrothal of one of the members. The supervisor can seldom force such "traditional" events, but the opportunity to develop such traditions is ever present.

Stress Teamwork. The supervisor can build cohesiveness by stressing the importance of teamwork. She can personally set the style by accepting the basic principle that builds teamwork in professional athletics: I don't care who gets the credit as long as we win!

The supervisor who is thinking in terms of managing a group should indicate in verbal and nonverbal communication a commitment to the team principle: Do not worry about credit but do worry about the team reaching its goals. If the supervisor does seem unduly interested in taking credit for a contribution to the group's success, other members will soon follow suit, and the star system with every person for himself or herself may result.

The supervisor who is worried about credit may suggest to subordinates that they are working for the supervisor and his or her glorification. Such a person can provide them with some rewards, particularly monetary rewards, but ultimately can never give them the satisfactions that they can derive from teamwork. They will never work as hard for the supervisor as they will for the good of all.

Recognize Good Work. The supervisor can encourage his group to fulfill the social approval and esteem needs of the members. When a member pays another a compliment for a job well done, the supervisor can tell the person who paid the compliment that it was a good thing to do. A manager should be watching for positive reinforcement furnished by the members of the group for one another. He should note compliments, offers to help with work, social recognition of other members, and similar indications that members are considerate and appreciative of new employees as well as of one another. The alert supervisor will encourage such moves by adding his own compliment, offers of help, recognition through social invitation, or by praising the person who furthers group solidarity and by pointing out to him that his actions are of great *importance to the group.*

If the supervisor is not on guard, he will be excessively preoccupied with the high status members of his group. These are "good" people, who are responsible and can be counted on to always do a good job. If he attends to the low status members, those who are marginal in their routine work, it is usually to criticize or worry about how to improve them. He should spend more time fulfilling social and esteem needs of low status people than he does those of the high status members. A little time devoted to showing the marginal man, the potential "deadwood," that the supervisor thinks of him as doing a vital job (even though routine) and that he recognizes and respects him as a person, will go a long way toward increasing his output. The man who sweeps the floor can take pride in his job, but he is not likely to if no one recognizes and appreciates the work. The file clerk may be paid to keep files neat and orderly, but only part of the satisfaction potential of the job is realized if no one notices.

Set Clear Attainable Group Goals. Group cohesiveness is increased if everyone knows that the group has a goal, if they clearly understand what the goal is, and if they believe that it can be attained. The supervisor often breaks the production quota for the division into short-term production goals without making it clear to every person that the individual quota is but part of the larger group goal. Attaining a group objective further emphasizes the team nature of the task. One of the most powerful factors building teamwork in athletics is the fact that *teams* win or lose. A track coach has more difficulty building cohesiveness than a baseball coach has because even though the track team competes with other track teams a high jumper may win even when the team loses. The fact that the entire group wins or loses increases the group's cohesiveness.

Many groups in organizations do not clearly win or lose as do competing athletic teams, but much the same effect results from the group's having a clear goal. Reaching the objective is an indication of success, and success gives the group prestige and satisfies the esteem needs of its members.

The group may need long-term plans but the supervisor must also provide clear short-term goals. For most groups a goal that is several months away loses its attractiveness. A goal that may be reached within a week or two seems much more attainable. And groups only work for goals they think they can reach.

Of course, the goal to be attained must be clearly specified and understood. A vague statement of objectives is seldom useful. For example, a good job is the goal of every division of the organization. But how can members of a unit know when they have done a good job? On the other hand, if the goal is to change over to the production of the new part by June 10 and to be in full production by June 12, the unit has a clear objective against which to measure success. If the supervisor can report that the changeover is making excellent progress, and if everyone works together, the group may be able *to beat* the deadline, then the supervisor is exerting a positive pressure on the group that will increase its cohesiveness.

Give Group Rewards. Reaching a goal is rewarding, but the supervisor can emphasize the identity of the group, help build tradition, and stress teamwork by giving the entire group a reward for reaching an objective. Too often organizations gear their incentive system to the old view of managing individuals. Thus, individual incentives are stressed over group incentives.

Competition and mixed-motive communication within the group is encouraged by giving individuals salary increases and bonuses. Rewarding individuals for outstanding work is certainly an important way to increase organizational success. However, this practice encourages the "star" system and destroys team spirit. One must remember that organizations are largely dependent on people working together.

The wise supervisor will continue to use individual incentives to encourage productivity but he will also give group incentives. These may take the form of across-the-board salary increases when some noteworthy achievement has been made by his division, or they may be bonuses for every member when an important goal is reached. There may be other rewards aimed at the need for esteem and the recognition of workmanship such as letters of commendation for the group, plaques, dinners, or other social affairs in recognition for a job done well.

Should the supervisor receive personal recognition from the organization, such as a special award or letter of commendation, he is well advised to call a meeting of his group and reflect the recognition back on them. The old "I could not have done it without each and every one of you" speech may sound corny but it is given so often because it succeeds in building cohesiveness.

Keep Psychologically Close to Group Members. The supervisor who wants to build her unit into a highly cohesive team must associate with her subordinates so that she can understand their point of view. If she does this, she can anticipate their reaction to new proposals and can interpret their position to her superiors. If she does not keep psychologically close to her subordinates, she may find herself fighting them. Inevitably there will be times when the directives of higher management will come in conflict or seem to come in conflict with the group's goals. When this happens the supervisor must decide whether to fight for her unit and try to change the directive of higher management or whether she must change the group's goals to bring them in line with the directive. In short, will she be for the group or the company? The first-line supervisor is the person who faces this knotty problem most often.

LEADING THE MEETING

Characteristics of a Good Leader. A leader needs to bring to the job a commitment to the meeting and the desire to conduct a productive session. She needs to have the time and energy to devote to the task. She should enjoy participating in a discussion and be a good speaker. She should know the dynamics of groups. She should know how even temporary groups begin to form cohesiveness and structure. In addition, she needs to develop some specialized skills that are required to lead a meeting. These skills include planning an agenda, creating a climate that assures widespread participation, controlling the talk so it is orderly and all participants are given a chance to be heard, and steering the group by using the agenda. She should be able to make spur-of-the-moment adjustments and allow some detours if they seem useful; she must be careful, however, not to let the meeting drift too far off course.

Duties of the Leader. The leader should introduce any members who do not know one another. She draws out the silent participants. She keeps one or two members from monopolizing the meeting. She watches the time and the agenda and keeps the meeting on track and on time. She often must relieve tensions at the beginning. She must handle comments and questions in such a way that people are encouraged to make more contributions.

Techniques for Leading the Meeting. The leader has three basic techniques to use in managing the meeting: these are the question, the summary, and the directive. The first problem facing the leader is to get the meeting started. Questions are useful to get a discussion under way. She should quickly establish that the comments are to be short and to the point. If the first speaker runs on, the leader can ask a direct question of another member.

Perhaps the most frequent problem for the leader of the meeting is the tendency of groups to drift off the topic. Sometimes such discussion leads to important matters that appear on the agenda elsewhere and they can be taken up out of order without harm. The skillful leader recognizes when this happens and lets the meeting have its head. Frequently the digressions are time-wasting and she must bring the meeting back on the topic. Questions can be used to do this. She may ask: "Can we tie this in with the point about the quality control standards?" "Just a moment, how does this relate to the problem of slow deliveries?" "Let's see now. I'm a bit confused. Where are we now in relation to overtime?"

Summaries can also be used to give the meeting an overview of the last few minutes of discussion, and if the leader emphasizes the topic on the agenda she can tactfully suggest that the group is off the topic. She may also use the summary as a way to move to another item on the agenda if she feels the meeting is drifting because enough has been said on a topic.

Finally, the leader may simply assert that the group is off the subject and direct that they get back on the track. She may say: "We seem to be getting off the subject. Let's get back to Bill's point." "This is interesting, but it really doesn't help much in regard to the question of who is responsible." "I've been listening to the last few minutes here and wondering how it ties in. We have to get back to the basic question that Joe asked earlier."

The leader is expected to move the meeting along. She should watch for signs that a given item has been discussed enough. Quite often a loss of interest or drifting from the subject is a clue that the time has come to stop talking about a topic. The summary is the most useful technique to keep the meeting in progress. The leader can round off the consideration of an agenda item and lead naturally to the next topic by giving a summary. She may also use questions and ask whether enough time has been devoted to the topic and whether the group would like to move on to the next item.

From time to time during the course of the meeting the group may need to make decisions. The leader can help the members if she steps in at these points and indicates that there seems to be a consensus as to what should be done or if she asks for an indication of consensus. Questions are helpful at this point. She may ask: "Are we in substantial agreement on this point?" "Can we all agree that this revised production schedule is the one we want?"

She can also help the majority reach a decision by suggesting a vote. In a small meeting this vote can be taken very informally by an expression of agreement or disagreement or simply by nodding and shaking heads. In larger meetings the leader should clearly state the issue and then ask for the affirmative and negative votes. She may take a voice vote or ask for a show of hands or a standing vote. Some organizations have provisions for secret ballots or for roll-call votes on extremely important issues. The leader must always announce to the meeting the results of the vote.

Handling Difficult Situations. One of the most common and awkward problems for the leader of the meeting is the member who talks too much. If the leader is too brusque in cutting him off, she may embarrass the other participants and sound antagonistic.

Sometimes the leader can ask a yes-no type question of the talkative member and then quickly direct an open-ended question to another participant. For example:

Leader:	*(breaking in)* Just a minute, Joe, would you be willing to drop that account completely?
Joe:	Now, I didn't say . . .
Leader:	I just want to be clear on this. Would you be in favor of that?
Joe:	Well, no, but . . .
Leader:	*(interrupting)* Bill, I wonder how you feel about this matter?

Sometimes the person who is dominating the meeting is speaking at an abstract level; he can then be stopped by a question asking for specific information or for an example. The following dialogue is illustrative:

Joan:	There are altogether too many people around here who are not pulling their weight. We just have too much deadwood. Too many of our people are just putting in their time . . .
Leader:	*(interrupting)* Excuse me, Joan, but could you give us an example of what you mean?

Summaries can be used to stop long-winded contributions. Recapitulations are expected of the leader, and if she breaks in to summarize, the dominant member will often sit back and give her the floor. If the leader concludes her summary by directing a question to another member, she can tactfully cut off the talkative participant.

Sometimes the leader will simply have to direct the member to stop talking. She might say: "That's an important point. Let's get the reaction of some of the rest of us on that." "Just a minute, you have raised three or four points. Before you go further I would like to spend a little more time on this question of responsibility. What do the rest of you think about that?" "I'm going to ask you to stop there for a minute and hold your next comment. All of the group has not yet had a chance to be heard on this point. Let's hear from them and then we will come back to you."

A less spectacular but equally difficult situation is furnished by the member who does not talk up. The leader will have to use questions to deal with this person. She should address him by name and ask a direct question. The best form of question is the open-ended one, because if she asks a question that can be answered with a *yes* or a *no,* she is likely to receive a one-word answer. When the leader is first drawing out a participant she should be careful to ask questions that the person can answer. She should not ask for specific information or examples unless she knows the member has the answer handy. The wisest course is to ask for an opinion. Questions such as the following can be used to draw out a quiet member.

> Bill, what do you think about this proposal?
> Bill, where do you stand on the quality control matter?
> Bill, we haven't heard from you about this yet. What do you think?

If members of the meeting come in conflict, the leader must take the responsibility of handling the situation. *She should not take sides.* If she is questioned about her opinion, she can relay the question to the group. "That is a tough one. Can someone take a crack at it?" She may also reflect the question back to the questioner. "Let me ask you how you would answer the same question?" If the leader answers questions about substantive measures, she is quite likely to be drawn into the conflict. Once a part of the fight, she loses control of the meeting. It is difficult to lead and take an active part. The manager who does both may monopolize the meeting.

When several members come into conflict the leader should interrupt and focus the attention of the meeting on the group procedure rather than on the individuals involved. Remind the group of the areas of agreement. Admit that intelligent people differ and that the group wants everyone to express his or her opinion. Emphasize the importance of the ideas rather than the personalities involved in the conflict. Remind them that differences about ideas are important to the successful functioning of the group. If the leader can insert a note of humor (not sarcasm or irony) to relieve tensions, she should do so.

If it becomes clear that the conflict is important to the group's welfare, the leader should place it on the agenda and help the group confront it and work it through.

SUMMARY

Organizational status puts the manager in a one-up position in many organizational meetings and the supervisor is often expected to take the lead. As a manager it is your responsibility to decide when and where to have a meeting, how much time to give to it, and the nature and extent of the preparation for it. As a manager you need to develop skill in controlling the channels of communication in a two-person conference. The directive strategy is often a good one in the conference to gather specific and uncontroversial information. The nondirective approach may be the best during certain portions of an appraisal interview and in counseling sessions. Some mixture of the directive and nondirective strategies is often useful in interviewing potential new employees.

Another ability the manager needs in leading two-person conferences is skill in asking questions. The three major kinds of questions are the "yes" or "no" response question, the forced-choice question, and the open-ended question. Questions may also be *leading* in that their form contains or implies the desired answer. *Permissive* questions leave the choice of answer largely to the respondent. *Loaded* questions contain an attack or a charge on the respondent's behavior or character.

The competent modern manager must not only know how to manage individuals but also how to manage a team. A first principle of team management is that the more cohesive the group the more efficient the communication within the group. Cohesiveness creates a climate that encourages feedback and feedback, in turn, aids communication. In the cohesive work group every person knows his or her role and is secure in it. People are not threatened by the admission that they do not know or understand and they can thus let the message source know of their misunderstandings, confusions, and lack of information.

Among the important communications which contribute to the social climate of a group are those that deal with tensions, with disagreements, and with conflicts. Tensions, disagreements, and conflicts create socially punishing communication climates. Yet disagreements are essential to good task decisions. Conflicts too can be productive overall if they bring out hidden agenda problems or cause the group to face up to important decisions and confront and work them through. Of course conflicts can also be destructive.

Conflicts often result from the dynamics of role structuring. Groups find conflicts in the social dimension difficult to deal with. Often members take flight from conflicts in ways which make the problem worse. The best way to manage conflict is to confront it and work it out.

A manager can encourage cohesiveness in the work group by giving the group an identity, by building group traditions, by stressing teamwork, by recognizing good work, by setting clear and attainable goals, by giving group rewards, and by keeping psychologically close to the members.

The manager must often assume the duties of group leader in business meetings. These duties include planning the meeting and the agenda, creating a communicative climate which assures productive communication, controlling the talk so it is orderly and all participants have a chance to talk, drawing out the silent members, cutting off the too-talkative participants, keeping track of the course of the discussion, and not letting the discussion get too far afield.

QUESTIONS FOR DISCUSSION AND REVIEW

1. What communication problems does a manager face that are different from those of a subordinate?
2. How may a manager control the channels of communication in a two-person conference?

3. What are the types of questions available to a manager in an interview and how can they be put to strategic use?
4. Discuss the communication implications of the role of manager as team leader.
5. How is cohesiveness related to communication within a work group?
6. What are some typical blocks to adequate feedback in work group communication?
7. How can a manager help to build a positive social climate in a work group?
8. How can a manager communicate to encourage group cohesiveness?
9. What are the characteristics of a good leader of a group meeting?
10. Explain how a leader could handle three difficult situations that frequently come up at meetings.

REFERENCES AND SUGGESTED READINGS

Bormann, E. G. and N. C. Bormann. *Effective Small Group Communication,* 3rd ed. Minneapolis: Burgess, 1980.

Brillhart, J. K. *Effective Group Discussion,* 3rd ed. Dubuque, Iowa: Wm. C. Brown, 1978.

Likert, R. *Motivation: The Core of Management.* New York: The American Management Association, 1953.

Stewart, C. J. and W. B. Cash. *Interviewing: Principles and Practices.* Dubuque, Iowa: Wm. C. Brown, 1974.

11

The Oral Presentation

---------- **Laboratory Application** ----------

Now that you are a manager, you will be called upon for oral presentations that are frequently elaborate and complex. Some of your previous experience as a leader in social, educational, religious or other groups may be useful, but other background or information needed will be completely new to you.

A presentation is very different from a talk. Usually you will give a talk because someone has asked you to provide information about a topic in which you are an expert. In giving a talk you will "make a few remarks" without any special audio-visual support and then throw the meeting open for informal questions. In a "talk," the stress is on informality and information and such communication is seldom an important part of the organizational decision-making.

A presentation also differs from a public speech. More and more members of the leadership community give public speeches to large groups within the organization for inspirational purposes. Public speeches are an important way to communicate the organization's saga. Managers also give public speeches to outside groups largely for public relations purposes. Often the inspirational, public relations, or public service speeches are ghostwritten and they typically do not use multimedia material as a basic way to communicate. The fact that a member of upper management relies on someone else to write the speech, often someone from the public relations department, provides a clue as to how important managers consider their giving a good impression is in their public speaking. Managers tend to give public speeches to outsiders for the same reasons their firms invest money in institutional advertising. "You represent *the company.*"

Presentations also differ from oral reports in that a report is usually not as important as the presentation. Audio-visual materials are optional for oral reports. Multimedia material plays a central role in the presentation. You will give a presentation in a situation where only carefully prepared audio-visual materials can do the job that needs to be done in the time allotted. Our emphasis in this chapter is upon presentational speaking. We emphasize presentations because if you learn the principles of preparing and delivering the important messages, you will learn the same skills and information you need for the less complicated and important oral reports that you will have to give.

Presentations are among the more important formal messages available to the organization. You may be asked to give a presentation by a member of upper or middle management who has the organizational status and responsibility to be able to give you the assignment. When you reach a suitable level of management you may have enough authority to make the decision to give a presentation. Presentations require much time and effort in their preparation and require a formal decision in order to assign organizational resources to their development.

The same presentation may be given several times to different audiences, but the most common situation is one in which you prepare and give a message to a specific audience for a definite persuasive purpose. Your audience for the presentation may be a single person (the chief executive officer); usually it will be a small group (the Board of Directors, the Department Heads), or, occasionally, it will be a large group (the 25 quality control inspectors, the annual stockholders meeting.)

You will give the presentation, for the most part, to peers or superiors in important situations. Decision-making tends to move up the organizational levels of management. Lower management works up proposals and makes presentations to middle management. Further refinements and study result in middle management making presentations to upper management for final decisions.

Although you can read a public speech written by your organization's public relations firm, when you are asked to give a presentation the situation changes. You face a situation where failure is often damaging and success important to you personally. You will probably have help from content specialists and audio-visual experts in preparing the presentation but you cannot rely on a ghostwritten effort. You will have to be on top of the material, able to answer questions and defend your position.

You will be giving the presentation to offer yourself, a sales proposal, a program, or an important budget or organizational change to others who have the power to accept or reject the substance of your message. The entire proposal may be accepted or rejected in the meetings initiated by your presentation. Your purpose succeeds or fails in the form in which you presented it. The results of the presentation are often immediate and clear. Decisions may come in a few minutes and frequently within a week and they are often in terms of yes or no, go ahead or forget it.

Under these circumstances it is no wonder that presentations are the most carefully prepared, structured, developed and tested messages you will be asked to give. Specialists and other managers may review your presentation before you give it. You should rehearse several times (in front of an audience, if possible) before making the actual presentation.

ASSIGNMENT: An Oral Presentation

If there is time your instructor will assign each student an individual organizational presentation to deliver to the class. The presentations will be eight to ten minutes long and will utilize multimedia aids to carry the bulk of the clarification and support for the message.

Since an oral presentation is a major production, your instructor may assign you to a production unit or team which prepares and gives the presentation.

──────────────── **Theoretical Rationale** ────────────────

PREPARING THE PRESENTATION

When you give a presentation to others in your organization you do so because you have specialized knowledge and are in the proper organizational position to do so. Your problem in preparation is not so much finding something to say as it is cramming everything you need to say in the most effective way possible into the short period of time available.

As a specialist you will know all the ins and outs of the question and since the presentation focuses attention on you there will be much pressure to prepare the best possible message. If you are not careful you will become message-centered. A message-centered speaker dwells on the details of what he or she will say. Without being aware of it you may prepare your message as though there is an ideal presentation and it is your duty to approximate that ideal. Many of the presentations we have observed in the organizational setting appear to have been aimed at the speaker! The manager has decided to develop a message that fellow specialists will admire for its understanding of the topic, for its technical skill, and for its completeness. For most others, it is deadly, dull detail.

In the early stages of preparation it is all right for you to be message-oriented and try to develop an analysis of the topic that is complete and logical. Once you have such a message, however, you often find that to do it justice you ought to have five hours instead of the fifteen minutes you have been allotted. *You need to become audience-centered.* Throughout the book we have stressed the communication principle that you must analyze the other people with whom you are communicating whether in two-person conferences or small group meetings. Nowhere does this principle apply more strongly than in the preparation of an oral presentation.

After you have thought through what an ideal message for a specialist would look like, you need to select from that message those parts that fulfill the needs of your audience and adapt those parts to your listeners. The second stage of preparation involves careful analysis of your listeners and judicious selection of material for them. When you begin to think of your listeners you often find that much of your five-hours' worth of material will be unsuitable for *their* needs and interests. In our work as consultants with organizations, we have helped many managers prepare presentations. We have found time and time again that they have prepared messages that fail to tell the listeners what they want and need to hear about; what they have told them, instead, is what the speaker is interested in. The audience is often bored by a highly technical discussion of details phrased in the jargon of the speaker's special interest.

You need to make a careful analysis of the individuals who will hear your presentation in terms of their organizational position, their informal roles within the organization, their pet interests and hobbies as well as their technical backgrounds and experience. You should also analyze their shared fantasies, their rhetorical vision, and the organizational saga to which they are committed.

ORGANIZING THE PRESENTATION

In order to organize your message effectively, you need to do several things: (1) decide on a central theme; (2) arrange your material; (3) decide on a pattern of presentation; (4) plan the introduction, body, and conclusion; (5) prepare transitions.

Central Theme. Many people have trouble organizing messages because they fail to analyze the material for their presentation into its parts and discover the major point they wish to make with this particular audience at this time. Admittedly, finding and developing such a central thesis statement is not easy. We can provide you with suggestions, but there is no recipe or formula for finding an appropriate central idea.

A good exercise is to sit down with your material available at your desk and write out several sentences, each of which expresses your central theme. If you find yourself writing a paragraph, maybe even a page in order to explain what your presentation is all about, you have not yet thought through your purpose and your analysis of the audience to the point where you can begin to select the material for the presentation.

A good central idea is worded as a complete declarative sentence. If you end up with fragments like "our employee information program," "our proposed work improvement program," or "our problem with the new interest rates," you have failed to specify such important limiting features as who, what, when, why, and how.

A phrase such as "our problem with the new interest rates" suggests in a vague way that the speaker will discuss interest rates and criticize the way the company is reacting to them. "The time has come for us to adopt a new policy in regard to corporate financing of capital improvements" pins down the point in better fashion. A phrase like "our employee information program" would allow the speaker to include everything remotely relating to that problem in the presentation. "Our new employee information program gives you important tools to make you a better manager" focuses the presentation on the needs of the audience.

When wording a central idea, make sure that it expresses a single idea only. Concentrating on one main idea gives your presentation unity and drives that point home with greater effect. If your thinking is still a bit fuzzy or if several important ideas are related in your mind, you will often find yourself writing long involved statements of purpose and theme. Here is a typical example: "If we want to protect ourselves in what promises to be for the foreseeable future a very volatile money market, we are going to have to adopt some of the new mechanisms for financing capital improvements such as have recently been tried successfully by several companies in our industry." Leave out reasons and explanations from your central idea.

Make sure your wording is specific. A speaker who says, "Today I want to tell you something about our proposed work improvement program" or "Today I want to consider with you the volatile money market and the rising interest rates," has not narrowed the scope of the presentation. If she has five hours worth of material, she is no further along in the task of picking out the material to be included because she could probably fit all of it under such vague central ideas.

When you have a clear, simple, and specific wording for your central idea, you can use that statement as a yardstick against which to measure all of the material available. When you find some ideas that do not clearly relate to your central idea, you should discard them. For example, suppose that you have a central idea like "Our new employee information program gives you important tools to make you a better manager." You have five hours' worth of material about the employee information program. Some of that material deals with ways in which the new system will make it easier for you and your subordinates in the personnel department. This particular material may be the most important and interesting to you personally but it does not clearly relate to your central idea and you should discard it.

Arranging the Material. Once you have selected the material you plan to use, your next step is to find some pattern of arrangement so you can decide what point to make first, what second, and so on. Again, some concrete paper and pencil planning is in order. A good way to plan your arrangement of the material is with an outline.

An outline forces you to decide how important the points you wish to make are in relation to one another. Ask yourself, are there two or three major points? Can the other points fit logically under the major points? Are there further minor points that fit under those of moderate importance? Asking such questions helps you to analyze the topic. By answering the questions about level of importance, you can allot time proportionately—more time to major points, less time to minor points.

An outline is really a picture or sketch of the points of your speech placed in order of importance so you can see at a glance how they relate. The conventions we use to indicate order of importance involve (1) the way we place the words on the page and (2) symbols such as letters and numbers that label each level of importance.

The outline places the more important ideas closer to the left hand margin of the paper. You place ideas of lesser importance that relate to the main points under them. The pattern looks like this:

Main point
    Supporting point
        Subpoint under supporting point
        Subpoint under supporting point
    Supporting point
        Subpoint under supporting point
        Subpoint under supporting point

To make quite clear that the points relate to one another in order of importance, we usually also label each point with a system of symbols.

While the system of labels may differ, the main thing is that you understand what they mean. In a course in communication, however, where you are learning outlining technique, your instructor will probably ask that all students use the same system simply to make it easier to communicate with each other. A commonly used system begins with Roman numbers for the main points (I, II, III), uses capital letters (A, B, C) for supporting points, Arabic numbers (1, 2, 3) for subpoints, and small letters (a, b, c) for further subpoints if necessary. For example:

```
I.
    A.
        1.
            a.
            b.
        2.
    B.
II.
```

When you have made your plan in an outline form you have answered some important questions about your presentation. You know the most important ideas you want to leave with your audience regarding your central theme and you know the order in which you are going to make your points. You will have thought through your argument and your position in detail during the outlining process. You will have done much of the hard thinking required for a good presentation.

A good outline is the product of hard thinking because when we begin with a mass of undigested material that we think relates in some fashion to what we want to talk about, it is difficult to see how all the bits and pieces can fit together. We often rely on past experience either of our own or of other speakers in getting started on the outlining process. There are certain standard ways of organizing messages that have been used successfully in the past and if we know these stock ways of arranging material we can often speed up the outlining process.

Pattern of Presentation. We provide here a list of the time-honored patterns of organization that have been used not only for presentations but also for public speeches and written messages of various kinds:

1. Classification (you find some list of topics of equal level of importance for each major point of your presentation, *engineering, machining, personnel,* etc.)
2. Space order (you arrange topics in terms of geography or architecture, *northeastern banks, midwestern banks, southeastern banks, Rocky Mountain area banks,* etc.)

3. Time order (you arrange topics according to earlier and later, *orientation period, distribution of materials, collection of materials, interpretation*)
4. Method of residues (analyze problem and list representative solutions, then object to and eliminate all but the last)
5. Problem-solution (begin with analysis of problem then suggest a recommended solution)
6. Proposition-support (state your case and then prove it)

Introduction, Body, Conclusion. When you have outlined the topic for your presentation, you have a framework on which to build. The framework must be filled in with the information you wish to present to the audience (the body of the presentation). Then you need an *introduction* and *conclusion* and *transitions* to tie the major points to one another and to your central theme.

Because your presentation is an oral message that involves personal relationships, you need to make some opening comments to establish rapport with your listeners, to give them a chance to remind themselves of who you are as a person as well as in your official capacity, and to focus their attention on what you are saying so you can get down to the business at hand. The technical name for these opening comments is an *introduction*. The purposes of an introduction are to catch the interest, focus the attention, and open up consideration of your central idea. The first minute or so of your presentation will establish important first impressions and may be more important than you think to the reception of your main ideas. You should plan your introduction carefully and rehearse it several times aloud.

The *conclusion* of your presentation is important; it rounds off your ideas and clearly indicates to the audience that you have finished. Conclusions tend to be summaries of the main ideas of your presentation. The summaries may be a brief concise listing of the main points or they may summarize the gist of your message in more artistic form. You may be able to use a brief anecdote, a quotation, a slogan, an adage, or a folk saying for summing up your presentation. Or you can conclude with an appeal to action or belief. Such appeals are often emotional and should be used sparingly and only when the speaker has the nonverbal competence to deliver them properly. In many organizational settings in North America emotional appeals are out of place in business meetings. Usually such pep talks or public speeches are given on inspirational or ceremonial occasions.

Transitions. Presentations that run for ten or fifteen minutes require *transitions* when you shift from main point to main point to help the listeners stay on course. In written messages the way the paragraphs are placed on the page can indicate how the ideas relate to one another (although in long reports and books transitions are useful, too). Oral messages require nonverbal or verbal indicators that you have concluded a major point and are now moving on to another major idea. Sometimes nonverbal transitions are enough. You can drop your voice, pause somewhat longer than for an end of a sentence, or gesture in a way that suggests the completion of one idea and the start of another. Often, however, it is better to use verbal guideposts to help the audience see where you have been, where you are at this point in your message, and where you plan to go.

Verbal transitions tend to be (1) summaries of the previous point, (2) forecasts of the next point, or (3) both a summary and a forecast. You could move from one point to the next with a summary such as the following: "The lesson of the past twenty years is clear. The trend in interest rates has been a steady one from relatively stable rates to ever more rapidly and widely changing rates." At the same place in your presentation you might use a forecast: "I turn now to the damage that rapidly changing and rising interest rates have done to our recent profit picture." Finally, you might both summarize and forecast as follows: "The lesson of the past twenty years is clear. The trend in interest rates has been a steady one from relatively stable rates to ever more rapidly and widely changing rates. I turn now to the damage that rapidly changing and rising interest rates have done to our recent profit picture."

In the final stages of preparation you should develop a working outline that you can use in the actual delivery of your message. The final outline should have an introduction, body, conclusion, and a plan for transitions. Figure 10 presents a model of an outline you can use as a basis for your own preparation of a presentation.

USING MULTIMEDIA MATERIALS

The preoccupation with time in many of the organizational sagas of North American businesses, industries, agencies, and institutions means that you will often be given definite time limits for your presentation. You may be told "You will have an hour and we hope that you will save at least half of that time for questions" or "We have set aside twenty minutes at the commencement of the meeting for your presentation."

Even with careful audience analysis and preparation it is often difficult to get a complex message across in twenty or thirty minutes. The oral presentation is a message form that arose under such time pressures when the technology for multimedia communication was evolving. Television and film provided innovations that allowed communicators to take great care and invest time and resources in

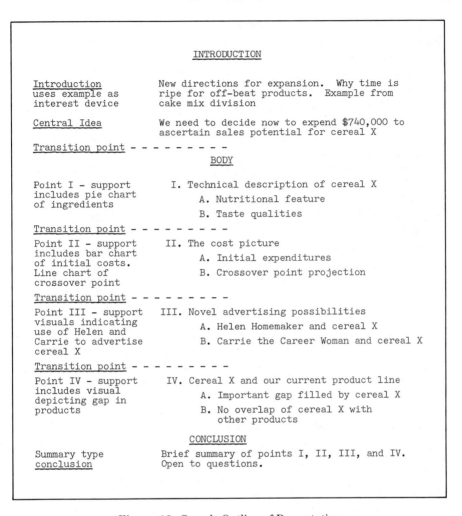

INTRODUCTION

Introduction uses example as interest device	New directions for expansion. Why time is ripe for off-beat products. Example from cake mix division
Central Idea	We need to decide now to expend $740,000 to ascertain sales potential for cereal X

Transition point - - - - - - - -

BODY

Point I - support includes pie chart of ingredients	I. Technical description of cereal X
	   A. Nutritional feature
	   B. Taste qualities

Transition point - - - - - - - -

Point II - support includes bar chart of initial costs. Line chart of crossover point	II. The cost picture
	   A. Initial expenditures
	   B. Crossover point projection

Transition point - - - - - - - -

Point III - support visuals indicating use of Helen and Carrie to advertise cereal X	III. Novel advertising possibilities
	   A. Helen Homemaker and cereal X
	   B. Carrie the Career Woman and cereal X

Transition point - - - - - - - -

Point IV - support includes visual depicting gap in products	IV. Cereal X and our current product line
	   A. Important gap filled by cereal X
	   B. No overlap of cereal X with other products

CONCLUSION

Summary type conclusion	Brief summary of points I, II, III, and IV. Open to questions.

Figure 10. Sample Outline of Presentation

developing brief, polished messages. The television commercial and political messages of the last two or three decades are short, carefully produced, persuasive presentations. The importance of these 30- and 60-second spot announcements to an advertising or political campaign assures that much money and talent is invested in their production. Over the years multimedia production specialists have developed the techniques for getting across ideas and persuasive materials quickly and effectively by means of sight and sound.

The television commercial message uses music, sound effects, dramatized segments, dance, graphs, charts, testimonials, animation, flip charts, and camera tricks to catch the audience's attention and make a point clearly and quickly.

The oral presentation is an organizational message that grew out of similar pressures and has adapted many of the multimedia techniques of television and film to the needs of managers. Skillful use of audio and visual materials enables you to communicate complicated statistical data efficiently. Pictures, demonstrations, and video and audio tapes can quickly clarify complex processes.

You need to think in multimedia terms when you begin to translate your outline into a presentation. That is, do not think only in terms of "What will I say?" but think in terms of "What media will I use?" "How can I picture, chart, visualize my message?" "How can I use sound to enhance and communicate ideas and mood?"

In most organizations you will have available a range of devices to help you present your ideas. The simplest, least expensive materials are those which do not require projection equipment and include the chalkboard, easel cards, flip chart, and flannel board. You can prepare charts, maps, diagrams, word lists, slogans, and so forth ahead of time on these devices and reveal them at the right place in your presentation. You can, for example, prepare a deck of easel cards and mask them with a blank card. As you go through your remarks you can remove the cards one at a time to reveal the visual material. You can use the chalkboard and flip chart as a large surface to write or draw or chart on as you speak.

When you move to devices that project either still or moving images on a screen you gain a great deal in versatility compared to flip charts and chalkboards. Projection devices require more preparation time and suffer from more technical failures. Bulbs burn out, extension cords do not fit plugs, and the film may not run properly. In terms of effectiveness and economy, the most useful of these devices is the overhead projector. With a projector you can prepare visuals in black and white or color and bring them to the presentation. Since they are smaller and lighter in weight than flipcharts and easel cards they are easier to carry about. You can place one visual over another and thus make comparisons and move from simpler to more complex ideas. You can also use the overhead projector as a substitute for a chalkboard by drawing or writing on the transparencies.

Other still projection devices include slide projectors that can show still pictures and film strips, and opaque projectors that will throw an image from a book (for example) on a screen, much as an overhead will provide an image of a transparency.

Motion pictures can also be projected on a screen. They are excellent adjuncts to a presentation but are often expensive to produce.

You may, on occasion, be able to find films or portions of films already produced that can make your point for you.

The development of inexpensive videotape recorders has made possible the preparation of television pictures to supplement your presentation without the investment of time and resources that film requires. If your organization has a video camera and recorder you can take pictures of production lines, work procedures, plant layouts, and so forth and insert them into your presentation to advantage.

For some purposes, an audiotape recorder is sufficient. Test your equipment ahead of time to make sure that the sound will reach all members of your audience.

PRESENTING DATA

Many organizations depend upon data processing systems for their factual information. Often the data are in the form of statistics, which you can use for making comparisons. By comparing how two things, processes, or results are similar and how they are different, an organization can decide which way it wants to go. Comparative data will show whether there is enough or too much of something; whether the division or unit is gaining, leveling off, losing ground in some regard; whether the unit is on time, late, ahead of schedule; whether sales in some regions are weaker than others, and so forth.

People preparing written messages often put statistical comparisons in the form of tables. When you are writing a report, a table allows you to provide many statistics in a brief amount of space. You can also arrange the table so the reader can make comparisons among a number of different things. As a result of the usefulness of tables in written messages you will probably receive most of your data in written tables.

But most tables in written messages are not suitable for oral presentations because they include too many statistics and too many comparisons. In our work with managers in business and industry we have found that they tend to simply copy a table out of a written report and throw it up on the screen. If you want to use a table, prepare one especially for your presentation. Make sure the table presents only one comparison and contains no more than twenty words or symbols.

We recommend that you present your data by means of graphs and charts. A line graph is an excellent way to quickly portray trends through time. Figure 11 is a line graph showing the trend in sales for Invention, Incorporated "last year," month by month. Line graphs can also be used to indicate one comparison. (Do not add more lines to make more comparisons.) Figure 12 adds another line to show the trend in sales for last year compared to the first eight months of this year.

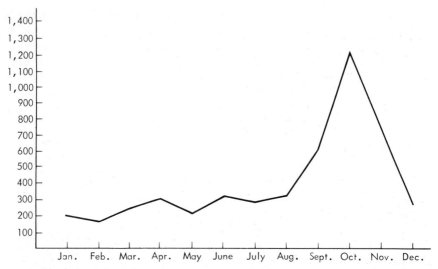

Figure 11. Sales for Invention Incorporated Last Year, Month by Month, in Thousands of Dollars

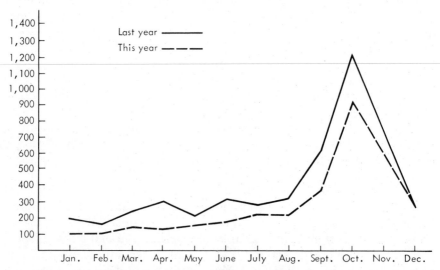

Figure 12. Sales for Invention Incorporated Last Year, Compared to This Year Month by Month, in Thousands of Dollars

Bar graphs are another means of quickly picturing comparisons. Figure 13 is a bar graph showing the sales "last month" in four different sales regions. As a general rule, the bar graph in Figure 13 is as complicated as a visual should be. You might add one comparison but more than one would be too complicated. Figure 14 is a bar graph showing a comparison of the sales last month with those the same month a year ago for the four regions.

The pie chart is a good way to graphically portray the parts of a whole. Figure 15 is a pie chart showing the proportion of total sales represented by each region. Notice that when you make a pie chart you should start with a radius drawn vertically from the middle and then going clockwise with the largest slice of the pie first and continuing with the next largest, and so on down to the smallest.

Graphs must be large enough for the audience to see and read whatever symbols they contain. You should be selective in deciding what data to picture in graphic form. Only a few of the most important comparisons should be used. Each visual should contain only two basic comparisons and a well planned presentation would not show the audience any graph for more than 20 or 30 seconds at a time.

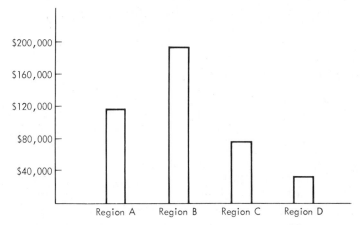

Figure 13. Last Month's Sales for Invention Incorporated by Four Major Sales Regions

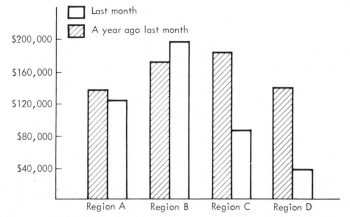

Figure 14. Last Month's Sales for Invention Incorporated Compared to Same Month Last Year for Four Major Sales Regions

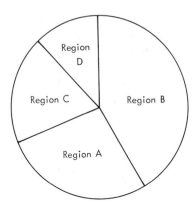

Figure 15. Percentage of Sales by Major Sales Regions Last Month for Invention Incorporated.

DELIVERING THE PRESENTATION

You will feel the pressures of organizational status and influence of nonverbal communication we discussed in Chapter 9 most strongly when called upon to make a presentation. Your nonverbal communication will be an important part of your believability and effectiveness as you deliver the message. The organizational communication context creates the expectation that a manager will be on top of the material, poised and in control during important leadership situations. There are few other public occasions in which you will be as much the center of attention as when you are giving a presentation. Your manner and platform personality become a vital feature of your presentation.

Your listeners will be more favorably disposed to your ideas if your verbal and nonverbal communication project confidence, openness, and thorough preparation.

In the culture of the typical North American organization the projection of confidence while delivering a talk, an oral report, a public speech, or a presentation is often a major problem. We expect a good public speaker to be poised and confident but we also expect that most people will suffer from "stage fright." In many organizations, once you are scheduled to give a presentation, your colleagues will treat you as though you are about to come down with a serious disease. They may joke about it or they may sympathize with you; often in nonverbal fashion they indicate that you are bound to become more and more nervous as the fateful day and hour approaches.

If you are anxious, your listeners will undoubtedly find out about it, largely through your nonverbal communication. Your hands may shake, your voice may quiver, and you may look away from the audience in an embarrassed way. Sometimes you may feel very nervous but your audience does not get that impression because your nonverbal communication is characterized by a poker-face and a stiff posture with few gestures. Anxiety can come across as boredom. In either case, whether the audience perceives you to be nervous or bored, the nonverbal dimension of your presentation can distract and detract from your message as well as from your authority as a manager and expert.

We all tend to get excited when we are about to try something we view as important. When much is at stake and we anticipate that success will be pleasant and rewarding and failure will be painful, the body responds by getting charged up for a maximum effort. We can think of the response as one of "fight or flight." We probably inherited the response from our prehistoric ancestors who often faced personal danger. Our bodily symptoms when we experience the fight or flight response vary from person to person but may include sweaty palms, increased heartbeat, dry mouth, and shortness of breath.

In earlier chapters we have stressed the power of words to arouse emotional responses unintentionally. We can overcome the often crippling effects of such word magic by recognizing how it works. Rather than call the feeling of excitement that normally accompanies giving a presentation by the negative term *fright,* we will call it *anticipation. Anticipation* implies looking forward to a pleasurable event. A person about to ride a roller coaster, start down a ski slope, or fly with a hang glider may have the same feelings of pounding heart, sweaty palms, and dry mouth as a manager about to give a presentation, but the rider, the skier, and the hang-glider may interpret the bodily responses as pleasurable excitement.

We do not have to succumb to the widespread nonverbal suggestion that the usual response to speaking publicly is fear. We should realize that almost everyone, including professional actors, entertainers, and speakers, experiences bodily arousal and excitement before appearing before audiences. Often the professionals testify that on those rare occasions when they were not keyed up before they went on, their performance was flat and below par. When they were keyed up, they did a better job.

A good way to manage the physical tensions surrounding the giving of a presentation is to develop positive interpretations of what they mean. You can daydream about the presentation in negative ways and see yourself freezing up, unable to speak, tripping over an electrical cord, or knocking over the overhead projector. If you fantasize along these lines you are likely to interpret your feelings as fear. Too bad that television and film comedy routines so often poke fun at the frightened speaker.

How about a different scenario? Why not choose to see in your mind's eye a successful outcome, the congratulations of those you respect, and the feeling of achievement that stems from a good presentation. If you begin to view your communication in positive fashion you can go a long way to overcoming the common bugaboo of "stage fright."

As we have been noting throughout the book, your primary duties as a manager are communicative in nature and you will undoubtedly have to give presentations. You would be well advised to make successful communication your hobby. Do not take flight from the emotional arousal that comes with public speaking. A well delivered presentation can be every bit as exciting and rewarding as a good ski run down a new hill covered with fresh snow.

In addition to the mental attitude and interpretation you bring to the presentation, you can take some concrete steps to assure the *productive use of tension* before and during the speech. One of the most important steps is to prepare thoroughly. A good way to feel in control is to know that you are well prepared.

Having planned and outlined your speech you need to flesh it out with examples, factual data, argument, analogies, and other supporting material. In the final analysis, this fleshing out consists of finding the right words and forming them into good sentences. One way to prepare at this stage is to write out your presentation. With a written draft of your message you can get other people to read it and make suggestions for revision and you can polish the language to make sure you are saying exactly what you wish to say. When you have a polished written draft you are faced with another decision. Should I read my manuscript or should I memorize it?

Reading a manuscript serves to overcome your worry about forgetting what you will say. You may need a written manuscript for other reasons as well. If your presentation will be reported in the news media or if you will have members of other units from the organization present who will go over your comments carefully, searching for loopholes or mistakes, you may want to write out and read your message. Subsequent discussions and arguments can be tied to exact quotations. You will also guard against a misstatement or an error in selecting a word or phrase by using, and sticking to, a prepared text. In many political campaigns the candidates run into difficulty because some phrase or comment in a speech or news conference becomes a matter of argument.

You may also need a manuscript if your multimedia development is elaborate and involves people who are helping you run slide or film projectors, models, mockups or videotape recorders. They may need a script to follow along so they can provide a film clip or a slide, or play an audiotape on cue.

A written manuscript for your presentation poses some problems in terms of nonverbal communication, however. When you read your presentation, the manuscript may serve as a barrier between you and your audience. Few people can read with the directness and lively sense of communication that they put into their best conversation. They do not sound natural; their voice drones on, failing to pause at the right places, failing to emphasize ideas. The manuscript itself becomes a distraction for the listeners. You may decide to use a speaker's stand to hide your manuscript and then grip the stand tightly with both hands except when you have to turn a page. You may lean on or hang onto the stand, thus failing to gesture at appropriate places. Of course you can put your presentation on note cards, but a 15-minute presentation will require a large stack of cards. The way you shuffle the deck, look at the cards, or possibly get them out of order may often distract the audience.

Careful and repeated rehearsal *with all multimedia support* is a must if you use a manuscript for your presentation. If you are personally running the overhead projector and slide projectors and other electronic devices, you need to learn where the trouble spots are and experiment with various ways to make the transitions from one machine to another without losing your place or leaving your manuscript somewhere where you cannot see it easily. Rehearsals will also give you a chance to develop effective vocal emphasis, directness, and proper patterns of pausing as you read your presentation.

If you write out your presentation and feel that the manuscript poses too many problems, you can memorize it and free your hands (and eyes) for other duties. You will find it easier to polish up your nonverbal communication with a memorized presentation than with a manuscript. You can stress your use of voice, timing, and gestures. Some people memorize very rapidly and if you are one of those lucky individuals, memorization is something to consider. For many managers, however, memorization requires a lot of additional time. With a memorized presentation you do run some risk of losing your place. When your remarks are memorized and you forget, it is difficult for some people to ad lib and keep going. They often cannot get started again until they remember the right words or are prompted. Finally, memorization, for a beginner, often results in a patterned use of voice and gesture that can be as much a problem as an unnatural way of reading.

For most of your organizational presentations we recommend a third way of preparation which is the extemporaneous method. In using this method you do not write out your presentation but prepare a careful outline and either write out the main points on the outline with some key words or phrases to jog your memory about supporting material or memorize the main points of the outline. You then rehearse the presentation by talking it out aloud from your outline several times.

If you prepare your presentation carefully in the extemporaneous manner you can forget a detail and still keep going, and you can adjust your presentation to the audience response. You can look at your audience and read their feedback and include material that springs to mind in the midst of your talk. You must be careful, of course, not to depart too frequently from your prepared outline or you will run overtime. When speaking extemporaneously you should keep track of time continuously. Keep your watch handy, or ask a colleague to give you time signals at regular intervals. The extemporaneous presentation also frees your hands for gestures and for handling the multimedia materials.

After thorough preparation another concrete step you can take to manage communication tension is to develop an audience-centered approach while you are speaking. We can aggravate our anxiety by being self-centered. If we are worried about how we look, whether our gestures are effective, whether we are making a good impression, we emphasize how much personal stake we have in the presentation. By focusing on the audience and on communicating with them, we take our minds off ourselves and our performance. Watch the individuals who make up your audience. Read their facial expressions, postures, and gestures for feedback on what they understand and agree with. Are some members of the audience getting excited by what you are saying? Are some getting involved, or do some look bored or sleepy? Do some appear confused? Becoming audience-centered also improves your nonverbal suggestion by communicating interest in your listeners and a willingness to help them understand your message.

Finally, you should act confident prior to and during the presentation itself. While waiting to speak, sit erect and look about with confidence. When your time comes, move forward to a spot you have picked out and when you reach that spot, look out at your listeners and begin in a firm, take-charge manner. If you need to set up multimedia materials, have a plan so that you do so with efficiency and with a minimum of time and effort. With a little rehearsal of the opening two minutes, you can get your presentation off to a good start. The uncomfortable part of communication tension often wears off after several minutes.

Look directly at your listeners. If you do not see them, you have no idea what they are doing. The unknown is often more frightening than knowing exactly what is going on. Some faces will prove easier to talk to than others and you might pick out some responsive, supportive people at the beginning, but be sure to look at everyone during the course of the first few minutes—not over their heads—*at* them.

Work something into your introduction to catch their interest, something that will bring a positive response. If you can get them to laugh, smile, or nod in agreement early, the positive response will be a tonic for you, will help them relax as you begin, and their positive impressions will feed back to you and make your speaking more enjoyable.

SUMMARY

Managers are usually expected to make presentations to other members of the organization or to the general public as representatives of their organizations. Presentations, which are among the more important formal messages available to the organization, require a formal decision in order to assign organizational resources to their development and delivery. Much time and effort goes into their preparation.

When you are asked to give a presentation, it is because of your special knowledge and your organizational position. That being the case you cannot rely on others to prepare the presentation for you. One of the most important managerial skills, therefore, is the ability to prepare and deliver organizational presentations.

In order to adapt your knowledge to the listeners you need to become *audience-centered.* After you have thought through what the ideal message for a specialist would be like, you should make a careful analysis of the listeners and cut, rearrange, reword, and in other ways adapt the ideal message to the specific audience and occasion.

Having analyzed your audience you need to organize your message effectively. An important organizational step is the development of a good central idea. When you have a clear, simple, and specific wording for your central idea you can use it as a yardstick to select material for your presentation. Having selected the material you need to find a pattern of arrangement. A good outline will help plan the arrangement of material for your presentation. There are standard patterns that have been tested over the years and proved effective that you can use to organize your ideas. Included among them are classification schemes, space order, time order, method of residues, problem-solution order, and proposition-support order.

After the body of the presentation is organized you still need to supply an *introduction* and a *conclusion* and to tie the major points within the message to one another and to the central theme with *transitions.*

Multimedia experts have developed techniques for getting across ideas and persuasive materials quickly and effectively by portraying their messages in sight and sound. One of the main distinguishing features of the business presentation is its essential character as a multimedia message.

In most organizations you will have available multimedia aids such as blackboards, chalkboards, easel cards, flip charts, and flannel boards for inexpensive presentation of charts, maps, diagrams, work lists, and so forth. Usually managers have available devices such as overhead projectors, slide projectors, and film projectors. The use of audio and videotape recorders can facilitate clarifying difficult concepts and complex information.

Most tables in written messages are unsuitable for oral presentations. The manager should present complex statistical comparisons by means of line graphs, bar graphs, or pie charts. Each visual should contain only two basic comparisons and should not be shown to the audience for more than 20 or 30 seconds at a time.

A good way to manage the physical tensions involved in giving a presentation is to develop a positive interpretation of what they mean. You should work on ways to make productive use of your tension prior to delivery by preparing thoroughly and anticipating success. Funnel the tension during the delivery of the presentation into positive nonverbal communication.

Careful and repeated rehearsal with all multimedia support is a must if you use a written manuscript or memorize your remarks but it is also valuable if you speak extemporaneously. We recommend the extemporaneous approach because it allows you to adapt to the situation and the audience during the course of the presentation.

We recommend that you project confidence before and during the delivery, look directly at your listeners, work something into your introduction to catch their interest and draw a positive response, and have fun with the opportunity to get your ideas across in a setting where they will have results.

QUESTIONS FOR DISCUSSION AND REVIEW

1. How does the organizational presentation differ from other speaking occasions?
2. What are the implications of the principle that "you should be audience-centered" on the preparation of the organizational presentation?
3. What are some things to look for when making an audience analysis?
4. What are the five things you have to do to organize a presentation?
5. What is the nature of a good central idea and how does it function to help organize material?
6. What principles of outlining would be useful in organizing a presentation?
7. What are the characteristics of a good introduction and conclusion and of clear transitions?
8. What are the major multimedia techniques and devices available for the manager who is preparing a presentation?
9. What are the main principles involved in presenting data on charts and graphs?
10. What are some productive uses you can make of tension before and during the presentation?

REFERENCES AND SUGGESTED READINGS

Clevenger, T., Jr. *Audience Analysis*. Indianapolis: Bobbs-Merrill, 1966.

Howell, W. S. and E. G. Bormann. *Presentational Speaking for Business and the Professions*. New York: Harper & Row, 1971.

Kemp, J. *Planning and Producing Audiovisual Materials*. San Francisco: Chandler, 1963.

Wilcox, R. P. *Oral Reporting in Business and Industry*. Englewood Cliffs, N.J.: Prentice-Hall, 1967.

Wittich, W. A. and C. F. Schuller. *Audiovisual Materials: Their Nature and Use*. New York: Harper & Row, 1967.

12

Persuasion

——————————————— **Laboratory Application** ———————————————

In Chapter 11 we stressed the idea that most important oral messages such as organizational presentations turn out to be, in the final analysis, persuasive. Managers giving presentations usually have a program, a policy, an internal change, a change of organizational objective, or some other plan that they want adopted and the success of the proposals depends upon the willing cooperation of others. As a manager you will find yourself facing many persuasive situations in your daily formal and informal communication in addition to those occasions when you make a presentation.

While the formal presentation may be the high point and climactic moment in a persuasive effort, most attempts at making substantial changes of behavior, opinion, or attitude are campaigns that consist of a variety of messages, short and long, informal and formal, written and oral. Most persuasive campaigns take place over a period of weeks or months, even years.

You may begin a persuasive campaign by planning a new way of doing things and thinking through the details of your plan carefully before you ever mention it to anyone. Recall the case study of Janet Perkins, the new sales manager for Invention Incorporated. Janet began with an analysis of the present sales programs, then worked out a detailed plan to institute new computer-aided market analysis in her department. She put the new procedure into operation on October 15, without undertaking a persuasive campaign to gain acceptance and support. What she should have done was plan a campaign. Such a campaign would begin with a thorough analysis of the audience. Janet made an excellent study of the facts of the situation but overlooked the human dimension. After analyzing the audience she should have selected the central themes of the campaign, the supporting ideas, and the general outline of how and when to introduce the ideas, to develop them, and to gain acceptance.

She needed also to evaluate what channels to use, when to step up her messages, when to peak the campaign, and so forth. Perhaps a wise way for her to begin would have been with some informal mentions of the new ideas in unthreatening situations. Janet might have talked with people in the sales force about an article in a magazine dealing with new developments in market analysis. She might have asked one of the salespeople to read it and give her an opinion about it. Next, she might have introduced the possibilities in a formal departmental meeting, followed by written memorandums to other managers, and to sales persons. In any case, since she was planning to make big changes, she should have thought in terms of a campaign to gain acceptance as an important part of making them.

Our point here is that persuasion takes place in all communication contexts. You can be persuasive in informal two-person conferences, in written letters and memorandums, in small group meetings, in the creative use of bulletin boards and newsletters or organizational newspapers, as well as in the formal presentation.

Persuasion requires the most careful and sophisticated analysis of the listeners of all communication. You need to learn as much as you can about what "makes them tick" if you wish to persuade them, whether your focus is on a total campaign or on a specific presentation for a given occasion. Our laboratory application is a case study discussion of audience analysis for a presentation. We chose it because it allows you to make specific application of the theoretical material. The same material could be applied to a case study of a persuasive campaign.

CASE STUDY ASSIGNMENT: The New Breakfast Cereal

John Jamison finds himself confronting a problem in communication that seems incapable of satisfactory solution. For two years he has supervised the development of a new product, an off-the-beaten-track breakfast cereal which John is convinced can be promoted and sold profitably by his company. Now the time has come to take the next step toward that goal. Manufacturing processes and techniques are reasonably well worked out and tested. Cost estimates of production are firm. A market test of the new cereal involving saturation advertising and marketing in two large cities, St. Louis and Minneapolis, has been readied.

To proceed, John Jamison must have the approval of the Board of Control of his company, a group of seven representatives of top management. He has been allotted twenty minutes for his presentation, and has two weeks to prepare. His mission on P-Day: to persuade the board to approve manufacture of the new product and authorize the expenditure of $740,000 to ascertain its sales potential.

John considers his mission impossible because of the amount of information he feels obliged to transmit to the board and the absurdly brief time limitation of twenty minutes. A quick calculation shows him that if he tells the board what they really should know concerning the new product, about eight hours of lecture with visual aids would be required. To say that John is frustrated as he tilts back in his chair and contemplates the immediate future would be the understatement of the year.

With a nagging sensation of time running out, John has exhausted his conventional alternatives and is seeking frantically for a miracle. He remembers a memo from The Training Division of a month or two ago that offered individual consultation to managers who are preparing presentations. Luckily, the one-page memo found its way into the bulging, dusty "Training" file instead of landing in the wastebasket. In a few minutes John has Paula Osterhus, an instructor in speech communication, on the phone, and Paula has agreed to join John at lunch in the company cafeteria.

Luncheon conversation between Paula and John takes several surprising turns, from John's point of view. He finds that his predicament of eight hours of material to present and twenty minutes to do it in is not exceptional, in fact it is the norm. He learns that success in coping with this problem has come, not from a masterly condensation of information into well-organized essentials, but from meeting the expectations of individual members of the decision-making group. For the first time he is made aware of the "pitfall of projection," the tendency we all have to design a presentation that would satisfy *us,* disregarding the preferences and prejudices of the people we will talk to. And he is led to appreciate that his first step in preparing his presentation is to analyze the motivations of the people who are to receive it. When he knows the priority of interests each board member has in any new product, he is ready to select from his mass of information what will be most persuasive to that person. This strategy of selection, rather than logical briefing, is the organizing principle recommended by Paula for one reason: in the past it has produced better results than any other procedure.

Back in the office, with a new set of guidelines, John sets about analyzing his persuasion problem, person by person. He has observed the board in action for several years, so when he begins to list statements about the dynamics of decision-making within the board, he has considerable information. He recalls that interaction among board members has been dominated by the three senior members, each with a vigorous and aggressive approach to group deliberation. John decides he will make his pitch to these three. The other four he sees as lieutenants of the big three. Hence, he need only convince his selected opinion leaders and his success is assured.

John begins motive analysis with Ralph Anderson, president of the Company and the moderator at board meetings. Ralph is "top status" man on the board in every way. He has the highest rank, the longest service with the company (he was one of the founders), and is older than the others. Ralph Anderson's training for his present responsibilities was "in plant," on the job, totally. As the company grew and expanded into new product lines, Ralph was solving associated problems of production. His particular talent was improvement of production techniques. Everyone knew that Ralph could figure out how to produce any product more efficiently, for less cost. Now in his mid-60s, Ralph has settled comfortably into thinking about the business operation in terms of the criterion that has served him so well throughout his career, "How can we keep costs down?" When previous new products have been presented to the board, John can remember how Ralph kept harping on his one recurrent theme, costs. "O.K." he would say, "show me how soon we can pass the crossover point!" meaning that point when a new product begins to show a profit.

Next John turns his thoughts to Homer Lydgate, head of the company's marketing operation. Homer is in his late 40s, a hot-shot up-and-coming executive who has become an influential member of the inner group through several breakthroughs in advertising and distribution. Homer was pirated from a rival milling company some six years before. His advertising caught the fancy of millions, and the decision to create a new salary bracket for Homer and start him near the top has paid rich dividends. Under his direction, company merchandising evolved from the dullest in the industry to perhaps its most novel and exciting. Naturally, Homer perceives each new product in terms of its advertising potential. Novelty is his hang-up. Sound but run-of-the-mill proposals have little attraction for him.

The third member of the influential trio is Marsha Everding, known throughout the company as the theory-happy character on the top-management team. As company comptroller, she manages the financial operation with high competence. She enjoys keeping up with new developments in data processing and computer technology. Her ideal is to run the company according to the most modern financial, engineering, and management theories, for only then, Marsha is convinced, can the company compete successfully.

One of Marsha Everding's favorite theories is that the company with the most complete product line, but one that is free of internal duplication, has a real competitive advantage that will build substantial profits over the long pull. Consequently, she fusses continuously about modifying manufacturing in the direction of making each product distinctive and, in the aggregate, covering the range of the market comprehensively. When a new product is being evaluated she has two questions: Does it overlap anything we are now producing? Is there a gap in our present line that this product can fill? If the person presenting the innovation answers the first question negatively and the second in the affirmative, to the satisfaction of Marsha Everding's informed and inquiring mind, then Marsha's initial apparent obstructionism usually changes to hearty support.

Already, John's presentation is taking shape. He devises a five-part strategy that serves as the organizing principle of his talk. Part 1 is brief, a two-minute, rather technical, description of the new cereal he has developed. Parts 2, 3, and 4 are of approximately equal length, none to exceed five minutes. One of these sections deals with the cost picture, with particular emphasis upon evidence that the crossover point should occur in less than average time. Another section develops the novel advertising possibilities of this unique and extraordinary cereal. The third part of the presentation shows that the company, with the addition of the new cereal to its already extensive product line, can meet every known market better than can any single competitor. The time remaining, perhaps three or four minutes of the allotted twenty, John will leave for questions and comments, for he has learned the hard way that not every doubt can be anticipated, and unanswered questions block favorable response. The question period then becomes the last step in his five-part plan.

Implementation of the strategy is relatively easy. From his eight hours or so of material John can select impressive evidence to drive home his three-pronged attack. He enlists the help of the audiovisual section of his company to prepare eight or ten simple, colorful visuals to be used with the overhead projector. He rehearses before a sympathetic and knowledgeable associate who comments frankly and suggests changes. When the production has "jelled," with all visuals and major content items in approximately final form, he rehearses some more, always before the videotape camera. His notes are discarded, and his timing is practiced until he knows that with only an occasional glance at the clock at certain checkpoints he can finish "on the button."

John does not memorize his talk, because he understands that only a professional actor can make memorized lines sound fresh and spontaneous. To be sensitive to his listeners, and particularly to the influential three, he must react to them continuously. So he practices in an informal, direct, and conversational style. Many words and phrases that seem to be effective are retained as the talk gains in ease and smoothness. But no paragraph is ever literally reproduced in a subsequent rehearsal. To communicate effectively in the small-group situation, John knows that he must preserve the extemporaneous character of his speaking.

When the appointed hour came for John Jamison, he was relaxed and ready. He felt that he had equipped himself to meet the needs of the occasion and more pertinently, to supply the facts of the case that would be most vital to his audience.

John felt a new and welcome confidence as he began his presentation. As Paula recommended, he watched the small audience carefully and paid particular attention to each of the three opinion leaders as he developed that part of his presentation aimed specifically at that individual. The section on the cost picture was particularly successful. Ralph Anderson was nodding approval before John had gotten halfway through the point. Feeling good about Ralph's approval, John sailed into his second point feeling a sense of pleasant excitement. Giving a good presentation might even be enjoyable.

John watched Homer Lydgate for his reaction to the novel advertising possibilities. He had worked up two visuals, one utilizing the old traditional advertising symbol of the food division of International Mills, Helen Homemaker, and another using Lydgate's new symbol for cake mix advertising, Carrie the Career Woman. John thought he had come up with a clever way to use these two symbols in advertising the new breakfast cereal. Lydgate apparently was buying the possibilities and John was thinking "This is almost too easy" when he shifted his gaze to the other members of the audience and found Marsha Everding frowning and shifting in her chair.

When he looked back at Homer, however, he saw that Lydgate was becoming more and more supportive and he forgot Marsha's frowning response. When he came to point three and started to concentrate on her pet interests he noticed that the frown was still on her face. As he proceeded, however, she seemed to be drawn into the analysis of how the new cereal would help round out the product line and John was feeling better about her feedback when he brought the presentation to a conclusion and asked for questions.

There was a short pause. Everyone seemed to be waiting for Ralph Anderson to give some sign one way or another. After a bit, Ralph asked several supportive questions that indicated that he was impressed with the projected crossover time and then said, "John, that was a good presentation. You got right to the point."

There was another pause. Marsha was shifting in her chair, apparently disturbed by something. She began asking about the advertising possibilities of the new cereal. John was caught off guard. This was out of character for Marsha. He framed an answer to the question, but he realized that he was not getting through. Finally she started to ask about his two visuals. She asked him if he would show the visual on Carrie the Career Woman again. Suddenly John remembered some messages he had been getting on the grapevine about the new influx of women managers organizing a support group. He recalled that he had been surprised to hear that Marsha was part of the group. She had been with the company twenty years and when she started, her degrees in business administration and management information systems gave her an unusual background compared to most women. When she became a member of top management she was something of a token woman manager but her no-nonsense manner and outstanding performance had overcome tokenism to some extent. Still, he knew that some shared fantasies had characterized her as a "queen bee" and he had never thought of her as a feminist.

As her questions continued, John realized that Marsha was not just irritated but downright angry about something to do with Carrie the Career Woman. She was talking about super-woman images and that they were more damaging even than Helen the Homemaker. John was at sea. He had not anticipated this. He had no answer to her attack on the advertising campaign. He tried to say that his visuals were only suggestions, that he was not a professional in advertising. Now the other woman on the board spoke up. The question and answer period was getting out of hand. Just then Homer stepped in and began to defend the campaign based on Carrie the Career Woman. Soon Marsha and Homer were arguing about the sexist nature of the company's advertising and John found that his presentation had inadvertently gotten tangled up in a conflict between the women in upper and middle management and International Mills's latest advertising campaign. Again, John had heard about it on the grapevine, but at the time he was preparing for the presentation, and had not paid much attention.

After a bit, Ralph Anderson stepped in and said that determining whether the company's advertising was sexist was an important matter. He, for one, wanted to examine this criticism in depth, but it was not the issue for the meeting today. The question was whether or not they should approve the new product. After a few minutes both Homer and Marsha calmed down and the meeting came back to the issue at hand.

A month later, after further discussions and after John had done some fence-mending with Marsha and others on the board, International Mills approved the new cereal. Paula had urged John to make a practice of evaluating a presentation after delivery. In thinking about what happened later, John decided that Paula was right when she stressed the complexity of communication. He had neglected to make a complete analysis of his audience. By concentrating on one person at a time he forgot to ask himself, if I take this approach to appeal to Ralph Anderson, will it have any effect on Homer Lydgate, or if I take this approach to Homer Lydgate, will it influence Marsha Everding? He also appreciated more fully Paula's warning about the power of words and symbols to arouse emotional responses. He thought he was simply reporting how innovative changes in the current advertising campaigns could include the new cereal. He discovered that for Marsha, the Carrie the Career Woman symbol was loaded with negative meanings while for Homer, it was a positive symbol.

QUESTIONS FOR CASE ANALYSIS

1. Did John's analysis of the motives of the big three reveal any deficit motivation?
2. Did John's analysis of the motives of the big three reveal any emotional tension motives?
3. Did John's analysis of the motives of the big three reveal any other-than-self centered motivation?
4. What organizational pattern did John use for his presentation?
5. How could an analysis of the shared fantasies, rhetorical visions, and participation in organizational sagas have helped John in his analysis of the audience?
6. In general, how would you evaluate John's ability at audience analysis?
7. How would you evaluate John's presentation in terms of persuasion?

(Read the rest of this chapter before you answer these questions.)

Theoretical Rationale

In our analysis of organizational communication we consider persuasion to be a prerequisite to other management skills. In other words, the manager is unable to apply his knowledge and implement his programs without the ability to purposefully influence the attitudes and behavior of those who work for him and with him. Skill in persuasion enables a manager to "get things done through people."

How does a person learn about persuasion and increase her ability to persuade? The first essential step is to assume the *process attitude,* to resolve that henceforth she will resist her impulse to "feel her way" in persuasion, and instead will detach herself and view what is going on as a process. She should identify the steps in the process, classify stimuli, describe responses, and attempt to explain them. *Being objective*—the first step toward learning about persuasion—is not easy, for all of us during most of our lives have avoided being systematic and analytical when initiating or experiencing acts of human influence.

A key principle applies the process attitude to motivation: *People do things for their own reasons, not yours.* When we recognize that persuasion consists of purposefully connecting our recommendations to the OTHER PERSON'S motives, the importance of this becomes obvious.

The force that prevents us from learning the other person's reasons (her motives) is within ourselves. It is the "Pitfall of Projection." Without thinking about it, all of us project upon the other person our own habits, interests, goals, and desires. Further, without realizing it, we tend to assume that the other person has experienced our experiences, that she has our vocabulary with the same meanings for words familiar to us, and that the facts we know so well are in her grasp.

How can the "pitfall of projection" be avoided? Not by simple good intentions. Often we hear, " You must put yourself in the other person's shoes." Realistically, this is clearly impossible. Another person is very different and incredibly complicated; the best we can do is to add up fragments of definite information about him, such as the words he uses and facts he must know.

If we are diligent and sensitive, we may perhaps occasionally experience a flash of insight that amounts to "getting something of the other person's point of view." When this occurs his responses suddenly make sense, and what was mysterious becomes obvious. It is a rich reward for our effort, and it affirms our resolution to be "other-person centered."

The difference in our perception of communication made by our gain of insight into the other person's view is always profound. When we appreciate the other person's point of view, the situation changes considerably. A cartoon best illustrates this. It shows two rats in an experimental box. One rat is saying to the other rat, "Boy, have I got this human trained! Whenever I push this lever, he gives me some food!"

KEY STEPS IN PERSUASION

Successful persuasion requires four tasks. Because these come in sequence we call them steps, or stages, in the process of persuasion. These are:

1. Gain and maintain attention.
2. Arouse selected desires (motives, habits, interests).
3. Connect desires to persuasive purpose.
4. Produce a specific response.

Gaining and Maintaining Attention. Obviously, we must gain a person's attention before communication can take place. Step one underlines the word "maintain" for good reason: The necessity of *working at* the holding of attention throughout the duration of the message is *not* obvious to most of us. We forget the nature of human attention, which above all else is intermittent. We listen for 15 to 45 seconds typically, then let our mind wander. A bit later we tune in again, and depending upon what we hear, stay tuned in for either a longer or shorter interval than we did before. A trend develops toward listening more and more or less and less, whatever the case may be.

Our naive assumption that because people pay attention when we begin to talk they will continue to do so is without foundation. The able persuaders employ carefully prepared devices to revive the attention of their listeners from time to time. Lively illustrations, examples, touches of humor, colorful language, all serve this purpose well. One main point is that attention does not "just happen." Purposeful effort and a variety of techniques are needed to do the job of maintaining attention.

Arousing Selected Motives. The important word in step two is "selected." We should select the motive, habit, or interest to be activated in a person being persuaded by as careful a motive analysis as time and circumstances permit. Much will be said later about motive analysis, the truly basic problem in the preparation of persuasion. The task confronting the persuader is that of finding what the people to be persuaded want that is or can be related to the persuader's purpose. By "what they want" we mean what they are interested in, what is important to them, what they find exciting or rewarding.

Beware of the "pitfall of projection" while reviewing interests of another person. Our own desires and preoccupations seem so "right" to us that we are inclined to assume that they are universal.

Your specific recommendation guides you in motive selection. Can you show the person to be persuaded directly and simply *how* what you are suggesting will help him get what he wants, do what he enjoys doing, achieve a goal he has set for himself? If so, and you are sure the motive is his, not a projection of yours, the choice is a wise one.

Connecting Motives to Purpose. People frequently neglect step three, "connect desires to persuasive purpose," because, having identified pertinent motives and having made their recommendation clear, they assume that the job is done. Nothing could be further from the truth. People must be shown, explicitly and specifically, just exactly how a recommendation will serve their purposes and advance their interests.

To do this "connecting" we recommend the device of "visualization." Visualization consists of picturing your proposal in action in the future, after its adoption and implementation. Naturally, the one being persuaded will want to know "How will things work out?" In concrete terms, with vivid examples, the persuader dramatizes the future, describing in detail the probable effects of his proposal. And always, the person to be persuaded is involved centrally in the visualization. Notice that dramatizing is the first communication step in the process of sharing a group fantasy and building a rhetorical vision. By means such as this, recommendations are unmistakably "connected" to desires.

Here as in the next step it is necessary to be more explicit and detailed than most of us are habitually. We trust people "to figure things out for themselves" to some extent. When we overestimate people's capacity to do this, the results are not always pleasant.

Producing a Specific Response. Step four, "produce a specific response," is usually neglected even more than step three. Too often, when we have gone through the first three steps we are ready to quit and go home. If we do, we will regret it. Human beings possess almost infinite capacity to do things the wrong way. Whenever one permits people who are "sold" on a general course of action to go ahead on their own and work out details of implementation, we can confidently anticipate disaster.

To complete the process of persuasion successfully, much guidance is necessary in the last stage. This is complicated by the nature of the required guidance, which may seem obvious and mechanical. The one being persuaded may feel that he is being treated in a manner unworthy of his position and his intelligence. He may say, "Don't you give me credit for figuring out *anything* by myself?"

Artistry in the execution of step four consists of suggesting details of implementation in such a way that the one we are persuading believes *she* is originating them. This is done most readily through questions. "How do you think we should get this started?" "Here's one thing we could do, but I'm not satisfied with it. Can you improve it?" "What do you think of this procedure? Will it work?" Adopting a "team" approach with many leading questions permits the persuader to produce the specific response without insulting the intelligence of the other person.

Applying the Four Steps. How should the reader apply the four-step process of persuasion? We suggest two ways: as a guide to the preparation of persuasion, and as a diagnostic tool for the analysis of persuasion.

Assume that you wish to submit a proposal to modify an important operation within your organization. You are to present it to a three-executive committee that will evaluate your proposal and accept or reject it. The plan you are recommending is in final form. You have the evidence to support it.

A good way to prepare your persuasive presentation is to plan how you will accomplish each of the four steps with this particular group of three people. Ask yourself "How will I . . .?" and, in terms of these individuals on this given occasion, work out the *best* way to accomplish each step. If you do this thoroughly, you will have a comprehensive and custom-built presentation. It will be *complete* because it will have been designed psychologically to carry the listeners through a complete thought sequence to the acceptance and implementation of your proposal.

As a diagnostic tool for the analysis of past and present persuasion, you can use the four steps in critical evaluation of your own persuasive efforts or the persuasion of others. After an attempt to persuade, ask, "How well did I gain and maintain attention?" "How well did I *select* what was important to my audience and get those desires in motion?" "How well did I connect my proposal to what they were interested in?" "Could they see unmistakably how their needs would be met by my proposal?" And finally, "How effectively did I guide the final response?" Answers to these questions will, typically, indicate that one or two of the steps were less well done than the others. Conscious evaluation will aid you in improving those weak points in future persuasion.

INFORMATION USEFUL FOR PERSUASION

Skill in persuasion is based upon knowledge of human beings and the resultant ability to predict their behavior; therefore we need to know all we can about people. However, much content of the behavioral sciences is peripheral to our interest. We find valuable information that is useful to the study in motivational psychology, applied logic, and semantics.

Psychology of Motives. Motivation psychology sounds complicated and academic. As implemented by the student of persuasion it can be made very direct and quite simple. A person can become proficient in motive analysis by building two lists, one of the ways that people tend to resemble each other in their responses, and the other, ways in which they tend to differ. Add items to your lists only when you are convinced that they are reliable and represent something significant.

Analyzing Motives. Knowledge about the similarities and differences in people comes from many sources. Popular publications abound in articles that are helpfully informative. Many books on motivation are available; several deal with people with an organizational background. Courses are offered in psychology; we recommend particularly those relating to motivation. And last, but not least, your own observation of yourself and your associates can contribute items to the lists.

We urge that the reader approach the study of motive analysis as a do-it-yourself project. All of us have some knowledge and a great interest in "why people are the way they are." Build on this with *systematic* reading and observation and keep adding to the lists of similar and different patterns of behavior. It is vital that you keep *written* lists, for if you trust your memory the potentially most penetrating insights may slip your mind and be forever lost.

The system of motive analysis presented later in this chapter will serve as a guide to the building of the lists. It will also provide a classification system that serves as a structure for motive analysis. Long lists of motives tend to be of little use because what we want to remember is usually lost in a mass of items. Our system places related motives together, and by doing so makes them more useful.

Motives may be envisioned as the "engines for persuasion." When a stimulus triggers a motive, energy is released to power a particular response. A response can be understood only in terms of the motives that energize it. Ultimately, the ability of a persuader to PREDICT RESPONSE of particular people under specified circumstances depends upon his or her knowledge of differences and similarities in their structures of motivation.

Defining Motives. We define *motives* as variable sources of energy to pursue selected alternatives. Two key words in this definition need explication. *Selected* suggests that a network of motivation *screens* one's input of stimuli, causing people to respond significantly to only a few of the sights, sounds, smells, etc., presented to their sensing and perceiving mechanisms. "Variable" suggests a wide range in *amount* of energy made available when a motive goes in pursuit of an alternative. An individual's motivation to "go after" an objective can vary from a barely perceptible impulse to a total effort that surmounts obstacles and endures.

Let us look at our own motives to see how this screening and control action takes place. All of us are confronted daily with hundreds of opportunities to become interested in things suggested to us, to spend time, energy, and money pursuing these alternatives. Yet, at least 95 per cent of the recommendations made to us by advertisers, propagandists, ministers, friends, teachers, and associates are ignored. Our motive structure, the network of our habits, interests, needs, desires, and goals, *screens out* the possibilities that are unimportant to us. We perceive only the proposals that catch our interest and command our attention. The others are suppressed so effectively that many of them are not *consciously* heard or seen.

Let us suppose that a recommendation "rings the bell." Perhaps a friend urges us to share with him a season ticket to the concerts of a symphony orchestra. One motive aroused is an *interest,* specifically in a certain type of good music. If the interest is strong, it may release sufficient energy to impel us to spend a considerable amount of money and rearrange a year's social calendar to permit attending 12 or 15 concerts. But if the interest is weak as compared with our devotion to basketball and hockey, available energy may well be insufficient to cause us to follow through on our initial impulse. Obviously, something within us tells us what attitude change or action we should implement, and further informs us as to how fast and how far we should go in carrying out an initial impulse. This control center we call "motivation."

Persuasion or Motivation? The terms "persuasion" and "motivation" are often misused in a way that causes confusion between them. Frequently an attempt to persuade is incorrectly referred to as "motivation." A typical misuse is this request: "Can you motivate Helen to accept the presidency of the union?" The correct usage would be, "Can you persuade Helen to accept the presidency?" Using the verb "motivate" to designate an attempt to communicate persuasively with Helen suggests that motives can be transferred or reasons important to Helen can be given to her. This cannot be done; her motives are already in residence.

But yet another confusion results from substituting "motivate" for "persuade." To illustrate: Suppose we are consulting with Joe Jackson, director of Sales Training for Y Company. After studying communication between his office and the Y Company Abrasive Products Division, we reach a tentative conclusion as to the cause of the difficulty that exists between the two departments. We report to Mr. Jackson orally. "Joe," we announce, "your problem is one of motivation."

Because of the dual meanings of "motivate," Mr. Jackson is understandably confused by the term's ambiguity. He has no way of knowing whether we are referring to (1) his efforts to influence his subordinates to do the job properly, or (2) to the motives present in the people who make up his sales force. Here is a perplexing and readily avoidable breakdown in communication.

"Motivation" should be used to refer to the structure of habits, interests, desires, and goals that is part of the personality of an individual. Any effort to purposely control his or her behavior *from the outside* by attaching a recommendation to those motives should be referred to as "persuasion." A simple sentence makes this arbitrary distinction clear and easy to remember: Motivation is *in* the person being persuaded.

To illustrate the utility of this distinction, let us return to our consultation with Mr. Jackson. Assume that we all understand and accept this arbitrarily restricted use of "motivate." When we label the problem as "one of motivation," he knows that, in our opinion, the difficulty stems from the values, needs, interests, and goals of his subordinates. If we had judged the cause to lie in the communication from Jackson's office to the sales force, he knows we would have labeled it "persuasion."

Deficit Motives. A substantial contribution to the theory of human motivation is the *sequential* arrangement of basic needs. These are sequential in that some needs are more "basic" in that these must be satisfied first. Only when the lower, more fundamental, needs are met reasonably well can higher level needs emerge.

Arranging these motives as rungs in a ladder suggests that activation of each level depends upon the gratification of needs below (see Figure 16).

Most elementary among the causes of striving behavior are *physiological needs:* primarily, food, air, and protection from physical harm; and secondarily, the relief of tensions that have a clear and direct physical causation, e.g., the need for sleep, for activity, and for sexual experience. When a person is severely deprived of satisfaction of one or more of his physiological needs, all other needs become insignificant. For example, until a supply of food he considers adequate is obtained, the hungry individual behaves as though he lacked security, social approval, or esteem needs. Moreover, his deprivation colors his thinking: He contemplates the future only in terms of food.

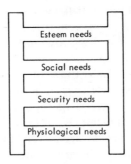

Figure 16. Ladder of Deficit Motives

But when there is ample food and other physiological needs are met, what happens? He begins to be concerned about security until he is no longer insecure. Subsequently, he tends to become preoccupied with his needs for social approval. When he has sufficient favorable attention he then becomes centrally concerned with his "image," the satisfaction of his esteem needs.

The names of the levels in Figure 16 suggest quite accurately the nature of the motives they represent. *Security needs,* sometimes called safety needs, refer to our strong desire for a predictable, organized environment in which we and our families and friends can look into the future without fear of disruptive change. Any circumstance that makes the future uncertain increases the pressure of security needs. *Social needs* become important when physiological and security matters are well in hand. Then the needs to "belong" with other people and to give and receive affection become critical. *Esteem needs* are two-fold: the need for self-esteem and the parallel desire for the high regard of others. Esteem needs will be strong only when a person has succeeded in meeting physiological, security, and social needs.

Why are these needs sequential? An implied key proposition that helps to clarify the sequential order of basic needs is this: *Satisfied needs do not motivate behavior.* This explains why in a given person at a particular time one of these four motives tends to be dominant, whereas those above and below it have little influence.

Why are these needs "deficit"? Why do we refer to our diagram as a "deficit" ladder? Two related concepts, *deficit motivation* and *gratification health,* will make this clear.

Motives in the ladder are universals. Their satisfaction is prerequisite to the functioning of a healthy personality. In any stable society these basic requirements are readily met. Consequently, a mature and well-adjusted individual will have few concerns caused by motives in the ladder. But a personality in conflict often becomes preoccupied with one need. Perhaps esteem, perhaps social, possibly security, even physiological needs may come to be of central importance to such a person. For example, adverse circumstances, such as the unexpected loss of a job, may cause a woman to "bounce back down the ladder" to the level of *security* which then—temporarily—becomes dominant. An urge from any of the ladder motives is *deficit motivation,* deficit in the sense that the subject has fallen behind and is trying to catch up. If she were well-adjusted, none of these needs would be of significant concern to her.

Gratification health views these same phenomena from a positive perspective. If a person succeeds in meeting her four deficit needs, then she is free of them and available for other interests.

Any hypothesis suggesting that a strong, well-adjusted, and resilient personality rests on a foundation of need-gratification is bound to conflict to some degree with the remnants of the Puritan ethic in American culture. We value "doing without," self-deprivation, denying ourselves the "good things" in life. The present writers assign all beliefs that need-frustration is good for the personality to the impressive accumulation of mankind's tragic mistakes. We contend that a person who has experienced a *minimum* of deprivation is better able to withstand severe deprivation than is another who has been regularly deprived.

To summarize, all people are motivated by the needs in the deficit ladder. There is a normal progression from the bottom to the top, with the ultimate movement out of the ladder to other dominant motivations. Well-adjusted adults have deficit motivations of substantial strength only in times of emergency. Then they soon progress up the ladder again and "over the top."

Energy expended in satisfying deficit needs lowers productivity. It is desirable for a person to move up the steps of the ladder as rapidly as possible. But his evolution is aided or handicapped by environment. There are direct and practical implications for supervisors and managers.

It is possible to plan a business enterprise so that satisfaction of security, social approval, and esteem needs will be easy—or difficult. We can help our people meet security needs by keeping them informed of what is going on and what is coming in the future. We can make it easy for them to make friends and get to know their associates on and off the job by physical arrangements, regulations and recreation programs, thus satisfying requirements for social approval. Esteem needs can be met in part by building into our organization a system that recognizes and publicizes achievement. Or, we can disregard these opportunities with the result that our employees waste their energy worrying about their lack of security; about insufficient human interaction; and about deficiencies in prestige. The manager will be wise to remember that employees divide their energy between worry over their selfish concerns and productive job-directed effort. Increasing one diminishes the other, and vice versa.

Emotional Needs. Earlier, we distinguished emotion from motive. Now we must combine the two, for we are approaching a category of motivation that has its origin in the emotional condition. The three emotional tension motives: mastery, social approval, and conformity spring from the primary emotions of rage, love, and fear. We will sketch in the theory of their development and consider in particular the problem caused when *one* of these motives becomes dominant.

Mastery motives appear as urges to excel, to succeed, to overcome obstructions, to compete, in general, to conquer situations in the face of difficulty. We can trace the development of these motives from *rage* behavior by showing that while for the infant rage initially comes only from physical restraint, soon verbal and other symbolic restrictions begin to have the same effect. The child's tantrum behavior is modified, too, with blind struggling responses evolving to a cunning thwarting of the people who impose restrictions. Eventually, the child develops many techniques for overcoming obstructions. A good example would be the scholar who works for years to overcome an obstruction to her understanding of a problem, propelled by a "remote" form of rage behavior that has become a complex mastery motivation.

Social approval motives seek favorable reactions of others, reach for attention, cause us to seek company when we are alone, help us conform to the customs and standards of our culture, and develop an appetite for sympathy. These have their roots in a basic *love* emotion. Examples of such behavior in the infant are movements to perpetuate stroking and cuddling. Later, the child responds to the presence of the person who gives him love. Still later, this response may occur when members of the family are together. The many satisfactions we find in group activities emerge from an elaboration of these "love stimulus" encounters. Here is the fountainhead of our powerful and universal needs for socialization.

A desire for social approval is not a weak or passive motivation at any level of maturation. The baby reacts vigorously and persistently when fondling is terminated. Children pester adults to the point of explosion in their quest for favorable attention. Adults do not wait for social stimulation to come to them; they seek it aggressively. Like mastery, the social approval motive releases an abundance of sharply focused energy.

An excess of basic *fear* emotion contributes to the prominence of the third emotional tension motive in a personality: conformity. Fear of punishment leads to patterns of withdrawal and avoidance that are essentially efforts to avoid pain. Punishment overstimulates the child. The experience becomes more memorable when punishment is accompanied by strong disapproval, for this associates punishment with blame. Repeated punishing episodes produce an irrational fear of criticism and the tendency to inhibit any unconventional acts that we call "social conformity."

Strong conformity motivation makes a person chronically apprehensive. In her childhood, fear was rewarding in that she avoided breaking taboos and resultant punishment by being continuously afraid. As an adult, she is still "running scared," seeking security by not permitting herself to stand out as "different" from the group in any way. She tends to "go to pieces" when she confronts unpredictabilities and insecurities that other individuals would consider routine.

Other-Than-Self Motives. By "self-centered" we mean "turned inward." Here the focus of interest and the major goal of expenditure of energy are enhancement of the ego. "Other-than-self centered" motivation subordinates the self (personal considerations) to the external process or person that claims our attention. The distinction can be stated in a paraphrase of the late President Kennedy: "If you are interested in what the project can do for you, your motivation is self-centered. If you are interested in what you can do for the project, you are experiencing other-than-self motivation."

In his book *Man's Search for Meaning* Viktor Frankl tells how he attempted to discover what kept certain inmates of concentration camps alive while most around them died. In each case he found a burning motive outside the self. One had a book to write, another an experiment to complete, a third had children he had never seen, so he refused to die until he had seen them. These men had forward-looking purpose in their lives, a condition that seemed to sustain them and release reserves of energy.

All of us have known people who "lose" themselves in their work. The writers recall a colleague in medical education who obtained the first electron microscope in his locality. He became obsessed with a desire to see more of the human cell than had been seen before. Considerations of self were put aside. He forgot to eat, slept irregularly, neglected obligations to the point that he was in danger of losing his job and his wife. Fortunately, he won his battle with the new device before he was fired or divorced. He contributed significantly to the art of using the electron microscope in medical research and gradually re-established a more practical balance among his motivations.

Engineers doing research for the exploration of space frequently become involved in their task in an other-than-self centered fashion. The problems of miniaturizing circuits, perfecting guidance and control systems, or achieving a "soft" landing on the moon often become dominant preoccupations. The reward to the participating engineer is the thrill of improving the process rather than getting a salary increase, if she has other-than-self centered motivation.

Teachers and managers become involved in the achievements of their students and employees. One sales manager came out of retirement because of the satisfaction he felt in helping younger people advance. He had unusual ability to discover potential in subordinates and to encourage its development. Although he received no material return from the success of the people he assisted, the need to help them was his central motivation and its achievement his highest reward.

Perhaps the most common other-than-self centered motivation is this interest in other people and their accomplishments. Family living develops this in abundance. When father discovers that his daughter's athletic career has become important to him, or mother finds that she gets great satisfaction from her son's development as a musician, or grandfather takes pride in the precocious antics of his grandchildren, other-than-self centered motivation is taking effect.

From your own experiences and those of acquaintances you can add many instances of motivation analogous to the above examples. The prevalence and importance of motives in the other-than-self centered category cannot be denied. It is unfortunate that so little has been written about them; only in the last few decades have they received much serious study.

Applied Logic. Applied logic is useful in improving the effectiveness of the reasoning we do in communication. Most of the writing on persuasion does not sufficiently deal with the presentation of a logically justifiable case, nor does it propose procedures for good reasoning. In the modern organization especially, people are not about to change their minds on important issues unless their better judgment approves the change. Yet the "tricks of the trade" approach to persuasion gets center stage. Although "gimmicks" and so-called psychological devices have some effect, we, as practical persuaders, must recognize that our first and probably most demanding task is to assist and survive the critical analysis of our proposal by those we wish to persuade.

Recent research confirms the power of "facts of the case" persuasion. Books on "how we think," training in problem-solving, games that teach the processes of logical reasoning, study and practices of briefing and outlining, all are useful in enabling us to produce better supported, more closely reasoned persuasion.

We must warn the reader against assuming that motives and reasoning are separate or unrelated. Actually, reasoning is often the best way of reaching a person's motives. Applied logic is highly effective in accomplishing step three of the process of persuasion, for it can demonstrate convincingly the connection between a motive and a recommendation.

Two steps are needed if persuasion is to be successful:

1. Good reasons must be provided to arouse selected motives, and connect active motives to a persuasive proposition.

2. A person's imagination must be fired so as to create excitement, overcome inertia, and thereby expedite change.

Although the "good reasons" (these include all facts and their sound interpretation) can be exciting in themselves, it is likely that non-logical devices will contribute relatively more to the firing of the imagination. And to get people to move, mentally or physically, requires some form of excitement, in addition to intellectual conviction.

If we fail to get people *involved,* they will probably never translate their good intentions into action.

Semantics. The study of language symbols and people's response to them can be called *semantics.* In this sense of the term, semantics can contribute much to applied persuasion. Subtle differences in word selection are often crucial to success or failure, such as the use of a neutral word instead of its emotive synonym. The advice most helpful to us in designing language for persuasion is the previously mentioned basic principle of all communication, "People, not words, have meaning." In choosing our language we speculate about what our listener will perceive. We ask ourselves what meanings he will read into our words and how he will respond to them. We then formulate our message in symbols calculated to produce the desired response.

Recognizing two distinctly different *kinds* of words helps the persuader to use language with greater precision and for increased effect. To a given person, REPORT words are those that carry (predominantly) information, without overtones of like or dislike, acceptance or rejection. To her certain other words and phrases are LOADED. These, although accompanied by referential information, can trigger an acceptance or rejection response that may or may not be linked to the primary information conveyed. People respond favorably or unfavorably to LOADED language. To REPORT language they respond more thoughtfully, without immediate direction.

In Chapter 7 we discussed inflammatory language as detrimental to good listening. Hence it is not surprising that for maximum clarity in exposition REPORT words excel. Failure in persuasion results from (1) use of words the persuader believes to be REPORT words but which, to the listener, are heavily LOADED; (2) use of intended *positively* LOADED language which turns out to be *negatively* LOADED to the listener, or vice versa; and (3) use of LOADED words for an intended effect, which the receiver interprets as REPORT language. Each of these unforeseen responses can result either from faulty audience analysis or from careless attention to semantic considerations, or both.

The notion that LOADING is determined in the mind of the person receiving the message is so often overlooked that we will illustrate the point. If you label a proposal "radical" to indicate disapproval, intending NEGATIVE LOADING, it is entirely possible that Mr. A may react to it as REPORT LANGUAGE, assuming that you meant simply to tell him that this is a little different from usual or routine proposals. Ms. B might well be attracted to the adjective "radical" because of her affection for offbeat, novel ways of solving problems. For her the term is POSITIVELY LOADED. For Mr. C it could be NEGATIVELY LOADED, due to strong rejection impulses springing from his hatred of "radical" political doctrines. Loading—or the lack of it—for any word or phrase is obviously the product of the receiver's unique personal experiences.

To what degree certain words are loaded depends on the context in which they are being used. "Moron" is negatively loaded in lay conversation, but is report language in a discussion among psychologists. Adjectives like "broad-minded" and "heroic" would seem to be positively loaded, but in the context of satire they take on negative connotations. Most executives respond favorably to "profit," whereas socialists take a dim view of any capitalist institution dedicated to "profit-making" activities. Mastering the nuances of language is a fascinating assignment if you wish to advance your command of the arts of persuasion.

Two obstacles to proper communication are a matter of semantics: ambiguity and vagueness. Ambiguous statements can be interpreted in two or more possible senses by the listeners. Consequently, they may choose a meaning different from that intended. Vague statements are those that do not clearly or precisely express the speaker's thoughts—no definite meaning emerges.

Both ambiguity and vagueness are problems in organizational communication, but the former produces more spectacular results. A report on a new vehicle states, "We cannot praise the brakes too much." One reader thinks this is total approval, another interprets it as an indication of serious deficiency. An inspector tells the foreman, "The difference between specified tolerance and variations in this part are critical!" Replies the foreman, "The difference is *not* critical!" What does each *mean* by "critical"? The foreman means performance testing. The inspector has in mind literal adherence to written, contractual specifications. An employee asks, "Do I turn this knob to the left?" The supervisor answers, "Right!" No intuition or deduction can help the employee to decide whether the supervisor meant "Right, turn it left," or "No, turn it the other way."

The sender and receiver of messages should realize how prevalent ambiguities are so that they can be on guard against them. How can this be accomplished? By checking the language against possible double meanings that could create potential confusion. The receiver, by making an effort to detect as many meanings as possible for the same units of language, accepting what seems to fit best, and by asking questions to resolve those that are uncertain. The sender, by *forcing* feedback to test the reception of her message. When the receiver reveals what *she* thinks the sender said, ambiguities become obvious and are easily corrected. Reducing ambiguous language to an absolute minimum should be a high priority item for any modern organization.

Vagueness can be minimized by using simple concrete terms and relying more heavily on examples. Instead of "substantial gain" state the definite amount and the base of comparison. When a person asks for clarification of a vague statement he should use the magic question, "Will you give me an example to show what you mean?" Thinking up an instance of application in itself sharpens and refines an idea. And because examples are specific and concrete they instill uniform meanings in the minds of people receiving the message.

Precision in communication is achieved by using concrete terms in preference to relatively abstract equivalents. Words the source might use to convey a thought may be visualized in an arrangement resembling the rungs on a ladder. Those near the bottom represent tangible realities, objects, and situations that can be seen, touched, and heard. These words are concrete. We call them low-level abstractions because they have definite meanings, and are not very abstract. At the top of the ladder are the high-level abstractions. These words, like "honorable," "substantial," and "freedom," represent a host of possible interpretations. Typically, these contribute vagueness to a unit of communication. Abstract words convey "feeling tones" and "impressions" rather than a clear picture and factual information. The moral of our ladder analogy is: Come down to earth. Almost always, the source will communicate more accurately (less vaguely) by using words that are as low as she can find on the ladder of abstraction.

SUMMARY

The first essential step towards successful persuasion is to adopt the process attitude. A key principle that applies the process attitude to motivation is that people do things for their reasons, not ours. In order to apply the principle, we must avoid the pitfall of projecting our own reasons and motives on the listeners and concentrate on gaining insight into how they are thinking.

Successful persuasion requires that the speaker gain and maintain attention, arouse selected motives, habits and interests, and connect desires to persuasive purpose in order to produce a specific response.

Motives are "engines for persuasion." We define *motives* as variable sources of energy to pursue selected alternatives. Motive analysis should be used to study the structure of habits, interests, desires and goals that are part of the personalities of the listeners.

The effort to purposefully control behavior from the outside by appealing to the audience members' motives is persuasion. Thus, persuasion and motivation are closely related but not synonymous. We ought not say the manager needs to *motivate* the workers when we mean the manager needs to *persuade* the workers. Managers have great difficulty implanting new habits, interests, or desires in people but have much more success attaching their recommendations to the motives already within their subordinates.

It is useful to think of human motives as arranged in a sequence from the more basic to the more symbolic and social. The more basic motives such as physiological and security needs have to be satisfied before the other needs such as the social and psychological become important to an individual. The needs are sequential because satisfied needs do not motivate behavior. At a given time, therefore, a subordinate may be feeling any one of the four basic needs. Energy expended in satisfying deficit needs tends to lower productivity in the organization. It is desirable to have people move up the ladder of deficit needs as rapidly as possible. As a manager you should do your utmost to plan your enterprise so the satisfaction of security, social approval, and esteem needs are easily met.

In addition to the deficit motives, people are often moved by emotional tension. The three emotional tension motives are mastery, social approval, and conformity. Mastery motives spring from the emotion of rage and impel the person to excel and succeed, to conquer situations. Social approval motives are based on love and drive the person to seek favorable attention from others. Conformity motivation is related to fear and causes a person to do as others do, to blend in.

A final important class of motives is the "other-than-self centered" motives. People who are moved by other-than-self concerns subordinate their personal deficit needs to external processes and people.

Reasoning and motivation are not separate or unrelated. Reasoning is often the best way to reach people's motives. *Applied logic* is highly effective in connecting the listeners' motives to the speaker's recommendation for action.

The study of language symbols and the way people respond to them can be called *semantics*. Subtle differences in word selection are often crucial to the success or failure of a persuasive presentation. For persuasive purposes we can divide the language of a message into *report* words and *loaded* words. Report words involve information with small amounts of emotional overtones. Loaded words trigger responses and emotions without the thoughtful weighing that tends to result from report language. Loading is determined in the mind of the receiver and a source may err in thinking the message is composed of report words when the receiver responds as though the language was heavily loaded. The degree of emotional loading in the language of a message is often a function of the context for the communication.

Two additional language obstacles to good communication are ambiguity and vagueness. Receivers can interpret ambiguous statements in two or more ways. Receivers find statements vague when they cannot decode clearly and precisely what the speaker was trying to say. They receive no definite meaning from the message. A persuasive speaker should compare carefully the listeners, the context, and the language to avoid ambiguity and vagueness when clear transmission of information is the goal.

QUESTIONS FOR DISCUSSION AND REVIEW

1. How might a manager go about planning a persuasive campaign in behalf of a new policy or program?
2. How can the manager avoid the "pitfall of projection" in planning a persuasive message?
3. What are the four steps in the process of persuasion?
4. How can a manager apply the four steps of persuasion?
5. What is the difference between persuasion and motivation?
6. What are the deficit motives and how can they be used in persuasion?

7. What are the emotional tension motives and how can they be used in persuasion?
8. What are other-than-self centered motives and how can they be used in persuasion?
9. What is applied logic and how might it be used in persuasion?
10. What are some important characteristics of language for the persuader?

REFERENCES AND SUGGESTED READINGS

Brembeck, W. L. and W. S. Howell. *Persuasion: A Means of Social Influence,* 2nd ed. Englewood Cliffs, N.J.: Prentice-Hall, 1976.

McClelland, D. C. *The Achieving Society.* Princeton, N.J.: D. Van Nostrand Co., 1961.

McGregor, D. *The Professional Manager.* New York: McGraw-Hill, 1967.

Maslow, A. H. *Motivation and Personality.* New York: Harper & Row, 1954.

13

Approaches to Management

———————— **Laboratory Application** ————————

As you become a more consciously competent communicator your management skills will improve and soon you may move into middle management. As a professional, you find yourself more and more preoccupied with learning management skills and techniques. As a middle manager you need to develop a philosophy of management and organizational communication.

We have already given you glimpses of how scholars have studied communication in general and organizational communication in particular, of how they have tried to develop theories of communication and have suggested various approaches and ways of improving communication within organizations.

Scholars have also studied organizations trying to develop theories to explain the way they develop and work. Working with the practitioners, they have tried to think through various approaches to management and develop coherent views of what managers should do, how they should view subordinates, and how they should conduct their work.

Your philosophy of management and your practice of organizational communication go hand-in-hand. As we noted in Chapter 8, managers will conduct an appraisal interview one way if they believe in management by objectives and another way if they believe in participative management. Even as you plan to join an organization at the entry level, you should find out what the overall organizational approach to management is there and decide whether you could be comfortable and productive within their theoretical framework

241

because theories and practices *are* directly related. Theory undergirds practice.

Your management philosophy as you work within the management structure of an organization will be closely related to the management and communication approaches of your organization. Indeed, these theories are an important part of an organization's saga and communication climate. People in organizations often consciously examine various approaches to management and communication, trying to change their organization's saga when they feel that a better approach than the one they are using exists. Many organizations have training divisions offering courses and workshops in management, leadership, and communication. There is a very large consulting industry composed of specialists in various approaches to management and communication. Managers who perceive that their organization is not doing as well as it should often hire consultants to help improve productivity, to persuade their employees to work harder, to improve morale, to improve communication, and so forth.

One of the more influential early approaches to consulting involved specialists in improving work procedures who would study a firm and make recommendations about how to raise production. In the early years these consultants were called "efficiency engineers," or "efficiency experts." These efficiency engineers did "time and motion studies" in order to improve the way people did their jobs. They often began with a study of plant layout and working conditions. They also studied the way workers did their jobs. The efficiency experts then made suggestions for rearrangement of assembly lines and for more efficient ways for individual workers to do their tasks. For example, they might observe a worker on an assembly line putting a part into an appliance. After careful study of the movements and the time the worker took to do the assembly job, they would work out a better way to do the task that involved fewer motions and less wasted effort. They then taught all the workers the more efficient procedures. Viewing womanpower and manpower almost as machines, these "time and motion" engineers were *not* popular with the workers.

A later influential approach emphasized the socio-emotional dimension of organizing. The countless cries of "*I* am *not* a machine" were heard. These consultants would suggest that managers should be less production oriented and pay more attention to worker concerns, allowing workers greater participation in decision making.

Organizations have spent many thousands of dollars in attempts to study their management and communication practices and change them for the better. As more and more money was expended, the leaders of the organizations began to ask for evidence that the consulting and training was resulting in improved productivity.

A number of investigators tried to study the relationship between the official institution of a new management philosophy or of an extensive program in management training and improvements in morale and productivity. The investigators found that it was difficult to sort out all the factors that go into organizational life in order to find out how much effect one thing such as a training program might have. One of the findings that did emerge was that brief training programs in management or communication often resulted in the trainee trying out the new ideas on the job for a short period of time and then gradually going back to the old way of doing things. The point is that you do not develop and practice a management philosophy in isolation. You tend to manage as those around you manage and if you decide that the general approach to management or communication should be changed, you will have great difficulty instituting such changes in isolation. You may try the new way by yourself for a while but the system will probably soon get to you and you will return to the established practices.

When it became apparent that successful change required widespread changes in communication, the conventional wisdom was that while it would be difficult for workers, or first-line managers, or even middle-managers to change management style throughout the organization, that top management could do so. Indeed, the argument ran that without top management's support such change was unlikely. After World War II many investigators who went into plants and factories discovered organizations that were run along the lines of the military. Consultants urged top managements to adopt a more democratic approach to decision making and management. Many top managements caught up in the latest thinking about industrial democracy decided to institute programs of change. They allowed the workers to make more decisions and to participate in managing their own units.

Many of the managers as well as the consultants were naive about the importance of the shared fantasies, rhetorical visions, and organizational sagas to which the workers and first-line supervisors were committed. They discovered that they could not change these matters easily from the top down. In a number of organizations, ironically enough, the end result was that top management was ordering the lower levels to participate in management decisions and become more democratic. The top management of a large assembly plant of an electronics firm asked several of the authors to help institute their new program in participative management. The top managers had hired an expensive consultant firm previously and the consultants had sold the plant manager on the importance of changing management style. The new program was failing, however, because the assembly line workers were not making the decisions they were supposed to make. When top management asked for help from the initial consultants who recommended the change, the consultants told them the problem was with the first-line supervisors who did not have the more complex management skills required to supervise workers in a democratic style. Among the missing skills was the ability to lead a decision-making group meeting. The training director approached us to help provide the first-line supervisors with group leadership skills such as those we discussed in Chapter 10.

We spent several days on the factory floor talking to workers and supervisors. We discovered the supervisors and workers had shared fantasies of the following type: "The plant manager and upper management of this plant are always making life miserable for us. They represent one of our biggest headaches in doing a good job. Nonetheless, despite what they do, we continue to turn out good work. This latest program in work improvement where we are supposed to have weekly meetings and make decisions and so forth is just a passing fancy of top management. They are not really sincere about giving us any of their power. All these meetings and other new regulations simply make life difficult for us, but if that is what they want, we will go through the motions. In six or eight months they will have forgotten about it and be on to something else."

We add these introductory comments about the role and nature of your personal management theory not to suggest that such theories of management and communication are unimportant or ineffective. We believe that it is important for you to understand various attempts to make sense out of organizing behavior and communication and to improve the quality of organizational life. What we want to emphasize is twofold—first, that while in our laboratory application we ask you to write up your personal philosophy of management and communication at this point in your career, as a student you should realize that when you, in fact, reach a management position, you will have to adapt your personal philosophy to the norms of the organization and of the informal groupings with which you work. Second, you will also have to communicate in terms of the shared fantasies in the organizational saga of the participants.

Our other point is that change can and does come to the organizing behavior of people but it is much more difficult to plan and manage than we often think. In our work with managers of organizations as consultants and teachers we are often struck by the fact that they want quick and easy solutions to problems of communication and management. These managers would like a recipe that would guarantee success in handling all problems—a too-talkative group member, a sullen subordinate, or a chronic communication breakdown. They would be pleased with a magic formula or phrase, five or six words that they could speak at the right time in an appraisal interview that would forever solve the problem of subordinates becoming defensive when their work was criticized. Managers want easy solutions to what they term "people problems," nonverbally communicating to us that people should not be so childish in the business world of grownups. But most of the problems we all churn over in our minds when we have trouble getting to sleep at night *are* people problems. There is nothing childish about paying attention to the needs of the people in your organization. Feelings matter; egos matter; anyone's sense of worth is involved at work as well as at home and elsewhere. Many people throughout the organization have to work long and hard with great communication ability to change norms, expectations, rhetorical visions and organizational sagas before changes in management style will run through units, divisions, or the entire organization.

ASSIGNMENT: Developing a Personal Philosophy of Management

After reading the theoretical rationale section of this chapter, you are to write a brief paper on your personal philosophy of management and communication. Recognizing that once you reach a position of management your approach will be influenced by the environment of the organization, still, it is useful to know the leading approaches and the major issues involved in the study of management and organizational communication.

─────────────── **Theoretical Rationale** ───────────────

THE IDEAL TYPE

Human beings design and create organizations. Sometimes organizations seem to just happen and the designing is done while the organization grows as was somewhat the case with Invention Incorporated. Sometimes the people planning a new effort design the organization ahead of time and in detail along the lines of ongoing successful institutions. If a group of people raise money and gain the right to start a professional soccer team they may set up an organization along the lines of established teams. They know that other organizations have a general manager, a coach with staff, players, and so forth. Before they ever begin the team they lay out the formal organization and then go out to hire people to do the jobs required by the formal positions.

How is it that the owners can plan the organization for a soccer team ahead of time? They can do so because people involved in organizing and managing soccer teams have developed an ideal type of organization for such an effort. The ideal type provides them with a blueprint to follow in designing the new organization.

Early students of organizational behavior sometimes assumed that there was only one ideal type and they set out to discover, by armchair speculation as well as by actual field studies of productivity and morale, the nature of that ideal. Sometimes they assumed that rather than an ideal type people could choose to adopt or not, there was an inevitable way of organizing and that by suitable study they could find the scientific principles governing organizing behavior.

THE CONTINGENCY APPROACH

Recently some scholars in organizational development, management, and communication have come to the conclusion that an organization that might be ideal for one setting and class of activity might not be suited for another. The technical term for this approach is the *contingency theory* or the *contingency model* of organizations. In this usage *contingency* means "depends on." Thus whatever is contingent will not happen unless those things it depends on to develop take place first. The theory argues there is no "one best way" to structure and manage an organization.

The approach suggests that only when you know the environment, the people involved, the jobs they do, their goals, and the pressures they get from other units, organizations, and the surrounding environment, can you tell what is best in a given situation.

An organization that is authoritarian in management style, in which managers stress formal status and authority, in which communication channels are clearly spelled out and informal communication discouraged, may be suited to military or para-military settings and purposes. Such an organization may also be useful for athletic organizations and for health care services that deal with crisis situations. An organization that is participative in style, in which managers downplay status and authority, in which workers make many decisions, and in which the informal channels become important, may be suited to research and development settings and purposes, to faculties of educational institutions, and to some service industries.

THE BUREAUCRATIC APPROACH

In nineteenth century Europe a number of countries developed large and efficient bureaucracies that seemed to observers to have an important influence on the course of world events. Prussia, one of a number of separate German states at the time, developed an impressive civil service bureaucracy and an equally impressive military establishment. Prussia subsequently dominated the German states and brought them into a unified Germany. Great Britain established dominance over an empire that included colonies around the world and maintained control with a bureaucracy that included both civil service and military elements.

The nineteenth century bureaucracies were organized along the lines of a pyramid. At the top was the chief executive officer and then came levels of upper management, middle management, first-line managers, and, at the lower level, workers or soldiers. The pyramid was subdivided into units that lumped together people who specialized in doing the same sorts of tasks. Orders were issued from the top and people at each succeeding level were expected to follow them. The formal duties of each position were clearly spelled out and the formal communication channels were emphasized. The organizational type stressed formal status; informal communication among members at different status levels was discouraged.

As long as the leaders of the military organizations and civil service bureaucracies could maintain discipline and *esprit de corps* they proved to be remarkably efficient. The leaders were trained to respond quickly to crises such as a rebellion by the natives. They gained efficiency by specialization. They allowed for the rapid turnover of personnel. The leaders could train people not only to specialize in work duties but also in administrative tasks. The result was an organization whose parts were essentially interchangeable. A British colonial officer could move from Africa to India and take up his duties immediately without special management training because the bureaucracy in India was organized along the same lines as the one in Africa. Over a period of years the organizations developed people of a certain type for various specialized duties to the point where they could be depicted in popular fiction. The German bureaucrat and the British colonel who had served in the colonies both became stock figures in novels and plays.

A management style evolved that was suited to the pyramid model of organization. Restrictions on informal communication and emphasis on status differences resulted in the people in the lower echelons having little solid information about what was going on in upper management. Lack of personal contact further added to the mystery. Freed from the restraints of hard news, the participants could easily share fantasies that depicted their leaders as angels or devils, incompetents or super heroes. Charismatic leaders who could inspire the workers or soldiers to blind obedience and superhuman effort were at a premium. The management style emphasized such concepts as *span of control* which related to how many people or how much activity an individual could supervise effectively. Managers were expected to supervise subordinates closely to assure compliance with orders. A noncommissioned officer who was supervising the building of a road or bridge and who picked up a shovel might well be reprimanded. His duty was to supervise, not to work. Managers were expected to make sure subordinates were punished for failures and rewarded for successes. They were also expected to discipline subordinates for failure to obey orders.

Workers or soldiers in such bureaucracies could probably have adopted without modification the slogan used by an automobile firm to sell cars on television in the 1980s—"We are driven!"

Early theorists in twentieth century organizational study stressed the bureaucratic or military model of chain of command moving from top to bottom, of specialization, of interchangeability of parts, and of task efficiency. Some writers refer to this approach to the study of organizations as the *classical* school.

Although a number of contemporary organizations still approximate the form of the hierarchical bureaucracy, many of the twentieth century theorists of organizational management and communication rebelled against the classical bureaucracy they found widespread in their culture. They recommended other ways to organize that they considered more humane and equally efficient. The lucrative practice of management consulting often consisted of the consultants recommending that organizations change from the form of classical bureaucracy to some other ideal type.

Despite the vigorous and long-standing critique of the pyramid design of organizations it remains a viable and important organizational structure. Indeed, theorists who developed the contingency theory may have been responding to a situation in which the pyramid continued to be used even after it was subjected to severe criticism and other ways of organization recommended to take its place. When they investigated the reasons for the continued use of the pyramid, some decided that for certain situations and circumstances, it might be the best type of organization.

You may, therefore, find yourself working in an organization organized along the lines of hierarchy and status. Perhaps the workers in your organization belong to a union, in which case they participate in two hierarchical organizations related to their jobs. The pitting of the union hierarchy against the hierarchy of management creates a complex work environment which the Prussian bureaucrat and the British soldier of the nineteenth century did not experience.

Some of those who criticized management as it was practiced did not reject the pyramid structure with its levels of management and division of duties but, rather, concentrated on the attitude of managers towards subordinates, their style of supervision, and the portion of the organizational saga that portrayed the decision making as flowing from the top downward.

THEORY X AND THEORY Y

Some criticized the classical structure because it encouraged an attitude on the part of management that portrayed workers as lazy, in need of discipline, and having to be continually goaded to work. One of the most popular of such critiques was provided by Douglas McGregor who suggested that managers in organizations might have one of two views of human nature. He labeled the first view *Theory X* and suggested it was the one encouraged by the typical hierarchical organization. He labeled the second view *Theory Y* and recommended it as a basis for reform of management practices. A number of other theorists also suggested a revised picture of the typical worker as an important reform of management attitudes, but McGregor's terms, *Theory X* and *Theory Y,* are widely used and you may well find your fellow managers using them in discussing management problems.

Theory X views human beings as motivated primarily by money and as essentially lazy. They try to avoid work and must be pushed by external forces. People are often unmotivated by organizational goals and must be supervised carefully to get them to do what the organization needs to have done. Most people are not self starters and have little self control.

The organization that has Theory X as an important part of its saga encourages a management style in which the supervisors keep a close eye on subordinates, give them individual monetary rewards for work well done, fine them or in other ways punish them for failure to follow directions, and clearly communicate what they are to do and when they are to do it.

Theory Y, McGregor's ideal for reforming management, sees people as finding work as natural as play and important to them. People are, for the most part, self starters who can do things on their own. Giving detailed instructions and providing close supervision is usually unnecessary and may often be counterproductive. There are no necessary conflicts between the goals of workers and the organization. Given a proper reward and communication system, people will make the organization's goals their own and become committed to organizational success. People gain satisfactions from a number of sources and not just money. Everyone in the organization is creative and imaginative and often workers have much untapped potential to aid the organization.

The organization with Theory Y as part of its saga encourages a management style in which supervisors allow subordinates to make decisions about their work, and take initiatives without close supervision. Theory Y managers provide a range of rewards in addition to money, encourage trust and upward and downward communication.

PARTICIPATIVE MANAGEMENT

Another line of analysis of the pyramid structure criticized the portrayal of decision-making as flowing from the top downward. The theorists began to advocate a new approach to supervision which is often called *participative management.* The participative approach to management requires a revision of the organizational saga as it relates to decision-making. The new portrayal pictures decisions as not coming from management and moving down the levels to the workers but, rather, sees the members of each unit making the decisions that are important to them. Managers move from roles as decision-makers and task masters to team leaders and facilitators.

Investigators in the early decades of the twentieth century went into business and industrial organizations to try to apply the methods of social science to improve productivity. As a byproduct of their studies of such things as lighting, rest periods, work arrangements and their effect on output, they discovered that the workers clustered together in informal groups. They further found that the norms of the informal groups often had a greater effect on productivity than efforts by management and efficiency engineers to increase output.

Some management theorists used the findings from field studies of organizations to argue that the old approach of supervising individuals was inadequate. The manager who was supervising individuals might analyze worker A and decide that he needed close supervision, careful explanation of objectives, and much praise in order to work hard and do a good job whereas worker B was a self starter and liked to be left alone and required little praise but occasionally needed to be sharply criticized. These theorists suggested that if members A, B, C, D, E were part of a close-knit informal group running drill presses and turning out the same part, the group norm for output was much more likely to govern their actual productivity than any individual style of supervision on the part of the manager.

Further investigations of team building in industry and management of groups found that when members of the groups directly involved in the work made decisions relating to working conditions and production techniques, the effect was greater morale and higher productivity.

The new approach to participative management, like the new

fantasy type of the creative, ambitious, and achievement motivated worker, was essentially a revision of organizational saga and not a reform of the pyramid structure. These theorists still saw the organization as structured in formal ways with specialized divisions, levels of management, and a chief executive officer.

The participative management approach grew in popularity after World War II and a number of authorities, consultants, and scholars developed variations on the theme. We will use Likert's Type IV ideal type of organization and Drucker's management by objectives to illustrate the way theorists recommended changes in management within the pyramid structure.

LIKERT'S TYPE IV

Likert was one of the early leaders in the study of groups and their effect on morale and productivity. Likert worked with the Morale Division of the United States Strategic Bombing Survey during the second World War and subsequently became the director of the Institute for Social Research at the University of Michigan. Under his leadership the Institute studied the question of what good management does to improve morale and productivity. Likert reported findings from studies in the late 1940s and early 1950s that indicated that workers whose supervisors were employee-centered were more productive than those whose managers were production-centered and that the supervisor's ability to manage subordinates as a group was an important factor in morale and productivity. Likert also reported that cohesiveness in the work groups was related to productivity. People in cohesive work groups cooperate more with one another than do members of groups with little group loyalty. Members of highly cohesive groups help one another and the work tends to flow back and forth depending upon the load; those workers who have finished a task will volunteer to help a fellow group member who is overloaded. Workers in highly cohesive groups take the initiative in helping each other, in solving problems and improving production.

Likert developed an analysis of four types of organizations running on a continuum with the bureaucratic saga similar to McGregor's Theory X on one end, and Type IV, resembling McGregor's Theory Y, on the other. Participative decision-making runs throughout the Type IV organization. The manager has complete trust and confidence in the employees and manages the unit as a team seeking to build cohesiveness. In Likert's formulation of Type IV the table of organization looks much like the classical bureaucratic table of organization. The essential difference between classical pyramids and Type IV organization is that in the latter, each unit is viewed as a group. These groups make decisions relating to their welfare, work, and objectives. Communication flows freely within these groups and the supervisor is essentially the team leader, facilitating group decision-making. The various groups, although arranged in a pyramid, are linked together by the person in the management position serving as a communication bridge to other units. When problems arise involving several units, people directly concerned meet together in a small group setting to solve the problem. According to the ideal, the result is a free flow of communication within units and laterally among members of different units as well.

MANAGEMENT BY OBJECTIVES

A second popular approach to management which provides more autonomy for the units and more participation in decision-making was developed in part by Peter Drucker and is called *management by objectives*. In an organization using management by objectives the saga relating to decision-making portrays the process as one where the supervisor and subordinate, communicating together, spell out their common goals, define who will be responsible for what, and then use these agreed-upon goals as a basis for evaluation of individual and group effort. As a middle manager, for example, if you were using this approach you would meet with your subordinates who were first-line managers and work out with them the objectives for each of their units. You would leave each unit free to reach its goals in any way it wished. Your major management responsibilities would consist of cooperatively communicating with subordinates to establish objectives and responsibilities and then subsequently evaluating their success or failure in reaching their objectives. The result of successful management by objectives should be a decentralization of decision-making similar to that accomplished by Likert's Type IV organization. Management by objectives, however, can take place within the pyramid form of organizational structure; the superiors at each level would be responsible for setting objectives and evaluating the accomplishments of subordinates.

THE AD-HOCRACY APPROACH

Recently some investigators and consultants have recommended an approach to management that involves a restructuring of the formal organization itself. These theorists suggest that organizations should no longer be bureaucratic pyramids but should consist of groups of people specialized in the necessary skills to do the work from which clusters of people form around projects and problems. When these clusters complete their tasks they disband and return to the main-stream to await the next assignment. We might draw an analogy to the white corpuscles in the blood stream that are available to meet a challenge or problem for the organism. When such a challenge comes, they collect at the point of attack and defend the body against infection. Once the challenge is met, they return to their holding position within the bloodstream.

Toffler called the new organizational structure *ad-hocracy* and predicted that future organizations would be of that form. An *ad hoc* committee is a small task-oriented group set up for a specific purpose; once they have done their job, they disband. By the 1980s there were a number of ad-hocracies in aerospace, electronics, construction, com-puters, and consulting industries, as well as in research and develop-ment organizations and governmental departments. The groups were often composed of specialists who were strangers to one another before they joined the group. These project teams might meet for a period of weeks, months, or years, and then be disbanded.

One of the leaders in presenting the new structure as an ideal type of organization, Warren Bennis, coined the term "Post Bureaucratic Leadership" to describe the management approach best adapted to the new structure. Bennis argued that bureaucracy was ill adapted to the needs of the late twentieth century. He saw four changes which encouraged the more fluid, adaptive, and temporary structures. First, the pace of change had speeded up since the hey-day of bureaucracy; second, bureaucracies had become unnecessarily cumbersome and large; third, technology was becoming so specialized and complex that the pyramid form no longer allowed specialists to work together effectively; and fourth, the changes in management thinking that emphasized more humanistic values in treating subordinates made bureaucracy out-of-date.

Proponents of the new form of organization often criticized bureau-cracy because the sagas associated with the pyramid form portrayed human organizations as operating like machines. Such a saga, they argued, resulted in treating people like parts in a machine rather than like human beings. Bennis characterized the new organizations as temporary systems based upon an analogy with organisms. When participants in an organizational saga see it as an organism, they believe that all parts are related to each other and that the whole is greater than the sum of its parts. After all, if something goes wrong with even a minor part of a living organism, it can affect the whole body. If you have an ingrown toenail you may walk in a way that favors the sore toe and this gives you a backache after a while that makes you irritable, making you upset with and upsetting to other people, all of which brings on your migraine headache!

The growth of ad-hocracies resulted in some new role functions and people soon became specialists in performing these functions. One set of role functions was often indicated by the label *consultant*. Consultants are specialists who owe allegiance to no organization but are available to any group that wants to hire their services and place them on a project team for a period of time until the problem is solved or the project completed. They are specialists for hire, who move from organization to organization.

The breakdown in the hierarchy that went along with the increasing use of temporary groups was also signaled by the label *associate*. Many organizations began to relabel some formal positions that had formerly been called "assistants" or "aides," changing them to "associate directors" or "associate administrators" or research "associates." The term *associate* suggests that the person is more equal in status with another associate, or even with the director, than is an assistant.

In some organizations the changes to ad-hocracy are only partial. They still have a table of organization and divisions of specialists and these parts function in the typical way of pyramid structures to do routine chores. In addition, they have project teams that draw from the line divisions for specialists. They meet rapidly changing circumstances with temporary structures, keeping the line structure for recurring needs.

Other organizations are essentially pools of talent from which teams are drawn to meet changing circumstances. Some architectural firms, for example, are moving to a concept of team architecture. When the firm gets a job, such as designing a civic center, the company forms a team composed of specialists in pertinent areas to develop the plans and supervise the construction. When the job is finished, these specialists return to the pool of available talent to await the next project.

As we saw in Chapter 2, the communicator's self-image and image of others influences the interpersonal communication. If you view human nature from the perspective of McGregor's Theory X you will communicate with subordinates in one way; if you view human nature from the perspective of McGregor's Theory Y you will communicate in a different way.

Likewise, your view of where decision-making should take place will influence your communication. If your position is that those with formal authority in the pyramid make the decisions, you will communicate in one way; if your position is that decisions should be made by those most closely concerned with the question, you will communicate in another way.

Since communication is closely related to management you will find that theoretical accounts of organizational communication are also important to your personal philosophy as a manager.

SYSTEMS APPROACH

A number of theorists have suggested that a good way to view an organization for the purposes of understanding the communication is as a social system. The *systems approach* to the study of organizational communication can be contrasted with the approach that analyzes an organization into its communicative parts and reduces their complexity into explanations based upon understanding the parts. When we reduce the study of communication to an analysis of the parts of communication, we assume that understanding the parts allows us to understand the whole. Scholars who view organizational communication from a systems perspective, on the other hand, assume that important features emerge from the interrelationships and patterns of the parts as they become a whole. As a result, the whole is greater than the sum of its parts. Scholars with a systems perspective also assume that the parts are influenced by the surrounding parts, that everything is interrelated. Thus, if communication goes haywire anywhere in the organization, the influence of that breakdown will ripple through the rest of the system. Likewise, if one subsystem of a larger system changes, that will impact on the other subsystems and the total system.

For example, in Chapter 12, the emergent subsystem of communication that consisted of the women managers at International Mills forming a support group, began to affect Homer Lydgate's marketing subsystem, and even had a rippling effect on John Jamison's new products subsystem.

We have noted that the systems perspective often makes the analogy of an organization with a living organism and that the bureaucratic perspective often makes the analogy of an organization to a machine. Some modern communication theorists also make a machine analogy but use modern computer and information processing systems as the basis for the comparison. They view the organization as an information processing system, viewing the organization in computer terms, focusing one's attention on information channels, networks, flow, and feedback mechanisms.

Some communication theorists have adopted a perspective that sees the organization as an emerging and evolving system of interpersonal roles, norms, and rules that govern the cooperative organizing behavior. They suggest that communication is the means people use to establish role expectations and standard operating procedures.

Other theorists have adopted a perspective that sees the organization as a system of organizing behavior and communication that is largely a set of symbolic actions which participants understand and perform because they have shared a common rhetorical culture. By their communicative interaction they share fantasies, rhetorical visions, and organizational sagas. These shared symbols and dramas provide the common ground they need to work, cooperate, and integrate their efforts. The organizational sagas provide missions, goals, objectives, self and group identification, prescribed ways of arguing, evaluating, problem-solving, and decision-making.

This book does not always reflect a coherent single perspective. With four authors one cannot expect complete agreement on such things. Most of this book is written from a general systems viewpoint. Some chapters emphasize the organization as an information processing system and others view it as a system of roles, rules, and customs. Through much of the book we have emphasized the influence of communication in terms of shared fantasies, rhetorical visions, organizational sagas, and the impact of symbolic action on organizing.

PRACTICAL CONSIDERATIONS

In our discussion of theoretical matters in this chapter we have presented a much more general and abstract account of organizations and communication than we have in previous chapters. These theoretical matters are important because they do have concrete and practical applications. At this point in your professional development in organizational communication, you would do well to spend some time as you study this chapter in thinking through some of the practical effects of your personal philosophy of management and communication as you develop it in your paper.

We will illustrate the way philosophical matters work their way into management training and communication style with several concrete applications.

The line of thinking that lay behind investigating the influence of employee-oriented supervision versus production-oriented supervision and tried to determine the best orientation for a manager soon led to management training. At first, the consultants and theorists were of the opinion that employee-oriented supervision was the best and they taught managers to be more involved in *human relations*. So prominent was this development that some have referred to it as a "human relations school of management." Further study seemed to indicate that heavy emphasis on human relations without some concern for task was less effective than a balance of concerns with subordinates as people and subordinates as workers.

A number of management consultants and trainers began to offer courses and workshops devoted to the question of the extent to which a leader should manage people as compared to the extent to which the supervisor should manage tasks. Prominent among these consultants

were Blake and Mouton who developed management training programs based on a multimedia aid they called a *grid.*

In the late 1970s the mass media stimulated a widely shared fantasy type in which a person evaluated the physical attractiveness of another on a scale from 1 to 10. A popular motion picture of the time was entitled simply "10." The title referred to the leading woman character, who represented, in the eyes of the leading man, the ultimate in female beauty and thus deserved to be rated a perfect 10. Blake and Mouton developed a somewhat similar system of rating, only the scale was from 1 to 9 and instead of rating physical attractiveness, their grid rates a manager's concern for people at one part of the scale and a manager's concern for production at another. Managers undergoing the training would fill out questionnaires and in other ways discover how they rated on the two dimensions of (1) concern for production and (2) concern for people. On the basis of such estimates, for example, you might come out with a rating of 4 for your concern for production and one of 8 for your concern for people. You would then be a 4,8 in terms of the management grid.

The management grid provides a visual depiction of all points in space defined by coordinates such as 4,8, or 7,3. Trainers, however, tended to concentrate on the corners of the grid and the midpoint in setting up their suggestions for improving management styles. The 1,9 managers were those who were running country clubs, and who saw their tasks and the purposes of their units as incidental to having a good time and keeping social relations happy. The 9,1 managers, on the other hand, stressed their roles in planning and directing the work of subordinates and viewed the social dimension as unnecessary. Managers who were 1,1 were clearly incompetent, but the 9,9 supervisors were ideal.

We have discussed the management grid as a visual aid to help managers in self analysis by comparing their position according to an ideal position. Many consultants, however, added the contingency notions that management style should be viewed in the context of a given organization and that the right management style depends on (is contingent upon) such things as the favorableness of the situation and the difficulty of the task.

Fiedler, for example, developed a contingency approach to leadership (management) that suggested that when a situation is extremely favorable in terms of organizational authority, earned leadership, and the goal is clear and the right way to reach it is evident, then the manager should be authoritarian. Under such conditions a more participative style of management (democratic form of leadership) is likely to waste effort. When the situation is extremely unfavorable the organization is facing a crisis and authoritarian leadership is again indicated. When the situation is moderately favorable the democratic style of leadership or management is best.

The last three decades have seen many different approaches to management develop. You now have some idea of the options available. Even though you will have to operate within the reality of whatever organization you join, you can and should think about what seems most workable and comfortable for you.

SUMMARY

Your philosophy of management and your practice of communication go hand-in-hand. Indeed, management theories are an important part of an organization's saga and communication climate.

People planning to start new organizations can often design them ahead of time by following the pattern of other similar organizations. Out of previous organizing communication they develop an *ideal type* of what a good organization should be like. This idealized structure allows them to hire appropriate personnel and get started. Early students of organization behavior sometimes assumed that there was only one all-purpose ideal structure that would serve for all organizing behavior.

Recently some scholars have come to the conclusion that the discovery of what is the best type of organization depends on the environment, the people involved, the jobs they do, their goals, and other important factors. The technical term for this approach is the *contingency theory* of organizing.

Early theorists in twentieth century organizational studies stressed the *bureaucratic model* of chain of command moving from top to bottom, of a pyramid formal structure, of specialization, of interchangeability of parts, and of task efficiency. These theorists of the bureaucratic model are sometimes called the *classical school.* Despite the vigorous and long-standing critique of the pyramid design of organizations, it remains a viable and important organizational structure.

McGregor provided one critique of traditional management with his formulation of two basic types of management, *Theory X and Theory Y.* The organization with Theory Y as its management approach encourages subordinates to make decisions about their own work and take initiatives without close supervision. Managers who practice Theory X view human beings as lazy and motivated primarily by money. Managers in Theory X organizations supervise subordinates closely and use carrot and stick approaches to get employees to work hard.

Participative management involves an organizational saga about decision-making that portrays the workers making the decisions that are important to them. Managers move from roles as decision-makers to being team leaders and facilitators for group decision-making.

Likert classified organizations into several types and then recommended what he called a *Type IV* approach. In a Type IV organization the participants view each unit as a group and managers see themselves as essentially managing groups. The groups participate in decision-making and although arranged in pyramidal form, they are linked together by formal positions which serve as communication bridges to other units. The result is a free flow of communication within units and laterally among members of different units.

Another approach to management that provides autonomy for units and participation in decision-making by employees is Drucker's *management by objectives.* In Drucker's approach the supervisor and subordinate communicate extensively to spell out common goals, to define who will be responsible for what, and to decide how the subordinate's work will be evaluated. The employees are then allowed to determine the way they will reach the agreed-upon goals without close supervision.

Some investigators and consultants have recommended restructuring the formal organization into patterns other than the traditional pyramid. They recommended *an ad-hocracy,* an organization consisting of pools of people who are specialists in different areas. Management's task was essentially to draw out clusters of people from the talent pools to staff specific short term and long term projects. When these clusters or *ad hoc* groups completed their project they returned to the talent pools until they were assigned to new projects.

A number of theorists view an organization as a system. They assume that important features emerge from the interrelationships and patterns of the parts as they become a whole. They see the whole as greater than the sum of its parts. Within the *systems perspective,* some see the organization as an organism; others as analogous to a cybernetic system; others as an evolving system of roles, norms, and rules; and still others as symbolic systems of shared fantasies, rhetorical visions, and sagas.

Although management theory is often general and abstract, it has *practical considerations.* Among the leading training programs for managers that apply these theories is the human relations school of thought which emphasizes participant management and employee-oriented supervision. Some consultants use the contingency theory in their management training programs. The contingency approach to leadership, for example, suggests that the appropriate style depends on such things as difficulty of task and how favorable the situation may be for the leader.

QUESTIONS FOR DISCUSSION AND REVIEW

1. What are some of the communication problems related to training programs for managers and other attempts to improve organizational performance?
2. What was the *classical* or *bureaucratic* approach to organizational study?
3. What is the *contingency* approach to organizational study?
4. What is the *Theory X and Theory Y* approach to management and how does it influence organizational communication?
5. What is *participative management* and how does it influence organizational communication?
6. What is Likert's *Type IV Organization* and how does it relate to communication?

7. What is *management by objectives* and how does it influence organizational communication?
8. What is the *ad-hocracy* approach to organizational structure and how does it relate to communication?
9. What are some of the systems perspectives on organizational communication?
10. What are some practical considerations that grow out of various theories of management?

REFERENCES AND SUGGESTED READINGS

Bennis, W. G. "Post Bureaucratic Leadership." *Transaction.* 6 (1969), 33–54.

Blake, R. and J. Mouton. *Building a Dynamic Corporation Through Grid Organizational Development.* Reading, Mass.: Addison-Wesley, 1969.

Drucker, P. *Management for Results.* New York: Harper & Row, 1964.

Fiedler, F. E. *A Theory of Leadership Effectiveness.* New York: McGraw-Hill, 1967.

Johnson, B. M. *Communication: The Process of Organizing.* Boston: Allyn and Bacon, 1977.

Likert, R. *The Human Organization.* New York: McGraw-Hill, 1967.

McGregor, D. *The Human Side of Enterprise.* New York: McGraw-Hill, 1960.

Toffler, A. *Future Shock.* New York: Random House, 1970.

14

Communicating the Big Picture

──────────────── **Laboratory Application** ────────────────

In Chapter 5 we laid out the basic rationale for the study of organizational sagas. We noted the nature and importance of shared fantasies, fantasy types, and rhetorical visions for the organizational saga.

Our emphasis in Chapter 5 was on your role as a newcomer to an organization trying to find out what the organization feels like from the inside. By analyzing the shared fantasies and the official comments about mission, purpose, plans, and goals, you were able to appropriate the organizational culture and understand the rules and norms of daily organizing behavior.

Here our focus shifts to the application of the symbolic convergence theory to the way managers can communicate to shape and sustain the organization's saga.

Although the culture of the United States is dominated by organizations, many of them pyramids, there are only a few positions at the tops of the pyramids. Not many live out the "American Dream," a fantasy that involves a dedicated and worthy human being who wants to "succeed," who works hard, has the talent, and is a decent person, and who climbs to the "very top" because America is a land of opportunity.

As we carry through our imaginative dramatizing of your future in the organization we probably should stop short of suggesting that you have now reached the pinnacle of the organization, the position of *chief executive officer*. If you speak the phrase aloud, *chief executive officer,* your ears should by now be sensitive to the heavy emotional loading it contains. Each word fairly rings with status, power, and authority—

chief, with its tribal overtones of the head personage, *executive,* with its connotation of doing, managing, executing, and *officer,* a term that calls up all the images of military elitism and control. Many specialists in the study of organizations use the phrase *chief executive officer* as a general term to indicate people who have reached the top organization position, whether the institution is involved in profit-making business and industry, in education, in health care, in religion, or in charity. Some such catch-all term became necessary because people use so many different labels for the top positions in their organizations.

Some organizations have *presidents,* some *directors,* some *provosts,* some *generals,* some *secretaries,* some *chiefs;* some have *chairmen* or *chairwomen* or *chairpersons;* some have *heads.* The fact that we use so many different terms for the top status spot indicates it is symbolically crucial to our internal communication. When we pick a term to name the position at the top of the pyramid, we say something important about that position, about our organization, and about ourselves. In a sense, picking the right term for the top position is like Janet Perkins changing the name of the position that had been formerly filled by Mary Harmon; the position had been called *secretary,* but Janet changed it to *administrative assistant* because Billie would not take the job, although the formal position did not change, only its name. Billie was happy to be an administrative assistant and would probably have been even happier to be an *administrative associate.*

Interesting enough, people tend to shorten the phrase, *chief executive officer,* to *CEO.* Of course, people in organizations often use shorthand ways of cutting down long words and phrases in order to save time. Still, reducing the highly connotative terms to letters of the alphabet serves another function. Just as it is somehow easier to talk of MS rather than multiple sclerosis, so it is less blatant to refer to the CEO than to the chief executive officer. To repeat the message of Chapter 4, in our culture, many have ambivalent feelings about status, leadership, and dominance.

When people take great care and effort in deciding on the proper term with which to label something they are involved in purposive persuasion, that portion of communication we will call *rhetoric.*

Rhetoric has one everyday meaning that suggests that a message is just words, words, words—not really amounting to much substance. You may hear someone refer to a speech as "mostly rhetoric," or "mere rhetoric." What they have in mind is that the speaker was just talking and did not really mean what she said. We often talk of "campaign rhetoric" in the same way. The assumption is that candidates will make promises and say things during the campaign that are essentially meaningless. What we mean by *rhetoric* is something much more complex and important. By *rhetoric,* we mean the highest level of conscious competence in communication. It involves a person's understanding of the situation in terms of the needs of the listeners, the community (in this instance the organization), the material and technological surroundings, and the occasion. It also requires that a person carefully draft purposive messages and campaigns to achieve communication objectives.

Our study of the sharing of group fantasies indicates that members of a zero-history leaderless group discussion often begin to share fantasies in what seems to be an accidental and unplanned way. Some member dramatizes a script that popped into his head as he was daydreaming along and he liked the idea and told the group. The group got caught up in it and soon they had built part of their group culture because one member said what popped into his head and it caught their fancy. There was no rhetoric involved. Groups that stitch their social reality together in such unconscious, haphazard, and accidental fashion may end up with a culture that is unpleasant, unrewarding, and unproductive.

People who are rhetorically competent and sensitive can plan the scripts they develop for their groups, communities, and organizations with an eye to the group cultures, community visions, and organizational sagas they wish to create. We have gone on at some length about the label *chief executive officer,* and whether or not you will ever reach that position, because the way you label the position and dramatize the acts of the person who holds it, is an important part of the rhetoric of upper management.

We are now going to let you in on a secret, one that many organizational sagas never mention; as a matter of fact, many members of upper management never admit this even to one another. In most organizations, *the CEO does not make the decisions!* Not only that, but the actions of the CEO usually have little effect on what the organization does.

The power of the symbolic convergence theory of communication stems from the human tendency to want to understand events in terms of people, even preferably *a* person, making decisions, taking actions, and getting results or failing. We seldom understand events in all their complexity; in order to understand them, we have to see them acted out by actors. When we share a dramatization of an event, we have made sense out of what prior to that time was a confusing state of affairs.

As we write this we are in the midst of a presidential political campaign. The country is in a recession, many people are unemployed, inflation is at a high level, and there is a problem relating to importing oil from foreign countries, several of which are internally unstable. Any one of these matters is incredibly complicated. Specialists in economics, industrial relations, foreign trade, sociology, psychology, and a host of related disciplines argue, analyze, conjecture, and generally have difficulty sorting out what is going on. For the citizen voter, a drama in which the president has taken action that resulted in the rise of unemployment thus making him responsible for it, cuts through all the confusion and complexity and provides an explanation for what has happened. It is much easier to get angry with a president than with, say, a volcano that erupts and causes billions of dollars worth of damage to say nothing of lost lives.

The point is that, knowing that people have a tendency to latch on to the main actors to understand the happenings, you do not have to be the CEO in order to have an important role in communicating the big picture to the others in the organization. If you are part of upper management many of your vital duties are *rhetorical.* To some extent, middle and first line management participate as well, but the rhetorical cultivation of the organizational saga largely falls upon upper management.

ASSIGNMENT: Saga Building

Your instructor will assign you to a project team (another chance to experience some of the pushes and pulls you will experience if you find yourself working for an ad-hocracy.) Your instructor will have you select either an actual or a simulated organization and have you make rhetorical plans to develop a suitable saga in terms of mission-statements, goals, or fantasy themes to improve morale and over-all productivity.

———————————**Theoretical Rationale**———————————

SAGA AND THE CREATION OF ORGANIZATIONAL COMMITMENT

Recall our earlier discussion of organizational communication climate in which we pointed out that on the surface, the organization would seem to be a cooperative context that would encourage value-added communication games. We also noted that in our consulting and study we have found a high proportion of competitive and mixed-motive communication. In our studies of zero-history simulated organizations, we have discovered that cohesiveness develops first in the basic work groups, both formal and informal, and then moves upward to commitment to larger divisions and only later do individuals at all levels come to feel a commitment and a sense of belonging and loyalty to the organization itself. In our experience, less than half of the simulated organizations exhibit strong evidence of widespread commitment to the organization itself although typically, several of the small groups become highly cohesive. We have pointed out the forces within organizational systems that encourage competition and empire building in Chapter 9. When several units or groups become cohesive in an organizational system where the members have little commitment to the welfare of the overall community, the communication climate encourages competition and infighting.

After we had run a number of simulated zero-history organizations we became intrigued by the question of why some achieved a high level of commitment on the part of most of the members to the organization, while others did not. After further study we found that one important answer was that those organizations in which most people were committed to the whole had people who communicated the "big picture" to the members. These people kept the total organization symbolically before the membership. They were rhetorically sensitive to the need to make the organization an important part of the consciousness of the employees. It was this group of people who kept mentioning, reminding, dramatizing, the social entity of the organization and the commonality of being part of the organization. One of the common fantasy types takes the form of the "we are all in this together and we sink or float together" analogy. Legend has it that Franklin said to the declarers of independence that we must all hang together or we most certainly will hang separately.

A group of people communicating the big picture is necessary for organizational commitment but not sufficient to assure such cohesiveness. What is further required is that the group communicating the big picture succeed in generating an organizational saga to which a major portion of all members are committed. Commitment to the organizational saga means that the rhetorical visions of communities within the organization not be in conflict and that their shared fantasies fit in comfortably with the overall saga. When we have observed organizations in which two or more substantial groups of people are pushing opposing or differing sagas, we have also discovered an organization full of conflict and warring camps.

The people who are in a unique position to communicate the big picture and create a consciousness of community and commonality among the members are those at the top. One of the major managerial duties of upper management is the rhetorical one of identifying the organization, dramatizing it in graphic terms, and keeping the saga alive and appropriate to changing internal and external circumstances.

Personifying the Organization. One important way in which the upper management team can create a feeling of commitment to the organization is by reminding the members that they are part of a larger community. Since human beings need to have complicated events portrayed for them in dramatic terms, the management team has to provide the membership with a symbol that represents the organization. They have several rhetorical strategies available to them to create a unifying symbol. One strategy is the rhetorical figure of speech called personification. With personification you take an abstract concept or an inanimate object and give it the qualities of a human being. You might say, "Fear is walking the corridors of Invention Incorporated whispering in the ears of the workers that they are about to lose their jobs." You might say, "That angry old man, Mt. St. Helens, is suffering from indigestion again and about to belch." Upper management could personify the organization in such terms as, "Information Systems is the Merlin of the computer industry. Information Systems has again performed a feat of magic in capturing the public's attention with its new inexpensive home computer system."

When upper management uses personification to identify the organization they must repeat the same characterization over and over again if they hope to get the members to share in the dramas and identify with the character. If the personification is to become part of the organizational saga they must keep pushing the same basic symbols. If Information Systems takes as its personification Merlin, the magician, then it might have a caricature of Merlin as part of its advertising campaign to the general public and use the same depiction of Merlin in internal communication. Organizations have utilized a number of real and imaginary characters as symbols to stand for the total community. We can all learn a good deal about saga building from organized athletic teams; such organizations almost always have a personified symbol that serves to identify the team—often a personified animal, a tiger, bear, wolf, gopher, or a wolverine. They might personify a bird such as an eagle, a cardinal, or an oriole. They might personify a natural phenomenon of great strength such as a tornado or a cyclone.

Probably the most important rhetorical strategy available to upper management is to create a *persona* related to a member of the organization. *Persona* comes from Latin and means mask or character. As we use it here it refers to the public character, the mask or facade of a person as that person is revealed in shared fantasies. The persona is an interpretation of what kind of person an individual is in terms of past

and future behavior. Your persona in the shared fantasies of subordinates is different from the impression you make on them in here-and-
now situations such as a business meeting or a two-person conference.
The more closely people interact with an individual who is a persona in
many public shared fantasies, the more they may decide that "she isn't
like that at all." The persona of an actress may be that of a "sex
symbol" while those who know her personally may decide that she is
probably not much interested in sex at all. The persona of a sports
figure in many shared fantasies may be that of a clean living, clean cut
young man who is active in many charitable causes. The intimates of
the man may decide that he is selfish and vicious, uses drugs
excessively and, when drunk, beats up friends as well as strangers who
irritate him.

In an organizational setting, the same individual may appear in a
variety of dramatized interpretations of events and very different
personae may be associated with that individual. We have already
noted that Janet Perkins appeared as a character in some diametri-
cally opposed scripts. The scripts did not disagree on the basis of what
Janet had said or done, but they did interpret why she did these things,
and the kind of person she was, quite differently. For a community of
women including workers and managers, Janet was a persona who
had courageously stood against the entrenched sexism of the management of Invention Incorporated and who was leading the fight to
make affirmative action meaningful. For the salesmen, her persona
was that of a castrating witch, a hypocrite who hid an essentially
masculine personality under a facade of female dress and flirtatious
mannerisms.

The most important *persona* for the rhetoric of upper management
is often that of the Chief Executive Officer. Earlier in the chapter we
analyzed the various terms used to label the position at the top of the
pyramid. Such labels serve to characterize the *persona* of the CEO.
Their selection is of vital importance to the shared fantasies about who
makes what decisions when for what parts of the organization.

Upper management must decide how they will characterize the
decision-making of the CEO. They may dramatize the CEO as a person
who makes all vital decisions, a decisive persona, almost godlike in
understanding, never making an error. Such a rhetorical decision
implies a fantasy type where subordinates bring suggestions, problems, troubles that seem insurmountable to the summit. At this place,
which they may choose to depict as almost sacred turf, the LEADER
listens and ponders and then, as though inspired, makes the proper
decision. The subordinates are portrayed as reverently aware that they
are in the presence of an extraordinary human being. The general label
for the fantasy type of leader as inspired decision maker is *charismatic*.

An organizational saga that characterizes the leader as charismatic results in separating the CEO from lower echelons of the organization. If many members of the organization became well acquainted in face-to-face informal communication with the individual who is portrayed as charismatic, they would be likely to start dramatizations that cut the CEO down to more human size. Such a rhetorical decision thus requires stress on status, emphasis on mystery, and separation from the rank and file except on staged occasions when the persona enacts a prepared script designed to reinforce the general portrayal of the persona.

Upper management may decide to characterize the decision-making of the CEO as participative in style. They may dramatize the CEO as a persona who assembles a team of top-notch people and allows them to take initiative, make decisions, and utilize their full potential. The persona is of an individual who knows talent and how to provide the environment for its maximum development. The persona is an inspiration, a facilitator who trusts others, and gets the best out of the people because they want to give their best rather than being forced to do so.

We keep saying that upper management can decide these rhetorical questions because the person who becomes Chief Executive Officer may be more or less skillful at the communication the position requires and even those CEOs who are rhetorically sensitive can exert only a limited influence on communication decisions. In the end, the team makes such decisions.

The persona of the CEO is one of the most important unifying symbols for the organizational saga. Upper management in its role as cultivator of the saga needs to make communication decisions about how to create and promote that persona in order to build commitment and cohesiveness. We stressed in Chapter 13, which covered various approaches to management such as participative management and management by objectives, that they required extensive changes in the organizational saga in order to be implemented. The drama of decision-making is vital to the persona of the CEO. Equally important is the selection of personal characteristics for the persona. Would it be better for our organization if the CEO were sophisticated, intellectual, artistic, or "old shoe," of the common people? You may think, but what if the person who *is* the president of the organization is a sophisticated, intellectual individual with a strong interest in the arts? How can upper management portray her as an "old shoe"? If she founded the company or was an early and important CEO, the odds are that her personality, appearance, and so forth had a lot to do with upper management's decision about how to characterize her. They would probably have characterized her in ways that suited her background, training, personality, and appearance. Once the organizational saga is established and upper management determines the persona it wishes to use as CEO, the odds are that, when they have to select a new CEO, they hire someone who is typecast for the role. During political campaigns we often hear about whether or not a candidate has a "Presidential aura" and commentators suggest that looking and acting like a President is an important part of a candidate's appeal to the voters. The point is that substantial numbers of citizens have a shared rhetorical vision that includes the persona of THE PRESIDENT and these citizens know what a good President should do and say.

One of the most important duties of the chief executive officer is that of portraying the unifying symbol of the organization. Some organizational sagas put upper management in a double bind because they contain fantasy types in which the boss makes all the important decisions, takes actions, compiles a record of accomplishments and is the mover and shaker of events. The trouble comes because the managers and the boss share the fantasies and try to enact them. As a result, the CEO tries to keep on top of developments in all divisions of the organization. Subordinates brief the CEO and press for a definitive decision. The CEO may agonize over what to do even though the briefings indicate quite clearly that one decision is preferable to others. Meantime, the necessities of the situation require the CEO to play the role of public persona. Important people must be met, entertainments given, speeches, press conferences—everywhere he or she goes the aura of the organization follows. Many organizational sagas of upper management portray the decision-making and "taking action" as more important than the rhetorical dimension of the position. They thus characterize the persona development and use as ceremonial functions, or symbolic functions, necessary but somehow unfortunate, for they take the boss away from the "real work," the important matters.

Various upper managements respond to the double bind in different ways. One way is to spend more hours trying to do it all. The fantasy type of the hard-working American president is widely shared, and almost always shared by the presidential team. Much of the additional time is probably wasted in the CEO's boning up on technical matters that a nonspecialist could not master in the time available. Somewhere in the upper management team there must be an individual or a small group of people who make the difficult decisions or they will go unmade. The saga may describe the CEO as the person who makes the tough decisions. The fantasy type is caught in President Harry Truman's phrase about the American Presidency, that "the buck stops here." In fact, however, some other person or group of people may make the tough decisions.

Even the decision-making by upper management may be symbolically more important to the people involved than it is in terms of any appreciable impact on the organization or the behavior of members of the community. Specialists in public administration have discovered that Presidential teams enter the White House and surrounding office buildings for periods of four to eight years and have remarkably little effect on the way such institutions as the Army, Navy, Air Force, State Department, and Congress operate. They may decide to cut budgets and trim unnecessary agencies, but somehow, the decision does not change things very much. The Presidential persona may declare war on poverty and stand in the South Bronx and promise that things will change for the better, but at the end of the term, poverty in the country and in the South Bronx has been remarkably unchanged because of Presidential decisions.

One school of literary observers of the managerial scene suggests that upper level decision-making is meaningless. Tolstoy's famous novel *War and Peace* makes the point that in the fight against Napoleon, the Austrian generals made plan after plan, all to no effect, while the wise Russian general made no plans or decisions and waited for the army to decide what it would do.

While we do not go so far as to suggest that upper management decision-making is meaningless, it is not necessarily more important to the good of the organization than the communication of the big picture and the development of a healthy and effective organizational saga.

When upper management is caught up in the saga of CEO decision-making, they often respond without much plan or rhetorical sensitivity to the demands on the CEO as symbolic persona. They do what has to be done without estimating its effect on the various audiences involved and the impact on various audiences of dramatizing the CEO in certain scripts rather than others.

How can upper management go about laying the groundwork for the use of the persona of the CEO as a unifying symbol for the organization? As scholars became more aware of the function of shared fantasies in the creation of community, some found that rhetorically sophisticated leadership groups were "staging" events for persuasive purposes. Television is so clearly a dramatizing medium and its power to cause the sharing of fantasies is so obvious that many referred to such planned actions as "media events" or "pseudo events." These scholars seemed to be saying that pseudo events or media events were less real or authentic than accidental events. Our point is that all events, planned and unplanned, are potentially an opportunity for dramatizing and may or may not result in people sharing fantasies that provide a meaningful interpretation of them. Why the unplanned and accidental event should be more real or authentic than the planned is unclear once one understands the symbolic nature of human action. Professionals in mass persuasion of course discovered that if they wanted to get on television and they could not afford to buy time, they would have to plan to do or say something that would attract "in the public's interest" coverage.

During President Carter's term as president, Hugh Downs asked Rosalynn Carter on a television interview program called "Over Easy" the most important difference she noticed after coming to the White House. She answered that she found she had "influence" and illustrated what she meant with the example that after she was the President's wife, she could visit a nursing home and that visit would make news. She said that because of media attention to her visit, she could focus attention on a problem and affect public opinion.

Upper management can use the symbol of the CEO in similar fashion. They can have the CEO visit workers on the assembly line. Having planned the event they can then subsequently dramatize it along suitable lines to show concern for a problem, to encourage greater effort, and so forth. The persona is an important rhetorical asset and ought not be expended willy-nilly without some planning. For example, many CEOs of universities are used as persona for "outside" audiences. They appear at artistic events, serve on boards of corporate directors, meet with alumni, consult with governmental officials. They may also use their persona in cultivating the internal saga. They can chair meetings of the University Senate. They may visit classrooms, meetings of academic departments, and spend some time in the evenings at local campus hangouts just talking to students. We have heard several male university presidents evaluated by our colleagues over the years in such terms as "he's a great outside man but a poor inside man," and vice versa. What this evaluation means is that the "good outside man" upper administration persona has made good rhetorical use of the president in terms of building the organizational saga within supporting groups in the community (a very necessary function) but that he has, as a "poor inside man," failed in terms of using the same persona for internal cohesion (also a very important function).

As we write this the Chrysler Corporation, a major automobile manufacturing firm, is in great financial difficulty. The Federal government has given guarantees to help the corporation get necessary financing to stave off bankruptcy. The upper management of Chrysler has made the decision to use the persona of the CEO in a heavy media campaign to gain public support and to sell automobiles. The president of Chrysler corporation has been appearing for a number of months in television commercials played on major networks.

The commercials depict the persona of the CEO of Chrysler in human but relatively dignified terms. The persona is competent, not as smooth as a professional announcer but poised and articulate. A number of local business firms in our area have also used their CEOs in television commercials. Some of these have been more bizarre than dignified. The CEO of one local rug retailing firm has appeared in a series of commercials dressed in strange costumes as a gimmick to catch the viewer's attention. CEOs of some local automobile agencies' used car lots have also appeared in television commercials that portrayed them in less than dignified fashion.

What we have said about the persona of the CEO also applies to every position within the organization. However, the development of persona is increasingly important the more communicative distance there is between the individual and the audience.

The "I Am the Symbol of All of Us" Fantasy. One important unifying rhetorical strategy is to have the CEO portray the role of symbol for all of us. The essential rhetorical line is that whenever the CEO (or a department manager) receives recognition in the form of an award, an honorary degree, a laudatory story in a newspaper or magazine or a feature on television, the CEO publicly states that "I am only the symbol for the organization. This is really an award for all the good people at X corporation whose work this award really recognizes." When the persona of the CEO comments in this fashion, the honest expression of the rhetorical facts cement the bonds of the persona of the CEO with the abstract entity of *the organization.*

Dramatizing Success and Failure. Upper management must communicate the organization's long term and short term goals to all members. The long term goals provide a sense of purpose for the entire effort. The short term goals provide continual benchmarks so the upper management can let the members know how the entire organization is doing.

When upper management develops mission statements and long range plans, these documents may serve an important function by becoming part of the organization's saga. When the organization has worked for a number of years to accomplish its mission and upper management can refer to a long record of achievement in terms of the statement, it becomes part of the saga. The mission statement relates to the sacred past of the organization and thus tells the members what their future should be like. The mission statement tells insiders and outsiders who read it what is unique and important about the organization.

Many organizations have mission statements drafted in abstract, general terms. The periodic evaluations of how well the organization is accomplishing its mission tend to come at ritualistic or highly ceremonial occasions such as anniversaries of the founding, yearly reports to stockholders, addresses on the state of the Union, and commencements. The appropriate persona typically makes a ceremonial speech and discusses the mission and how well the organization is doing in terms of that mission for an audience of people often selected for symbolic purposes. These messages should be distributed to the membership after the event. The mission statement is difficult to dramatize, however, in terms of concrete organizational success or failure.

Upper management can spell out the organization's short term goals in specific and concrete terms. They can also set up deadlines at specific calendar dates. When they reach the deadline, upper management can check results against the short term goal. They should communicate to the entire membership how they have succeeded in terms of their overall common effort. They may schedule a victory celebration of sorts because the organization has done better than expected, or they may use posters, memos, and announcements in staff meetings to report that the organization has succeeded in reaching its target, or, of course, they may use the same channels to note that the organization has failed to meet its target. When the upper management presents the organization, even by implication, in terms of an individual trying to reach goals and succeeding or failing, they have personified the community and its efforts and made it easier for the rank and file to identify with the overall effort. Skillfully done, even the communication of failure and crisis can serve to bring the members of the organization closer together.

The Saga as Collective Memory. No small group can become cohesive until it begins to have a common history. Group members create their common history by sharing fantasies relating to their past. No population living together in geographical proximity can become a nation until they develop a history. Without a history, even masses of people with similar language and ethnic and racial backgrounds cannot become a nation. With a common shared history, even people of varied religions, languages, and ethnic backgrounds, separated geographically, can become a nation.

After the American Revolution of 1776 the most rhetorically pressing problem for the leaders of the new government was the creation of a nation. One tactic they tried was to cut their ties with their European past and project a glorious future. We still participate in some of that rhetoric in such phrases as "for us and our posterity." Another tactic that some leaders used to build a nation was to take selected portions of the history of Western Europe which the colonists brought with them and use them to stitch together a useable past. But in the end, neither a common glorious future by itself nor an adaptation of European history was enough. They had to manufacture a common history as rapidly as possible. They did this by taking the persona of the CEO, George Washington, and dramatizing it as the "father of his country," and portraying Washington as a boy who chopped down a cherry tree but told his father about it because he could not tell a lie. They also raised up a set of heroic personae who were symbolic of the fighting itself and a set of demigods who founded the country by writing a Constitution which was very nearly a sacred document.

An organization is no different from the small zero-history group that gradually shares fantasies about what has happened to them until they build up a past and their history becomes part of their group culture. Of course organizations typically last longer and have a more complex past to dramatize than do small task-oriented groups, so in some respects, a very old and large organization resembles a national community more than a small group.

Upper management may hire a professional historian to write a documented account of the founding, evolution, and development of the organization. Such an authentic history could become part of the saga if a portion of the members read it and invest a sentimental commitment to its dramas. But, for the most part, the organizational members share a collective memory composed of folktales, legends, rumors, and reminiscences of the past. Some of these memories dramatize events that occurred on specific dates and their extent and nature can be documented, while others may be vaguely portrayed as having happened sometime in the dim past. "I understand there was a time when old Mr. Johnson . . ."

Upper management can build commitment and communicate the big picture by carefully retelling parts of the history and by staging appropriate ceremonial events to symbolize important past events. The rhetoric of anniversaries is most useful for keeping a common history alive. One event that is suitable for such symbolic celebration is the occasion of the founding of the organization. Upper management can also use periodic special communications relating to times of crisis, disaster, natural or human, and times of unusual success to create a sense of common history.

All of this may sound too somber and solemn to you. But you ought not discredit the importance of these moments of solemn ritual to the saga building and maintaining of the organization. Not all saga building need be so formal, of course. Although human collectives need such uplifting rhetoric about themselves from time to time, they will often poke fun at solemnity and puncture pretense and hypocrisy. Spontaneous dramas about the past that are irreverent and satirical may start chaining through the informal communication channels. As a member of upper management you will often be caught off guard by some of these spontaneous shared fantasies. Obviously if the fantasy is negative and destructive and enough members value the organization, they will not share it in the first place. But good-humored, fond yet satirical fantasies can be useful as well as fun. If the spontaneous grass roots fantasy helps build a productive saga, you should support its transmission and encourage such fantasies becoming part of the organization's traditions.

Suppose that the upper management of an organization decides they should try to change the organizational saga from one that depicts management from CEO downward, to one of participative decision-making. While they are trying to do so, a production division plans a picnic. As the workers plan the picnic, they suddenly share a fantasy about testing upper management to see if they really mean to change their ways of supervision. They decide to invite a number of upper managers to their picnic.

The upper managers, having developed some rhetorical sensitivity, are aware of the potential symbolic impact of their attendance, both positively and negatively. They accept the invitation. During the picnic those in attendance organize a softball game and during the course of the game, in a spirit of fun, the workers challenge the upper managers to play a proper softball game at some future date. The managers accept, but tell the workers that they must decide the time, place, and publicity, if any, to be given to the game. If the game catches the attention of others in the organization and the overall depiction of the event in the shared fantasies that follow seems to contribute to the changing of the saga, the members of upper management could encourage an annual softball game between Department 246 and the vice-presidents.

Sagas and the Rhetoric of Motives. In Chapter 12 we discussed human motivation in general terms. The organizational saga that a member shares and becomes sentimentally attached to provides specific actions for the playing out of these general tendencies. Motive analysis is important for a specific presentation or for a short term persuasive campaign, but for long term member effort, the motives embedded in the shared fantasies, rhetorical visions, and the organizational saga become compelling. Take, for example, our discussion of other-than-self centered motives. We noted the importance of such motives and supplied some of their general features.

Burton Clark, who has done extensive work in developing the concept of organizational saga, has studied educational institutions for the most part. Certainly schools, colleges, and universities are a rich source of materials since their members tend to be selected on the basis of facility in the use of language and since there is such a high turnover of members—most students staying for four years or less. If the institution is to function successfully, the faculty must communicate the saga to the students rather quickly. We provided the example of a research scientist who was so involved with solving a problem he focused his time and attention almost exclusively on that end. The specific nature of the way the motive expressed itself was supplied by the organizational saga and the fantasy type of the research scientist with which the scientist identified. He was living out one of the most celebrated dramas of the faculty at an institution dedicated to research and the discovery of basic knowledge. When he made his contribution to the use of the electron microscope, the organization provided him with the rewards suitable to such a great success.

The motives implied by the dramas serve to impel the members of the organization to strive for certain things and to ignore or downgrade others. Recall the studies of workers that indicated that the shared fantasies of the informal groups provided the motivation for the workers to produce at a steady rate despite efforts by management to speed them up, to increase productivity.

The organizational saga contributes greatly to the quality of life for the participants in it. It may move them to great productivity or to feelings of warmth and affection for others in the unit. It may also discourage productivity and create a climate of backbiting, hatred, jealousy, anger, and frustration.

One educational institution was fortunate in that the state legislature provided it with more funds than did the legislatures of surrounding states. The result was that the administration was able to hire some extremely promising young research scholars. Once having joined the faculty, they were placed on a schedule of automatic raises that assured that they would continue to be paid more than most assistant professors with their experience.

The organization's saga, however, contained a fantasy type whose shorthand label was "the golden chains." It expressed and contributed to the symbolic climate that was frustrating and unpleasant for the new faculty members. According to the drama of the golden chains, young promising research scholars accepted positions at X college because of better salaries. Having recently graduated from universities with major departments in their areas of interest, hired because of their "great promise," when they began work, they found X an institution that provided a poor climate for basic research. Without the supportive climate, many failed to publish and thus failed to earn the national reputations they and others had expected for them. Soon they became disturbed by their own inactivity and decided that they must leave for an institution where they could do more research but when they tried to find a new job, they discovered they would have to take a big cut in pay. They had become used to their current standard of living and, bound by "the golden chains," they remained at X college. As time went on they became more disgruntled and bitter but by now, their lack of productivity made it difficult for them to switch jobs so with their once promising careers coming to nothing, they waited uncomfortably in their golden chains for retirement.

McClelland has done considerable work in analyzing the motivation inherent in stories that workers tell in answer to questions about what they think is going on when they are shown pictures of typical work situations. He has also applied his system of motive analysis to folk tales and other stories.

McClelland suggested that the motives implied in scripts tend to fall into three major classifications: (1) achievement motives, (2) mastery motives, and (3) affiliation motives. If the fantasy type focuses on a protagonist whose objective is to accomplish something, such as the research scientist trying to develop new uses for an electron microscope, or a drill press operator who is creative in figuring out new ways to produce more parts in an hour and reduce breakage, the dominant motive is achievement—to *do* something. If the fantasy type involves a protagonist whose objective is to gain control, rise to the top, take charge and dominate the situation, the inherent motive is mastery—to be boss. If the fantasy type focuses on a protagonist whose objective is to make friends, have a good time socially, gain love, the dominant motive is affiliation—to be liked and to be with people.

Cultivating and Communicating the Organizational Saga. You should not read this chapter as a script with a predominant mastery motivation in which you as an upper manager can manipulate people in an organization by your control of the organizational saga. We do believe that if you can control *all* of the present fantasies being dramatized in an organization you can gradually control the organization's past, and if you can control the members' remembrance of the past, you can control the future. Thus the rewriting of the organization's history *will* change its future. The saga of International Mills portrayed it as an enlightened and humane organization with a strong public conscience and highlighted events in which the organization officially acted to support community efforts, charities, and artistic organizations. Should the new women's support group succeed in gaining widespread commitment to a rewrite of its history in terms of past repression of women and sexist practices, the impact on the future of International Mills would be substantial.

But you could not have such total control as we described above. An organization is an open communication system. Control of shared fantasies requires the restriction of communication to such an extent that no member could freely communicate with another. The point is that no group, in upper management, in the union, or elsewhere in the organization, can close off the system to such an extent that they can control the sharing of fantasies. As a matter of fact, when upper management tries to shut off the free flow of fantasizing, the result is often an increase in clandestine dramatizing and a tendency to share fantasies that portray the controllers as evil personae.

Rather than viewing the upper manager as controller and manipulator of the saga, a better analogy would be that of the upper manager as farmer, or cultivator of the saga. The agricultural analogy suggests that just as a farmer who understands the way plants grow and how to prepare and fertilize the soil can encourage both the production of foodstuffs and the growth of attractive, pleasant fields and flower beds, so, too, can the manager who understands the way fantasies are shared, and the way to encourage their communication and integration into the organizational saga, help create both a productive and satisfying communication climate.

When things are going well and when the plants are sturdy and thriving, when the sun is shining and there is plenty of moisture, probably the best thing to do is sit on the porch and watch the corn grow. We recall one manager who hired several of the authors to conduct a communication training program for his unit which was part of a large assembly plant for a multinational electronics firm. As we became better acquainted with him and his unit we discovered that he was a company troubleshooter, one of those corporate specialists assigned to units so torn with strife and unproductive that they were having a disastrous effect on the total plant.

He hired us after he had been on the job several years and he had been a good cultivator of the unit's communication climate. We discovered that the symbolic impact of giving his employees special training and transporting them away from the plant for several days in a continuing education center was more important to him than the actual content and impact of the training. Soon a number of managers of other units decided that they also should have communication training for their subordinates. His unit was dramatized throughout the plant as a trend setter.

When we visited the plant and went to see him in his office, we found it to be thickly carpeted, airy and light, but sparsely furnished. Instead of a desk he had a glass-topped table with a few items neatly arranged on it. His table was clean. There was not one piece of paper or any other indication that he was doing or had done any work recently.

When we asked him about his "clean desk," he replied that it was clean because he did not have anything to do. Indeed, he maintained that he could tell when he was doing his job as a manager well by how much he had to do; the better he managed, the less he had to do. When we visited him he did not have anything to do, he said, because the unit was composed of able people who kept things running smoothly. He was wisely sitting on the porch and watching the corn grow.

The skillful cultivators of farms and gardens will plant some things that, despite their best efforts, will not grow and thrive. Other plants will appear and thrive without even having been planted by the farmers. The gardeners may decide to encourage the unexpected plants, or they may try to root them out. All their efforts will have a better chance of succeeding if the cultivators know something about how the plants grow and yet, those they try to root out may keep coming back, often tougher and hardier than before. They may decide to shape the shrubs and trees by pruning, trimming them to achieve a more pleasant effect, but those they prune and try to shape differently may persist in trying to grow in their own way in spite of their efforts to control them.

You will experience some of the same frustrations and the same satisfactions as the farmer as you try to cultivate a productive and satisfying communication environment by working and tilling the organizational saga. You may help draft mission statements that gain no support from the rank and file; they dramatize them as meaningless and a waste of time. Sometimes you will portray the CEO persona in certain ways and the dramatizations will fail to chain through the organization. A negative spontaneous fantasy such as the "golden chains" one may spread quickly and even though you try to stamp it out, your efforts will only add to its power and influence. Even a promising saga entry, such as the annual softball game, may begin to move into a vicious competition of "us" against "them," and all your attempts to prune and reshape it into other, positive directions, may not succeed. When you are dealing with human beings, as you must in all organizations, you must stay as philosophical as all wise farmers and gardeners who have to await the fortunes of wind and weather no matter how much expertness they acquire.

For all that, farmers and gardeners who understand the principles of agriculture and botany do often have higher yields of foodstuffs and more beautiful flower gardens than those who do not understand these matters. Irrigation, protective covers, smudgepots and wind machines help farmers battle those elements not actually under their control, and you, as an upper manager, now have insights into the complexity of organizational communication with which you can hope to intervene in constructive ways. Even the best of farmers know they are in a chancy business; each attempt to grow a crop is a gamble. The hailstorm hits good and bad farmers alike. Droughts and floods are never programmed. Sickness at a crucial time can mean that the farmer does not get into the fields at a critical time. Rains must come when they are needed. And sometimes, when everything was done that could be done and all signs looked good, the plants still do not thrive and the wisest agronomist can find no good explanation for it. Just as often, and just as mysteriously, a crop will exceed all expectations. The neighbors all say, "You did an exceptionally good job of farming," but the farmer, being very honest with himself, has no idea why things went so well.

Upper management sometimes finds itself in a similar situation. Sales go up and the profit picture is excellent and they have no idea what happened this year that was different from the past. Farmers and managers can both probably be forgiven if when they are praised under such circumstances they do not hasten to say "Thank you all the same but it is a great mystery to us why things went so well this year. We don't think it was anything we did, but if it was, we don't know what it was. If we did, we would try to do it again next year."

When all is said and done, the drudgery and routine of preparing the ground, planting, weeding, harvesting—the fascination of farming often stems from the gamble, the unexpected, the sudden changes in weather, the crop that was better than expected, the puzzle over why something that looked "in the bag" did not work out as planned. We feel much the same way about the study and practice of organizational communication, much as the good farmer feels about his work. If we had been able to write a book of recipes for all your communication problems as you move from entry-level newcomer to upper management position in your organization, and if a step-by-step following of this or that list of directions would always assure your success, we would have found the study of communication, particularly within organizations, much less fascinating and rewarding than it remains. There are never easy answers to complex problems in complex contexts. It is the gamble of trying something that looks promising but might not work in an important presentation, the attempt to encourage a spontaneous fantasy and incorporate it into the organizational saga, the challenge of the unexpected, and the mystery of why something did or did not happen that makes the study and practice of communication fascinating.

SUMMARY

The term *Chief Executive Officer* (CEO) is a general label for the top position in an organization. The fact that we use so many different terms to refer to the top status spot indicates it is symbolically crucial to the internal communication of an organization.

When people take great care and effort in deciding on the proper term with which to label something, they are involved in purposive persuasion, that portion of communication we will call *rhetoric*.

A group of people communicating the big picture to the others in such a way that they succeed in generating an organizational saga to which a major portion of all members are committed is necessary for widespread commitment to the organization. The people who are in a unique position to create consciousness of community are those in top management. One of the major duties of upper management is the rhetorical one of identifying the organization, dramatizing it in graphic terms, and of keeping the saga alive.

One important way for upper management to create feelings of commitment is to dramatize the importance of the organization through such devices as personification, or the creation of a unifying persona. The most important persona for the rhetoric of upper management is often that of the Chief Executive Officer. Upper management may decide to characterize the CEO in such terms as charismatic or participative, as mysterious or "old shoe."

A major communication task of the chief executive officer is to portray the unifying symbol of the organization. Often upper management shares fantasies in which their decision-making duties are more important than their rhetorical duties relating to saga building. Such fantasies often cause management to neglect the important symbolic communication involved in building a productive organizational culture. We do not go so far as to suggest that upper management decision-making is meaningless, but we do argue that it is not necessarily more important for the good of the organization than the communication of the big picture and the development of an overall feeling of cohesiveness and commitment.

Upper management may adopt a number of unifying strategies including having the CEO portray the role of symbol for all members of the organization, spelling out the mission of the group, setting long and short term goals, and evaluating organizational success or failure in terms of such planning and goals.

No organization can become cohesive until it develops and shares a collective memory. The organization's saga contains narrative accounts of shared events, successes, and failures. For the most part the organization's members share a collective memory composed of folktales, legends, rumors, and reminiscences of the past. Upper management can build commitment by retelling parts of the history and staging appropriate ceremonial events to symbolize things that have happened to the organization.

The motives implied by the dramas that compose an organization's saga serve to impel the members of the organization to strive for certain things and to ignore or downgrade others. McClelland has done considerable work in analyzing the motivation inherent in stories and classifies them in terms of their content as containing achievement, mastery, and affiliation motives.

We do not believe you can control all the fantasies dramatized in an organization. If you could you might be able to control the organization's past and by doing so, control its future. But an organization is an open communication system and unexpected fantasies keep chaining through subsystems. Rather than viewing upper managers as controllers and manipulators of the saga, we believe a better analogy would be the manager as cultivator of the saga. The manager who understands the way fantasies are shared and the way to encourage their communication and integration into the organizational saga can help create both a productive and satisfying communication climate.

QUESTIONS FOR DISCUSSION AND REVIEW

1. Explain how rhetoric relates to the communication of upper management in terms of building and sustaining a saga.

2. How is the organizational saga related to building organizational commitment and cohesiveness?

3. How may upper management personify the organization in order to encourage worker identification with the company?

4. How may the persona of the Chief Executive Officer be used in managing an organization's saga?

5. How does the way an organization's saga portrays upper management's role in decision-making influence communication?

6. How can upper management dramatize the organization's successes and failures in order to communicate the big picture?

7. How can the saga as collective memory function to build cohesiveness?

8. In what way do the fantasies that make up the saga of an organization relate to employee motivation?

9. To what extent can upper management control the sharing of fantasies and commitment to an organizational saga?

10. Why is the agricultural analogy a useful one in terms of upper management creating and maintaining a productive organizational culture?

REFERENCES AND SUGGESTED READINGS

Baldridge, J. V. "Organizational Change: Institutional Sagas, External Challenges, and Internal Politics," in J. V. Baldridge and T. Deal, eds. *Managing Change in Educational Organizations.* Berkeley: McCutcheon, 1972, pp. 123–44.

Clark, B. "The Organizational Saga in Higher Education," *Administrative Science Quarterly.* 17 (1972), 178–84.

Roy, D. "'Banana Time': Job Satisfaction and Informal Interaction," *Human Organization.* 18 (Winter 1959-60), 159–65.

Sykes, A. J. M. "Myth in Communication." *Journal of Communication.* 20 (1970), 17–31.

Index